Online Dispute Resolution in China

This book provides an up-to-date and comprehensive institutional analysis of online dispute resolution (ODR), with a focus on the developments in China as well as their doctrinal and practical implications globally.

In the book, a wide range of ODR mechanisms, including online arbitration, online litigation, online mediation, crowdsourced ODR, blockchain escrow services, and more, are thoroughly examined and compared through an original analytical framework that highlights the evolutionary trajectories of dispute resolution in the digital era. The author leverages several empirical studies and her experience working with the Supreme People's Court on formulating the rules for online courts. She presents an insightful, panoramic overview of ODR practices across Chinese courts, arbitration commissions, and online businesses, including detailed case studies and critical analyses of major digital platforms such as Taobao and the internet courts, which informs not only a new conception of justice adapted to the internet society but also different developmental paths for both established and emerging methods of ODR.

This book will appeal to scholars, practitioners, and policymakers with an interest in online dispute resolution, online courts, law and technology, as well as digital platforms and the internet economy.

Wei Gao is Associate Professor at Peking University Law School. Her main research interests are in international economic law, arbitration, and the intersection of technology with law. She has published extensively in Chinese, English, and German.

Online Dispute Resolution in China

Institutional Analysis and Legal Practice

Wei Gao

Routledge
Taylor & Francis Group
LONDON AND NEW YORK

First published 2025
by Routledge
4 Park Square, Milton Park, Abingdon, Oxon OX14 4RN

and by Routledge
605 Third Avenue, New York, NY 10158

Routledge is an imprint of the Taylor & Francis Group, an informa business

British Library Cataloguing in Publication Data
A catalogue record for this book is available from the British Library

ISBN: 978-1-032-97623-5 (hbk)
ISBN: 978-1-032-97624-2 (pbk)
ISBN: 978-1-003-59451-2 (ebk)

DOI: 10.4324/ 9781003594512

Typeset in Times New Roman
by Apex CoVantage, LLC

Contents

Figures

Tables

Preface

In recent years, the rapid development of the internet industry and the gradual formation of various online dispute resolution (ODR) systems have garnered significant attention. My interest in ODR began in 2009, upon my return to China after completing studies in Germany and Switzerland, when I joined Peking University Law School for postdoctoral research. At that time, the China International Economic and Trade Arbitration Commission (CIETAC) had just issued its online arbitration rules, suggesting that this could be a novel area within international arbitration, with technological advancements potentially bringing new developments. However, the anticipated progress of online arbitration did not unfold as predicted. It would take nearly a decade for online arbitration to gain significant momentum in China.

What also piqued my interest was the flourishing of private dispute resolution mechanisms on e-commerce platforms, particularly Taobao. This prompted my initial understanding of ODR and led me to pose the following questions:

- What exactly does ODR encompass?
- From which perspective and with what analytical framework should we approach the success and failure of different ODR mechanisms?
- How do private dispute resolution mechanisms provided and organized by platforms operate and function?
- Why has the online variant of international commercial arbitration not yet thrived as an effective mechanism for resolving international disputes?
- Why has China been able to rapidly advance online litigation within a short period?
- How does China's practice compare to that of other countries?

These questions, along with the reflections they inspire, have gradually shaped my thinking on ODR over the past 15 years.

This research specifically addresses China's unique context, which is crucial due to its vast online population and leading platforms, offering rich data and research opportunities. China boasts the world's largest online community and an extensive judiciary network. This book endeavors to make a significant contribution by offering a rigorous and critical account of China's rapidly evolving ODR mechanisms in a global context. For instance, its in-depth analysis of China's integration of technology into the legal system is an underrepresented perspective in current international scholarship. This research is timely, as it provides a reference for other countries looking to modernize their legal systems and serves as a case study for large-scale technological integration into a judicial system.

Unlike much doctrinal legal research on this topic, this book's strength lies in its interdisciplinary approach, blending legal theory with empirical data and socio-economic analysis. This approach allows for a deeper understanding of the impact of ODR in China, not just from a legal standpoint, but also in terms of its broader implications on society and the economy. Moreover, it delves into the origins and latest developments of primary dispute resolution mechanisms in cyberspace, making it an invaluable resource for providing a comprehensive picture of ODR mechanisms and their evolution from an institutional analysis standpoint. This is further enriched by incorporating practices and opinions from the expanding Chinese ODR field, including academics, legal practitioners, and industry experts. Additionally, the analysis is strengthened by practical examples of the use of new technologies for ODR, such as blockchain technology in digital enforcement, smart courts, intelligent enforcement, and the use of big data in online litigation.

It must be noted that this book represents a staged reflection on the subject of ODR. Preparing a book on this topic is akin to describing a landscape while looking out the window of a moving train – events tend to move faster than one can describe them. During the course of completing this book, I observed that some situations discussed in the literature have changed, some ODR service providers no longer exist, and many early judgments have been superseded, with new situations continuously emerging. Despite these changes, this book is a summary of my understanding of the development of ODR to date. I have endeavored to convey what ODR is from my perspective. The subject matter of this book is institutional analysis, and in writing it, I have tried to capture the dynamics of institutional change rather than focus solely on legal details, although there is no shortage of specific legal analyses. These legal details – provisions and cases – are the flesh and blood supporting the legal system. Despite the rapid development of the internet industry, many of the concepts and ideas presented in this book capture the characteristics of the system at a certain stage. Should the proposed analytical framework withstand systemic changes over time and possess a degree of foresight, it would have more than fulfilled the aims of the research.

I often reflect that for every individual, including every scholar, the most daunting task is to describe the era in which they live. The rapid development of society can be overwhelming, leaving little time for deep reflection. However, being part of the history of institutional change allows us to have an emotional understanding of everything happening around us. Scholars must rely on their insights and wisdom to offer the most accurate portrayals of the world. I hope that readers of this book, and those who study the formation of law in the internet age, share this perspective.

I extend my heartfelt gratitude to the editors and staff at Routledge for their exceptional support and professionalism throughout the preparation and production of this monograph. I am especially thankful to Dr. Lu Xu for his thoughtful suggestions and constructive feedback on multiple early drafts. I also wish to acknowledge my research assistant, Tianchan Ren, for her dedicated efforts. All remaining errors and oversights are entirely my responsibility.

Wei Gao 高薇
October 2024
Beijing

1 Online dispute resolution

An institutional analysis

Changes in perceptions of ODR

From online ADR to ODR

The rise of online dispute resolution (ODR) stands out as one of the most intriguing and significant global phenomena in recent times. At the widest conception, ODR can potentially encapsulate any form of dispute resolution wholly or partially facilitated by the use of online methods or information and communication technologies (ICTs). Since its introduction in the 1990s, the modes of ODR have evolved dramatically.[1] Beyond the most common forms of ODR, such as online arbitration and online mediation, various innovative ODR systems have continued to emerge in cyberspace. These include domain name dispute resolution systems, rating and feedback programs, escrow services, automated programs, digital certificates, crowdsourced ODR, etc. Initially conceived for e-commerce disputes, ODR has expanded to include more sophisticated and consequential mechanisms, such as smart contracts and smart courts, addressing a widening range of disputes, including civil and criminal court cases.

More recently, international regulatory authorities such as the European Union (EU),[2] the United Nations Commission on International Trade Law (UNCITRAL),[3] UN Trade and Development (UNCTAD),[4] and the Organization for Economic Co-operation and Development (OECD)[5] have become increasingly involved in devising and promoting new forms of ODR.

1 Ethan Katsh, "Online Dispute Resolution (ODR): A Look at History," in *Online Dispute Resolution: Theory and Practice*, eds. Daniel Rainey, Ethan Katsh, and Mohamed S. Abdel Wahab, 2nd ed. (The Hague: Eleven, 2021), 10.

2 European Commission, "Online Dispute Resolution," accessed August 31, 2024, https://ec.europa.eu/consumers/odr/main/?event=main.statistics.show.

3 "UNCITRAL Technical Notes on Online Dispute Resolution," April 2017, https://uncitral.un.org/sites/uncitral.un.org/files/media-documents/uncitral/en/v1700382_english_technical_notes_on_odr.pdf.

4 UNCTAD, "Technology and the Future of Online Dispute Resolution Platforms for Consumer Protection Agencies," October 19, 2023, https://unctad.org/publication/technology-and-future-online-dispute-resolution-platforms-consumer-protection-agencies.

5 OECD, "Recommendation of the Council on OECD Legal Instruments Consumer Dispute Resolution and Redress," 2024, https://legalinstruments.oecd.org/public/doc/185/185.en.pdf.

DOI: 10.4324/ 9781003594512-1

Although ODR has been around for more than 20 years, its concept or definition is far from universally accepted and has even become increasingly contested.[6] The parable of the blind men and an elephant comes to mind here, where each person tends to focus on the distinctive part of the large object closest to them. Judges think about ODR when they preside over online litigation, while arbitrators talk about online arbitration. For ordinary internet users, ODR is most visible as consumer dispute resolution on platforms like eBay or Taobao.

Interestingly, the latter aligns closest with the origin of ODR, whose initial goal was to provide a new and improved means of resolving disputes related to online activities. ODR aimed to fill gaps where justice was lacking or where traditional methods were unsuitable or inefficient for handling online disputes. The original purpose of ODR was not to replace or challenge the existing legal system or even alternative dispute resolution (ADR) mechanisms.

Early designers of ODR often attempted to mimic the traditional ADR process. The human tendency to seek similarities in new things based on our perceptions and imaginings of what already exists is evident when managing the intersection between law and internet technology. The desire to apply traditional legal concepts to cyberspace and adapt industrial-era laws to the internet society often proves challenging and futile. In ODR, this tendency manifests in the initial efforts of some mechanism designers to create an online mirror image of offline processes, replicating as much as possible the essence of traditional methods.

Nevertheless, attempting to replicate ADR in the cyber environment will gradually prove less feasible. Traditional dispute resolution fits into an existing socio-economic environment that is substantively different from the new environment of cyberspace. Adapting and transplanting existing dispute resolution mechanisms into this new environment raises the "embedding" problem, which will be analyzed further in Chapter 2.

More importantly, ODR itself has begun to develop features that are distinctly different from traditional dispute resolution, such as eliminating the need for face-to-face interaction, automatically recording all data, and relying on machine rather than human intelligence. These features, once considered shortcomings due to their differences from traditional methods, are now seen as potential strengths.[7] For example, the lack of face-to-face communication was initially viewed as a drawback, as it sacrificed the richness of in-person interaction. But asynchronous communication offers notable advantages, including allowing time for research before responding. Similarly, data logging can enhance the quality of dispute resolution and prevent future disagreement. Finally, machine intelligence can increase efficiency through automation, enabling ODR systems to handle an astonishing number of small disputes.

6 Leah Wing, "Mapping the Parameters of Online Dispute Resolution," *International Journal of Online Dispute Resolution* 9, no. 1 (2022): 3, https://doi.org/10.5553/IJODR/235250022022009001001.

7 Daniel Rainey and Alma Abdul-Hadi Jadallah, "ODR and Cultural Components of Dispute Engagement," in *Online Dispute Resolution: Theory and Practice*, eds. Daniel Rainey, Ethan Katsh, and Mohamed S. Abdel Wahab, 2nd ed. (The Hague: Eleven, 2021), 241.

Incidentally, it is unproductive, unnecessary, and impractical to artificially limit the scope of ODR to different criteria that have been developed or understood, despite notable attempts to do so in the past. The practice and development of ODR may well outpace such narrow or restrictive doctrinal understandings. For instance, the notion of ODR as online, out-of-court dispute resolution, which was popular for a while,[8] could not accommodate the growing importance of the court in ODR practice over the past few years in multiple jurisdictions, as discussed later. Instead, ODR, under the broad conception of the application of ICT to dispute prevention, management, and resolution,[9] paves the most pragmatic and promising path forward.

In this regard, China, with its booming internet industry and ardent pursuit of technological applications across all aspects of society today, serves as an illuminating example of such pragmatic conception of ODR. The Chinese population takes for granted the use of various internet-based applications, including e-commerce websites and a variety of mobile phone apps in their daily lives, for services like taxi booking, food delivering, ticketing, and more. They are also becoming equally accustomed to using dispute resolution mechanisms integrated with the internet and technology to resolve disputes arising online, including online platforms' complaint systems, courts' online litigation apps, and online hearing platforms of arbitration institutions, with little regard to whether these novel mechanisms are alternatives to traditional dispute resolution methods or whether they belong to the conceptual framework of ODR.

While there is ample Chinese scholarship discussing various ODR tools and systems, as well as the legal issues involved, the impact of academic discussions on policy and lawmaking in China is limited. Designers of ODR, including online platform operators, arbitration institutions, and courts, are more focused on practical problem-solving for pragmatic reasons. They are adapting to and leveraging the impact of technology on dispute resolution, thereby promoting the development of ODR rather than merely perpetuating ADR. This shift in mindset reflects the recent evolution of ODR.

In summary, ODR has long surpassed the notion of being merely a category of online ADR. It encompasses all the dispute resolution methods mentioned earlier, with online litigation in particular becoming a focus of ODR practice and research. ODR is not simply old wine in new wineskins. Nor is it akin to the "emperor's new clothes" from Hans Christian Andersen's fairy tales, waiting for someone to expose it as merely a replicate or variant of traditional methods, but with emails or videoconferencing. Instead, ODR should be seen as the "ugly duckling" from another

8 Julia Hörnle, *Cross-Border Internet Dispute Resolution* (Cambridge: Cambridge University Press, 2009), 75, https://doi.org/10.1017/CBO9780511576102; Suzanne Van Arsdale, "User Protections in Online Dispute Resolution," *Harvard Negotiation Law Review* 21 (2015): 110; Maxime Hanriot, "Online Dispute Resolution (ODR) as a Solution to Cross Border Consumer Disputes: The Enforcement of Outcomes," *McGill Journal of Dispute Resolution* 2 (2015): 2.

9 Ethan Katsh and Colin Rule, "What We Know and Need to Know About Online Dispute Resolution," *South Carolina Law Review* 67, no. 2 (2016): 329.

of Andersen's tales, implying that we must wait for ODR to mature before we can recognize it for what it truly is, which is fundamentally different from dispute resolution in the offline society before.

Online courts as an important component of ODR

The early development of ODR globally was dominated by private ODR, while public sector involvement was minimal, especially that of the court. However, the landscape has changed considerably in the late 2010s with the advancement of online litigation in many countries, including the USA, the UK, Switzerland, China, and others.[10] The COVID-19 pandemic that swept the world from 2020 was an important impetus or catalyst, but not necessarily the determining factor.

Using the USA as the first example, the Michigan legislature pioneered in 2001 through passing "Enrolled House Bill 4140." This bill amended the Judicature Act of 1961 by adding Chapter 80, titled "The Cyber Court," which regulates the jurisdiction, trial procedures, and other aspects of the Cyber Court. By the end of 2019, nearly 70 courts in the United States had introduced online dispute resolution mechanisms.[11] According to an estimate by the National Center for State Courts, at least 40 states in the United States are exploring the integration of ODR into their court systems, while 35 states have operational ODR programs or plan to implement them in the near future.[12]

In the United Kingdom, the first online service offered by the court, Money Claim Online (MCOL), began issuing claims in 2002.[13] In 2016, a major review of the civil courts of England and Wales envisioned online court as the most crucial element of future reforms.[14] Although the proposal by senior judiciary for a single Online Solutions Court was ultimately rejected by the government,[15] some specific initiatives incorporating the understanding of online court and principles of ODR have already been implemented. One of the most successful schemes, the Online Civil Money Claim, intended to eventually replace

10 Julien Chaisse and Jamieson Kirkwood, "Smart Courts, Smart Contracts, and the Future of Online Dispute Resolution," *Stanford Journal of Blockchain Law & Policy* 5, no. 1 (2022): 64–65.

11 American Bar Association, "Online Dispute Resolution in the United States," September 2020, at 2, https://www.americanbar.org/content/dam/aba/administrative/center-for-innovation/odrvisualization report.pdf.

12 Statistical data acquired by Ebner and Greenberg, through correspondence with the National Center for State Courts of the United States in 2018; see Noam Ebner and Elayne E. Greenberg, "Strengthening Online Dispute Resolution Justice," *Washington University Journal of Law & Policy* 63, no. 1 (2020): 82.

13 House of Commons Constitutional Affairs Committee, *The Courts: Small Claims, First Report of Session 2005–06* (HC519, December 6, 2005), Ev29.

14 Lord Justice Briggs, "Civil Courts Structure Review: Final Report," Judiciary of England and Wales, July 2016, https://www.judiciary.uk/guidance-and-resources/civil-courts-structure-review-final-report/.

15 Terence Etherton, "Rule-Making for a Digital Court Process: The Civil Procedure Rules 20th Anniversary Conference, 2019," in *The Civil Procedure Rules at 20*, ed. Andrew Higgins (Oxford: Oxford University Press, 2020), 57, https://doi.org/10.1093/oso/9780198863182.001.0001.

MCOL, has issued over 472,000 claims since its launch in March 2018 through February 2024.[16]

Among civil law countries, taking Swiss as an example, the digitization of the Swiss judicial system has unfolded in three phases. The first phase involved the small-scale electronic transfer of parts of the litigation process beginning in 2005, exemplified by the eSchKG online debt enforcement project launched in January 2007 and the Swiss government's e-government reform, with the first Swiss e-government cooperation framework agreement coming into effect in 2008.[17] The second phase proceeded with the commencement of the Electronic Signature Act in January 2017, which systematically introduced the first ODR rules in the Swiss judicial system and transformed fundamental functions such as online filing and service of documents. The third phase, which began with the official launch of Justitia 4.0 in 2019 and continues to the present day, has seen the Swiss justice system undertake a comprehensive shift toward digitization, with the core objective of achieving safe digital justice. Justitia 4.0 is developing a system for electronic communication within the judicial system and access to files. Meanwhile, the amended Civil Procedure Code, with its newly added online court provisions, will come into force on January 1, 2025.[18]

An observation drawn from the developments in the aforementioned countries is that, while the idea of integrating ICT into the court system has been around for a long time, online litigation that complements or replaces traditional methods has only begun to develop substantively in the latter half of the 2010s.

One reason for the accelerated growth of ODR in the private sector is the demands of business development and competitive pressures. If ODR service providers fail to provide better services, users will switch to other competent service providers. The public sector, however, has been able to resist offering ODR services without fear of user migration because there is no alternative. Nonetheless, there is increasing pressure on the public sector to provide online mechanisms, not because of competitive pressures, but due to what has been termed the "expectation of mobility" problem. This arises when consumers' experiences with one

16 HM Courts & Tribunals Services, "Fact Sheet: Online Civil Money Claims," February 27, 2024, https://www.gov.uk/government/publications/hmcts-reform-civil-fact-sheets/fact-sheet-online-civil-money-claims.

17 European Commission, "eGovernment in Switzerland," February 2016, at 11, https://joinup.ec.europa.eu/sites/default/files/inline-files/eGovernment%20in%20Switzerland%20-%20February%202016%20-%20Edition%2010_0%20-%20v3_00.pdf.

18 The Swiss Civil Procedure Code (currently in force since September 1, 2023, Swiss CPC) only contains rules on electronic service and does not provide for rules on online hearing. However, the latest revision of Swiss CPC (expected to enter into force on January 1, 2025, Swiss CPC 2025) has added new provisions on online hearing. Articles 141a and 141b of Swiss CPC 2025 provide for basic principles and requirements of using electronic equipment for audio or video transmission. Article 170a, Article 187.1, and Article 193 of Swiss CPC 2025 respectively stipulate requirements on examination of witness, inquiries by expert, and questioning of parties and the evidence given by videoconference. See Swiss CPC (all editions), accessed August 31, 2024, https://www.fedlex.admin.ch/eli/cc/2010/262/en.

product shape their expectations of other products. For example, people accustomed to eBay and Taobao ODR services will eventually question why their local small-claims court is so inconvenient and inefficient compared to the dispute resolution mechanism of internet platforms.

Over the years, the work of courts has been increasingly shaped by digital technology. The use of computers and the internet has become routine in courthouses and courtrooms. Case management has become more efficient and digitized. Electronic evidence is legally accepted, and legal databases are available online, often free of charge. However, most of the technological integration into the court system over the past two decades has been driven by the desire to improve "efficiency," typically in response to financial considerations, such as budget cuts.[19] Rarely has there been a focus on providing new tools and resources to manage disputes. ODR mechanisms organized by private companies, however, have overcome physical, geographical, and even psychological boundaries in dealing with disputes.

Dispute resolution in courts is experiencing three significant technological and methodological transformations due to the online conduct of court procedures and the substantive introduction of technology into the judicial process. Firstly, there is a shift from physical to virtual or semi-virtual environments. Fully online platforms, or hybrid platforms that integrate in-person presence with online activities, are breaking down the traditional physical boundaries and specialized spaces that have characterized court processes for centuries. Individuals can now use the online court platforms to evaluate their legal position, communicate with other parties, and have their disputes adjudicated by a third party without the need for physical court appearances or adherence to court hours. This advantage of ODR process was initially realized in small-claims cases but is progressively being applied to other contexts.

Secondly, there has been a shift from human intervention and decision-making to an automated matching process. ODR introduces algorithms into the judicial decision-making process. These algorithms can enhance fairness by curbing human discretion, increasing consistency and reducing bias. However, they can also perpetuate biases, hindering the quest for justice.[20] Much depends on the ability to define the values underlying the algorithm's design and to rigorously monitor its operation. Additionally, courts are placing greater emphasis on the "user experience" when designing software, which is a new area of focus for court program designers. New methods are also being deployed to evaluate the user experience, with feedback being incorporated into the design and modification of the software.

The third and final shift of ODR in court is from a dispute resolution model that focuses on certainty to one that emphasizes the prevention of disputes through the

19 Briggs, "Civil Courts Structure Review," [5.36] and [6.66]; Catrina Denvir and Amanda Darshini Selvarajah, "Safeguarding Access to Justice in the Age of the Online Court," *Modern Law Review* 85, no. 1 (2022): 28, https://doi.org/10.1111/1468-2230.12670.

20 Pauline T. Kim, "Data-Driven Discrimination at Work," *William & Mary Law Review* 58, no. 3 (2017): 860.

collection, use, and reuse of data. As courts increasingly rely on digital technologies and ODR systems, they are recognizing data as a core element of dispute resolution. Data and digital platforms will play a key role in enabling court systems to operate in a new realm: preventing disputes and continuously improving litigation processes through data analysis.

There is still much work to be done in terms of improving ODR systems. In the public sector, the implementation of ODR is still affected by technological capacities, system interoperability, scalability, automation, business intelligence, cost efficiency, and vendor independence, among other factors. These challenges often stem from a combination of internal functional issues, such as limited budgets, restrictive policies, overly complex operational workflows, lack of trained personnel, and resistance to change, as well as external factors, such as language barriers and the rising cost of software development.

Contents of digital justice

Access to justice is one of the fundamental principles of the rule of law. The relationship between digital justice and ODR has been widely discussed in the literature.[21]

The Access to Justice Movement in the United States of the 1960s focused on lowering litigation costs for low-income litigants and levelling the playing field for those who previously could not reach the courts.[22] However, this approach remains court-centric. It is argued that the goal of ODR is to design new processes and institutions that are usable both in and out of court.[23] In discussing the relationship between online litigation and justice, Susskind suggests adopting a broader perspective to understand the notion of access to justice as a four-layer model: legal health promotion, dispute avoidance, dispute containment, and authoritative dispute resolution.[24]

In the European context more specifically, the establishing ODR mechanisms must consider the impact of these mechanisms on the requirements of Article 6, "Right to a Fair Trial," and Article 13, "Right to an Effective Remedy," of the European Convention on Human Rights (ECHR). A study for the Council of Europe's Committee on European Legal Co-operation (CDCJ) in August 2018 analyzed the compatibility of ODR with the right to a fair trial, including the challenges and opportunities that ODR presents, such as greater access to justice and enhanced

21 J. J. Prescott, "Using ODR Platforms to Level the Playing Field," in *Legal Tech and Future of Civil Justice*, ed. David Freeman Engstrom (Cambridge: Cambridge University Press, 2023), 287, https://doi.org/10.1017/9781009255301; Denvir and Selvarajah, "Safeguarding Access to Justice," 25.

22 Ethan Katsh and Orna Rabinovich-Einy, *Digital Justice: Technology and the Internet of Disputes* (Oxford: Oxford University Press, 2017), 40–41, https://doi.org/10.1093/acprof:oso/9780190464585.001.0001.

23 Katsh and Rabinovich-Einy, *Digital Justice*, 41.

24 Richard Susskind, *Online Courts and the Future of Justice* (Oxford: Oxford University Press, 2019), 113, https://doi.org/10.1093/oso/9780198838364.001.0001.

due process.[25] Furthermore, it explored whether ODR could provide new avenues for redressing human rights violations under the ECHR.

Generally speaking, the requirement of "access to justice" in the field of ODR can be understood as necessitating that the dispute resolver possess a "toolbox" for resolving disputes and that these tools are practically accessible, providing parties with the opportunity to resolve their disputes. A distinction should be made regarding the requirement of access to justice between different ODR tools, such as arbitration, online litigation, or private ordering, based on their inherent characteristics and values. These discussions suggest that the relationship between ODR and justice warrants further examination. Some practices from Chinese ODR can provide valuable insight in this context.

In the area of arbitration, it is important to distinguish between consumer disputes and commercial disputes among businesses. To date, the use of arbitration to resolve consumer disputes remains a matter of debate, with different jurisdictions having different laws and regulations. In the United States, large corporations routinely require consumers to resolve disputes through arbitration by imposing arbitration clauses that prevent consumers from pursuing class action lawsuits. Meanwhile, in China, the mandatory arbitration clause used by the Ofo app, a bicycle-sharing service, caused considerable controversy. Limiting consumer remedies through online contracts was seen as a form of "digital injustice," especially when arbitration is impractical or too costly, yet a valid arbitration agreement prevents litigation. In adjudicating of such consumer disputes, the Chinese court can give weight to concerns that such arbitration clauses "have the effect of excluding or restricting the rights of the consumers and are unfair and unreasonable to the consumers."[26]

In international commercial arbitration, leading international arbitration institutions have released special rules for online arbitration in response to the COVID-19 pandemic. Arbitrators and staff at these arbitration institutions hold divergent views on conducting online arbitration. Some arbitrators appreciate the online approach for its capability and convenience, particularly regarding the choice of time and place. Others value the in-person experience, especially for complex international disputes, where convenience or cost for organizing in-person hearings is rarely of any concern, except in extraordinary circumstances, such as when witnesses could not attend hearing because they were barred from entering a country. It is evident that the future of international arbitration will involve a hybrid of online and offline activities. The capacity of arbitration to deliver fairness and justice, and to achieve the desired outcomes for parties in large, complex international commercial disputes, depends on both the inherent values and characteristics of the arbitration system and the integration of technology into practice.

As online arbitration becomes a reality and a necessity, concerns regarding the validity of arbitration clauses under the existing legal framework or the applicability

25 European Committee on Legal Co-operation, "Technical Study on Online Dispute Resolution Mechanisms," August 1, 2018, https://rm.coe.int/cdcj-2018-5e-technical-study-odr/1680913249.

26 Civil Code of the People's Republic of China (in force since January 1, 2021), Article 496.

of the law diminish in significance. Instead, it becomes imperative to establish a new legal framework to facilitate the development of online arbitration. Currently, China is contemplating the inclusion of the digitalization of arbitral proceedings in the draft proposal for a new arbitration law.[27] While the legislative process is likely to lag behind the development of practice, the requirements for fairness and justice in online arbitration can still be achieved within the existing legal framework without amending current laws. For instance, when enforcing a foreign arbitral award under the Convention on the Recognition and Enforcement of Foreign Arbitral Awards, a Chinese court could assess whether the award complied with the due process provisions of Article 5, paragraph 1 (e) of the Convention, even if the process was wholly or partly online.

Besides arbitration, the utilization of ODR in litigation presents a distinctive perspective concerning the conception of digital justice. Initially, ODR was introduced to resolve simple, low-value disputes or to overcome geographical barriers, thereby reducing costs for the parties involved. These proceedings are conducted online, either synchronously or asynchronously, in many cases without legal representation, thus further reducing the costs for the parties. However, the introduction of even the simplest, most minimalist ODR processes reflects a changing understanding of the role that technology can and should play in the delivery of legal services. Conversely, even truly "simple" cases may not be necessarily simple enough for the ODR system to handle, as comparing complexity with the traditional, often adversarial, litigatory methods might be unhelpful.[28] Thus, as courts begin to adopt ODR, a fundamental question arises: "Is court a service or a place?"[29] The answer to this question depends on the path taken by different jurisdictions to define and realize digital justice. A representative stance in common law jurisdictions would prioritize adversarial justice, whereas China would place greater emphasis on the concepts of "diversified dispute resolution," placing litigation as services in combination with mediation, examined in Chapter 5.

Finally, as technology is integrated into dispute resolution, the landscape of dispute resolution is evolving and expanding. The core focus is shifting away from the activity of "resolution" per se to the design of software at the pre-resolution stage, the analysis of data at the post-resolution stage, and the prevention of disputes. Whereas dispute resolution is a reactive mechanism available to aggrieved parties, dispute prevention relies on tracking, predicting, and preventing disputes. Although dispute prevention may not directly contribute to "access to justice," it can reduce the incidence of injustice and alleviate the barriers to bringing disputes to justice. In this context, the understanding of technology and ODR has shifted

27 Arbitration Law of the People's Republic of China (amendment draft), Article 30, accessed August 31, 2024, https://zqyj.chinalaw.gov.cn/h5/readmore?listType=&id=4518.

28 Norman W. Spaulding, "Online Dispute Resolution and the End of Adversarial Justice?," in *Legal Tech and Future of Civil Justice*, ed. David Freeman Engstrom (Cambridge: Cambridge University Press, 2023), 261–62, https://doi.org/10.1017/9781009255301.

29 Susskind, *Online Courts*, 95.

from an emphasis on convenience to an emphasis on the collection, use, and reuse of data to prevent disputes from arising. Dispute prevention is no longer on the periphery of dispute resolution activities; it is becoming part of dispute management and a core element of ODR.

Since data recording and the analysis and utilization of such data are central to dispute prevention, the key questions are who has access to the data and who is responsible for dispute prevention. Problems can arise when platforms use algorithms for dispute prevention, especially if data is used for the benefit of the company at the expense of the users.

In 2010, Facebook conducted an experiment to determine if it could influence the outcome of an election by selectively promoting information about specific candidates to targeted user groups.[30] This case exemplifies the immense power that large platforms, with access to extensive data on millions of users, hold and the potential for this power to be used and misused. This naturally leads to discussions about the need for regulating private platforms. Beyond the private, for-profit nature of these platforms, it is worth noting that dispute prevention suffers more from the absence of transparent rules and oversight mechanisms than does the field of dispute resolution. One of the main challenges in the new and expanding field of online dispute prevention will be the formulation of appropriate guidelines for dispute prevention activities and the monitoring of their enforcement. The design and implementation of both dispute resolution and dispute prevention in ODR will ultimately determine the effectiveness and accessibility of justice.

By synthesizing all the aforementioned elements, it is contended that various ODR mechanisms can fulfil different values in the delivery of justice. Although individual mechanisms must still meet the general criteria for dispute resolution, such as fairness, transparency, and accessibility, it is crucial to acknowledge the unique values that each ODR mechanism brings to the table. The justice that ODR can ultimately deliver should be viewed from the perspective of the entire ODR system, rather than focusing on the individual mechanisms. The whole is greater than the sum of all its parts. A vision of "systematic access to justice" should be the goal and aspiration of ODR.

Challenges and opportunities for ODR in China

Platform monopoly and private ODR

Extensive literature has explored the various private dispute resolution mechanisms that have emerged online. As a private order form on the internet, dispute resolution mechanisms on online platforms often have commonalities, especially when their business models are similar. For example, Taobao's ODR bears notable similarities to eBay's regarding reputation mechanisms and crowdsourced

30 Jonathan Zittrain, "Facebook Could Decide an Election without Anyone Ever Finding Out," *The New Statesman*, June 3, 2014, https://www.newstatesman.com/science-tech/2014/06/facebook-could-decide-election-without-anyone-ever-finding-out.

ODR. Chapter 3 will delve into the specifics of private ODR systems, including those in China. However, it is important to first examine the issue of platform monopoly that has garnered considerable attention in major economies in recent years.

The evolution of economic patterns has increasingly influenced people's daily lives. During this economic transformation, the tracking of user information has progressed from simple cookies in the early stage to sophisticated technological tools, culminating in the formation of big data. Consequently, platforms have significantly enhanced their ability to access, exploit, and reproduce user data. In essence, platforms control information and data, and the provision of public goods and public life in the information society heavily depends on them. Hence, it may be said that the basic gateway to "social life" is effectively controlled by these platforms. For some digital giants with monopoly power, this control impacts the public interest and leaves users vulnerable to exploitation and manipulation.

Dispute resolution organized by online platforms initially represents private autonomy. However, the exponential growth of power platforms raises a new question: If large digital enterprises assume characteristics akin to public institutions, should the requirements for their ODR be adjusted accordingly? The answer to this question depends on the ongoing debate about how to classify large internet platforms and regulate their actions.

The digital giants of today's world are primarily based in either the United States or China. To foster the development of the digital industry, the United States has adopted a laissez-faire approach, refraining from heavy intervention in the digital market. Similarly, China has also taken a cautious and lenient regulatory stance toward the internet industry, rather than enforcing competition law stringently. However, global antitrust policies are changing. Major economies have recognized that strengthening platform regulation offers several advantages, including promoting digital market development, enhancing innovation and fair competition, and safeguarding consumer interests. As a result, initiatives bolstering antitrust enforcement, improving legal norms, and enhancing regulatory capacity have become priorities among the economic and legal tasks of the Chinese government.

In the United States, antitrust concerns, marginalized for years, have returned to the forefront of political discourse. The platform economy is characterized by a strong network effect, a natural tendency toward monopolization, and the provision of goods and services that significantly impact the public interest. Consequently, the regulation of public utilities has once again come into the spotlight. In recent years, there have been heated discussions on the public character of platforms and the need for regulation, ranging from proposals to classify platforms as "information monopolists"[31] and "common carriers" of information[32] to analyses

31 Tim Wu, "In the Grip of the New Monopolists," *Wall Street Journals*, November 13, 2010.

32 Bill Davidow, "Is Apple a Common Carrier?," *Forbes*, April 20, 2011. The concept of common carrier can be traced back to England in the 15th century. Later, the common law gradually developed the scope of common carriers to include all forms of carriers and transportation-related occupations.

of "platform neutrality"[33] and "search neutrality"[34] and advocacy for platforms as "essential facilities"[35] and "new public utilities."[36]

Some Chinese scholars argue that competition policy and anti-monopoly law hold the key to addressing the problem of platform monopolies. However, a more effective approach, it is submitted, would be to revise the anti-monopoly methodology and philosophy, by treating digital giants as new public utilities subject to a new regulatory framework.

Given the public nature of platforms and the responsibilities they should bear, it has been suggested that online platforms possess quasi-administrative powers. Regulation of them should draw from the experience of regulating public powers. This implies that ODR organized by platforms with a public character must also comply with the standards required for public ODR. These requirements may increase as platforms develop and become more integral to public life. However, the primary value of dispute resolution provided by platforms lies in offering users a timely, effective, and inexpensive alternative for problem-solving. Platform-organized dispute resolution does not need to meet the fairness and justice standards expected of judicial institutions.

Scholarship in the United States has highlighted a potential conflict between ODR and adversarial justice. ODR is perceived as a disruptive innovation initiated by Silicon Valley liberals underpinning notions such as access to justice, aiming to challenge the traditional establishment of judges and lawyers. This perception gives rise to both optimism and skepticism, similar to other disruptive innovations. A notable example is Uber, which purportedly promotes the interests of customers and cabdrivers against the corrupt monopoly of cab companies. Ironically, as Uber gained success, it increasingly began to treat consumers and drivers much like the very monopoly it "disrupted" did.[37]

The situation in China is fundamentally different in this regard. There is no discursive struggle, ideological antagonism, or competition between private ODR and

33 See Frank Pasquale, "Platform Neutrality: Enhancing Freedom of Expression in Spheres of Private Power," *Theoretical Inquiries into Law* 17 (2016): 487; Wei Gao and Yao Yang, "Chaining Cyber-Titans to Neutrality: An Updated Common Carrier Approach to Regulate Platform Service Providers," *Computer Law & Security Review* 31 (2015): 412, https://doi.org/10.1016/j.clsr.2015.03.003.

34 Daniel A. Crane, "After Search Neutrality: Drawing a Line Between Promotion and Demotion," *I/S: A Journal of Law and Policy* 9, no. 3 (2014): 397; Frank Pasquale, "Internet Non-discrimination Principles: Commercial Ethics for Carriers and Search Engines," *University of Chicago Legal Forum* (2008): 276.

35 Lina M. Khan, "Amazon's Antitrust Paradox," *Yale Law Journal* 126 (2017): 800; Tom Wheeler, Phil Verveer, and Gene Kimmelman, "New Digital Realities; New Oversight Solutions in the U.S.: The Case for a Digital Platform Agency and a New Approach to Regulatory Oversight," August 2020, at 34–36, https://shorensteincenter.org/wp-content/uploads/2020/08/New-Digital-Realities_August-2020.pdf.

36 For supporting arguments, see K. Sabeel Rahman, "The New Utilities: Private Power, Social Infrastructure, and the Revival of the Public Utility Concept," *Cardozo Law Review* 39 (2018): 1668. For opposing views, see Adam Thierer, "The Perils of Classifying Social Media Platforms as Public Utilities," *CommLaw Conspectus* 21 (2013): 274.

37 Spaulding, "Online Dispute Resolution," 252.

public ODR providers. Unlike in the United States, ODR in China is not driven by technology companies aiming to alter or challenge the judicial system. In China, the digitization of the court system is spearheaded by the courts themselves, with technology companies providing support as needed. Private ODR and public ODR work together to serve the larger, unified goals of dispute resolution and social governance.

Digitalization of the courts in China

Incidentally, the court occupies center stage in Chinese ODR. China is home to both the world's largest online community and the largest court network. Notably, the Supreme People's Court (SPC) operates China Judgments Online,[38] an expansive public access database hosting over 140 million judgments and other court documents, making it the largest repository of judicial decisions globally.[39] This pioneering spirit continues with initiatives such as China Court Trial Online, which has live streamed over 20 million trials and made more than 17 million recorded sessions available online. The integration of artificial intelligence in various aspects of the judiciary, from sentencing guidelines to judgment drafting, represents another compelling aspect of this dynamic transformation. In response, the SPC launched an extensive online court system encompassing all the more than 3,500 courts in China, covering civil, administrative, and criminal litigation. However, these developments have received relatively limited scholarly attention, particularly regarding their potential implications for enhancing access to justice and ODR.

From 2018 to 2023, China's court informatization advanced exponentially. The SPC first proposed the concept of the "smart courts" in July 2015, aiming to modernize trial systems and capabilities by fully utilizing technologies such as the internet, cloud computing, big data, and AI. This initiative sought to achieve highly intelligent operation and management of the court, ensuring fairness and efficiency and improving judicial credibility. In July 2019, the SPC announced its policy commitment to "one-stop, diversified dispute resolution," advocating for the integration of litigation and non-litigation procedures, allowing disputes to be resolved prior to litigation through diversified dispute resolution mechanisms.[40] Even during formal litigation, litigation and mediation are interwoven, with ongoing litigation encouraged to be resolved through judge-led mediation whenever possible.

It is notable that international scholarship on the topic of China's digitization of justice often focuses on the establishment of new institutions, such as the three

38 The seemingly official spelling used on the CJO website is "Judgements."

39 Lu Xu, *Chinese Legal Reforms: Transformations in a Decade* (Leiden: Brill, 2024), 83, https://doi.org/10.1163/9789004537125.

40 "Opinions of the Supreme People's Court on Building One-stop Diversified Dispute Resolution Mechanisms and One-stop Litigant Service Centers最高人民法院关于建设一站式多元解纷机制一站式诉讼服务中心的意见" (SPC Issue 2019/No. 19, July 31, 2019).

internet courts, which are the first of their kind globally, or the use of specific technological tools in the court system.[41] However, the Chinese judiciary's vision and strategy of "one-stop diversified dispute resolution" and smart courts construction, which integrate litigation with mediation, actually represent a more holistic approach aimed at modernizing court services and enhancing dispute resolution. The "informatization" of court and "smart courts construction" encompass a wide range of court work, including "smart trial," "smart litigation service," "smart execution," "application of judicial big data," and "use of blockchain technology in the judiciary." These developments should be examined holistically and doctrinally from the perspective of administration of justice.

The construction of online courts in China follows a top-down process under a top-level design. The SPC takes the lead in promulgating rules and guiding the four levels of courts to collaborate in implementation. The internal departments involved in these endeavors include not only the adjudication divisions, which handle trials and mediation, but also the case-filing division (*li'an ting*), which manage the entry of disputes into litigation and seek to reduce their number through various non-litigatory measures. Doctrinally, therefore, China's smart courts concept encompasses dispute prevention, dispute containment, and dispute resolution.

A series of regulations and policies to promote the digitalization of the court system has been promulgated to this end, including the rules for online operation, online litigation, online mediation, and the use of blockchain and artificial intelligence. The amended Civil Procedure Law of 2021 clarifies that all civil litigation can be conducted online by endorsing all online litigation activities with the same legal effect as their offline counterparts, thereby providing a solid legal basis for online litigation.[42]

There are two models for conducting online litigation in China's domestic courts. The first is the full-process online trial model. Currently, most cases in the three internet courts are fully online. Given that the jurisdiction of internet courts is limited to disputes involving the internet, the parties are generally expected to be able to participate online. The convenience and low cost of online litigation also encourage parties to choose this method. From an evidentiary standpoint, the evidence is typically generated and retained online. The internet courts rely on their inter-departmental data platform to facilitate the online submission of evidence, which is primarily in electronic form, largely eliminating the need for paper copies. The internet courts have established judicial blockchains where relevant evidence is uploaded for storage, fixation, and collection, addressing the issue of evidence authenticity online. The litigation platforms of the three internet courts

41 Huang-Chih Sung, "Can Online Courts Promote Access to Justice? A Case Study of the Internet Courts in China," *Computer Law & Security Review* 39 (2020): 105461, https://doi.org/10.1016/j.clsr.2020.105461; Liyuan Wang, "Application of Information Technology in Judicial Field: The Development Model of Online Litigation in China," *Computer Law & Security Review* 52 (2024): 105936, https://doi.org/10.1016/j.clsr.2024.105936.

42 Civil Procedure Law of the People's Republic of China, Article 16.

have also advanced technical infrastructure, such as face recognition, image recognition, and voice recognition, ensuring the smooth conduct of the entire online trial process.

The second model of online litigation is the "online and offline" hybrid model. Except the three internet courts, nearly all the over 3,500 Chinese courts have adopted this parallel approach, relying on the "People's Court Online Services" platform or the online litigation platforms developed by the courts themselves. Depending on the choice of litigants and the specific circumstances of the case, any part of the litigation process, including the courtroom hearing, can be conducted online or offline. The choice of one party as to online or offline participation does not preclude the other party from selecting a different option. If one party chooses online participation and the other prefers attendance in person, the proceeding will be a hybrid of online and in-person event.[43]

Meanwhile, the construction of smart courts in China has entered "phase 4.0," shifting its focus to artificial intelligence and big data management. The Chinese judiciary duly noted in January 2023 that a court in Colombia issued a judgment composed with the assistance of an artificial intelligence (AI) question-and-answer tool (ChatGPT), the first of its kind globally.[44] This development indicates that AI will gradually be integrated into future judicial work. In judicial trials, AI assists in judgment-making, with its core function based on "calculation" and instrumental rationality, which tends to prioritize reasonableness and efficiency. However, judicial trials also involve emotional and legal reasoning, as well as the experience of the adjudicating personnel, requiring clear analysis and value judgment – elements that may not align with instrumental rationality. The use of AI in judicial trials may weaken traditional judicial principles, such as autonomy and independence. Additionally, the construction of smart courts often involves technology outsourcing to data service providers to build AI and big data platforms, raising concerns about the reasonable handling of the vast amounts of personal information of litigation participants.

By 2021, the SPC announced that a one-stop diversified dispute resolution and litigation service system had been essentially constructed. More cases were successfully mediated before they were litigated, leading to the first decline of the court's litigation caseload in more than a decade.[45] The logistics of online litigation have become more streamlined and convenient, with all courts nationwide using the Mobile Micro Court (*yidong wei fayuan*) app. This app is interconnected with

43 Wei Gao and Lu Xu, "Online Courts in China: A New Hybrid Model for Access to Justice," *The China Review* 25 (2025).

44 Zhang Chen 张晨, "What Role Shall AI Paly in Judicial Adjudication 人工智能在司法审判中应扮演什么角色," *Legal Daily* 法治日报, March 30, at 2023, http://epaper.legaldaily.com.cn/fzrb/content/20230330/Articel06002GN.htm.

45 Ministry of Justice of the People's Republic of China, "Decrease for the First Time in Fifteen Years, What Leads to the Decrease in Civil Litigation Caseload? 持续增长15年后首次下降，法院受理民事案件数量为何如此之变?" March 9, 2021, https://www.moj.gov.cn/pub/sfbgw/zwgkztzl/2021nzt/qglh2021/qglh2021bgyqd/bgzgrmfygzbg/202103/t20210309_444937.html.

the court's mediation platform, preservation platform, commissioned appraisal platform, and trial flow and court fees payment systems across the country. This integrated system provides parties with 29 online litigation services, including case filing, inquiries, payment of fees, mediation, court hearings, preservation, and commissioned appraisal, all accessible through a single public service portal.[46]

In a broader context, China is striving to construct a new type of litigation process characterized by greater flexibility, enhanced efficiency, and a balanced approach to fairness and justice. It is not only the convenience and reduced cost of online proceedings that attract parties, but also the opportunity to engage in more amicable proceedings with guaranteed rights. Practices and understandings of justice vary from country to country due to differences in their established legal systems. Furthermore, it is very likely that the values and functions of litigation will change as digital processes are integrated with court procedures. For instance, the development of online courts in the United States has been decentralized, requiring each state to introduce, experiment with, consider, and implement different initiatives and innovations. China, in contrast, has adopted a nationally implemented, top-down approach. Studies in the United States have also shown that while ODR can reduce default judgments and promote justice, it may actually lengthen litigation and reduce efficiency.[47] This reflects the emphasis in the US judicial process on adversarialism and its role in achieving justice. Justice in the Chinese court follows a completely different philosophy, which will be further analyzed in Chapter 5.

New landscape of cross-border dispute resolution

International arbitration has long been one of the most prominent methods of settling international disputes. In its early stages, online arbitration was not as appealing as its promoters had anticipated. Some questioned the future of online arbitration, believed it naïve for arbitrators and lawyers to become accustomed to online arbitration. There have always been doubts regarding the feasibility of online arbitration, particularly concerning the arbitration agreement, arbitration process, and enforcement of the award.[48]

The COVID-19 pandemic, as an unexpected external factor, marked a turning point in the development of online arbitration. The operations of international arbitration institutions at physical offices were severely disrupted by the pandemic. Major international arbitration institutions adopted online arbitration as a crucial alternative mode of work and swiftly issued guidance documents and took steps to

46 The Supreme People's Court of the People's Republic of China, "Chines Courts Received Over Ten Million Cases Through Online Filing in 2020," April 2021, https://www.court.gov.cn/shenpan/xiangqing/296401.html.

47 J. J. Prescott and Alexander Sanchez, "Platform Procedure: Using Technology to Facilitate (Efficient) Civil Settlement," in *Selection and Decision in Judicial Process Around the World*, ed. Yun-Chien Chang (Cambridge: Cambridge University Press, 2020), 30–72.

48 Jasna Arsic, "International Commercial Arbitration on the Internet: Has the Future Come Too Early?," *Journal of International Arbitration* 14 (1997): 209.

promote digitalization. On April 16, 2020, 13 international arbitration institutions released a joint statement encouraging parties and arbitrators to explore the impact of the crisis and potential mitigation strategies through advanced case management. In response to the impact of the pandemic, China International Economic and Trade Arbitration Commission (CIETAC) issued its "Guidelines on Proceeding with Arbitration Actively and Properly During the COVID-19 Pandemic" in 2020, aiming to effectively mitigate the effects of the pandemic. The global arbitration community has now fully embraced digitalization. As major arbitration centers continue to use technology, some of their rules have been amended, and guidelines have been issued to accommodate the use of technologies. The impact of the pandemic on arbitration, much like its impact on the legal profession, is irreversible.[49] In a relatively short period of time, nearly half of 293 arbitration institutions in China have developed some online arbitration rules and service capacities, as examined in Chapter 4.

Additionally, online arbitration can be integrated with other dispute resolution mechanisms, such as online mediation, online courts, and various ODR tools or platforms, to achieve China's goal of diversified dispute resolution in cross-border dispute resolution. This approach is crucial both for facilitating the Belt and Road Initiative (BRI) and constructing China's one-stop commercial courts.

The BRI is a massive international endeavor by China aimed at enhancing regional connectivity and fostering a brighter economic future. Integral to this initiative is the challenge of resolving disputes among the diverse parties involved. Traditional methods of dispute resolution have proven complex and often inefficient, given the vast geographical spread and varied legal systems of BRI countries. In this context, ODR, particularly in its advanced forms with smart courts and smart contracts, emerges as a vital tool for addressing these challenges.

On January 23, 2018, the Central Committee of the Communist Party of China adopted the official policy of establishing BRI international commercial dispute resolution mechanisms and institutions, signaling a significant advancement in China's international commercial dispute settlement framework.[50] This initiative announced the creation of the International Commercial Court as a subsidiary tribunal of the SPC. This development is pivotal in establishing a comprehensive, one-stop mechanism for resolving international commercial disputes related to the BRI, with the International Commercial Court as the cornerstone of this new system.

The International Commercial Court integrates mediation, arbitration, and litigation to create a "one-stop," "diversified" international commercial dispute resolution platform. The SPC issued detailed guidelines for its operation, which took

49 Kathleen Lynn, "The Legal World Will Never Be the Same After COVID-19," *New York State Bar Association*, April 22, 2020, https://nysba.org/the-legal-world-will-never-be-the-same-after-covid-19/.

50 "Opinions on Establishing 'One Belt One Road' International Commercial Dispute Resolution Mechanisms and Institutions 关于建立'一带一路'国际商事争端解决机制和机构的意见," *Xinhua News Agency* 新华社, June 27, 2018, https://www.gov.cn/zhengce/2018-06/27/content_5301657.htm.

effect on January 30, 2024.[51] Subsequently, in March 2024, an enhanced version of the SPC's one-stop diversified international commercial dispute resolution platform was officially launched on the International Commercial Court's website.[52]

The "One-Stop" Platform of Diversified Dispute Resolution comprises four functional modules: mediation services, arbitration services, litigation services, and auxiliary services (for impartial evaluation and case scheduling). Specifically, this platform, based on the International Commercial Court website, integrates the SPC Litigation Service Network, the People's Court Online Preservation System, the People's Court Mediation Platform, the People's Court Internet Unified Identity Authentication System, the SPC Case Handling Platform, and the systems of ten international commercial arbitration institutions and two international commercial mediation institutions. After logging in, parties can choose from various dispute resolution methods and corresponding institutions based on their needs, including impartial evaluation, mediation, arbitration, and litigation.

China actively promotes close collaboration and integration between courts and commercial mediation organizations. For instance, the BRI International Commercial Mediation Center collaborates with the Beijing Fourth Intermediate People's Court. Similarly, the Shanghai Economic and Trade Commercial Mediation Center collaborates with the Shanghai First, Second, and Third Intermediate People's Courts, as well as the Pudong Free Trade Zone People's Court. There are notable conjoined efforts by Chinese courts, arbitration institutions, and mediation organizations in constructing the BRI cross-border e-commerce online dispute resolution mechanism, facilitating the establishment of an online dispute resolution center involving all three sectors.

The establishment of the BRI online dispute resolution center does not currently aim for the unification of legal regulations and their application among countries along the route. Instead, it integrates negotiation, mediation, arbitration, and other dispute resolution methods to meet the needs of the cross-border e-commerce market, providing fair and efficient dispute resolution and fostering judicial mutual trust among the parties. Led by China, the initiative encourages participation from countries along the route in formulating principles and rules in this field, aiming to enhance the development of cross-border e-commerce between China and these countries, thereby fulfilling the common aspirations of BRI countries.

The approach and perspective of this book

Often driven by perceived barriers or issues inherent in social interactions, theory development is formulated as a way to explain and predict behavior and dynamics in context. The word "theory" is derived from the ancient Greek verb *theorein*, which means "to view" or "to observe." Thus, *theory* can be broadly defined

51 Supreme People's Court, "Guidelines on the Work of the 'One-Stop' Platform for Pluralistic Settlement of International Commercial Disputes (for Trial Implementation) '一站式'国际商事纠纷多元化解决平台工作指引(试行)" (SPC 2023/No. 247, December 22, 2023).

52 https://cicc.court.gov.cn/pc

as "observation." This etymological background is significant, reminding us that theory is a specific way of viewing objects and relating them within a particular type of discourse.

In formulating the theory about the emergence of ODR, several important observations have been made about its development over the past decades. Conley Tyler's investigation of 115 ODR websites in 2004 found that 82 appeared to be operational, 30 had stopped functioning, and the status of the remaining 3 was unknown.[53] The report gives the impression that new players were constantly entering the field, with ebb and flow akin to any industry. Most ODR initiatives have yet to achieve market implementation, with many early providers no longer active. Pearlstein, Hanson, and Ebner followed up on such observations in 2010 and found that of the 57 service providers identified by Conley Tyler as having launched by 2004 in North America, only 14 remained active.[54]

The same trend can be observed in China. Various ODR systems have emerged in recent years, including cyber courts, online arbitration, online mediation, internal ODR systems, and the China Internet Network Information Center domain name dispute resolution procedure. Not all have succeeded. The most successful initiatives are the domain name dispute resolution procedure administered by the CIETAC and Taobao's consumer dispute resolution mechanisms. An early, less-successful example was CIETAC's online arbitration, which adopted the online arbitration rules in 2009. It was proclaimed as a major breakthrough in the promotion of ODR and demonstrated CIETAC's efforts to increase the speed and ease of its dispute resolution process in the new era of information technology. However, the online arbitration of CIETAC was not as successful as expected. While CIETAC's traditional arbitration maintained a caseload of around 1,500 per year,[55] very few disputes were referred to CIETAC Online Arbitration in the decade following the release of these rules.

Some private entities in China have launched ODR websites, such as www.odr.com.cn and www.odrbeijing.com, but these efforts have also proved unsuccessful, with few disputes submitted and subsequent closures. As the overall picture of ODR and its individual components evolved over the years, this early history and data fall short of answering the question, "Is ODR a success?"

In China, online arbitration, which had not developed well for a long time, has become a real alternative due to the COVID-19 pandemic. Dispute resolution mechanisms previously considered more successful on Taobao, such as

53 Melissa Conley Tyler, "115 and Counting: The State of ODR 2004," in *Proceedings of the Third Annual Forum on Online Dispute Resolution*, eds. Melissa Conley Tyler, Ethan Katsh, and Daewon Choi (International Conflict Resolution Centre, 2004).

54 Arthur Pearlstein, Bryan Hanson, and Noam Ebner, "ODR in North America," in *Online Dispute Resolution: Theory and Practice*, eds. Mohamed S. Abdel Wahab, Ethan Katsh, and Daniel Rainey (The Hague: Eleven, 2012), 446.

55 Jiang Huiling 蒋惠岭, Long Fei 龙飞, and Wang Li 王丽, "Studies on the Dispute Resolution Mechanism for the Belt and Road (I) '一带一路'纠纷解决机制研究(上)," *China Institute of Applied Jurisprudence*, March 2018, at 41, http://yyfx.court.gov.cn/upload/file/2018/06/27/15/36/20180627153647_46393.pdf.

crowdsourced ODR, have recently ceased their services. The ever-changing ODR practices demand a reconsideration of what is meant by ODR after three decades of development. More importantly, while much discussion has focused on promoting ODR to protect consumer rights online and creating a legal framework for achieving such goals, little attention has been paid to one seemingly straightforward yet deceptively difficult question: Among the various ODR mechanisms, why do some succeed while others fail? In particular, how is the development of ODR in China different from that in other countries?

For the first question about the success or failure of ODR development, there are various reasons. The era of ODR has largely paralleled the development of the internet and the physical market. The typical answer in such a context is often superficial, blaming the ODR program for not being well-designed or for failing to meet the particular demands of online users. Cortes identified additional challenges that hinder the growth of consumer ODR: financing ODR, lack of uniform procedural standards, reluctance to participate in the ODR process, and lack of awareness.[56]

Unsatisfied with such generalities, this book seeks to present a more principled theoretical explanation. To comprehend ODR development and the institutional evolution process, it will examine exogenous ODR and endogenous ODR from the perspectives of institutional economics and game theory. Under this framework, exogenous ODR is externally designed based on traditional dispute resolution mechanisms, while endogenous ODR has evolved internally with innovative methods. The answer to the aforementioned question can be traced back to this exogenous-or-endogenous dichotomy. This book will illustrate how endogenous ODR and exogenous ODR are embedded in concrete and ongoing social relations, ultimately contributing to the success and failure of ODR processes. The key issue determining the effectiveness of exogenous ODR is the challenge of embedding exogenous rules into a new environment. This provides a new explanation for the continued slow adoption of ODR that seeks to imitate offline practices in the vastly different context of the online environment. Regarding endogenous ODR, it is evident that private ordering developed earlier and has been more effective for a relatively long period because it is endogenous and socially embedded.

This analytical framework was first proposed in the author's 2017 article titled "The Success and Failure of Online Dispute Resolution." Since then, the practice of ODR has evolved further, but this analytical framework still holds considerable explanatory power, especially with further revision and refinement in the details and the analysis of new materials in view of the latest developments. For example, when this framework was originally proposed, online courts in China were not yet fully developed. Digitization of Chinese judicial practice has been ongoing for more than 15 years but witnessed considerable acceleration in 2017

56 Pablo Cortés, "Online Dispute Resolution for Consumers," in *Online Dispute Resolution: Theory and Practice*, eds. Mohamed S. Abdel Wahab, Ethan Katsh, and Daniel Rainey (The Hague: Eleven, 2012), 156.

and 2020, respectively. When online court is placed into the analytical framework, it should be categorized as a type of exogenous ODR. Meanwhile, it is necessary to distinguish between public ODR and private ODR and further analyze the problems in the process of endogenizing its exogenous system. This book is therefore a further advancement from the previous research in the theoretical study of ODR.

Technological advances are integral to the development of ODR. ODR theories now employ the concept of the "fourth party" to illustrate the idea that technology can aid the neutral, human third party in a dispute resolution process.[57] Some have also introduced the concept of the "fifth party," representing the provider of the technology.[58] Teubner describes the combination of law and technology as akin to nuclear fission.[59] Examination of these new technological developments and their implications further strengthens the analysis of ODR theory. The impact of technological factors on dispute resolution will be studied as part of the ODR "method," bringing examples and case studies throughout the book.

China's significant role in the global internet landscape provides invaluable context for this research, addressing notable gaps in international scholarship. This research specifically considers China's unique context, which is crucial due to its vast online population and prominent platforms, resulting in novel data and research opportunities. The research in this book takes a holistic approach, incorporating legal studies, institutional analysis, and economic perspectives. It integrates the main forms of Chinese ODR into a unified institutional perspective to examine their details and outline the direction and path of ODR's development, considering the institutional differences of these mechanisms.

Finally, while the characterization and embedding of individual ODR mechanisms are crucial under the aforementioned framework of endogenous and exogenous mechanisms, it is equally important to recognize that the field of ODR is constantly evolving. In many instances, a wider range of dispute resolution mechanisms can be utilized to resolve certain types of disputes than originally envisaged. These linkages between mechanisms are critical to understanding the ODR framework. For example, in specific consumer-related disputes, the platform's customer service, online arbitration, and online courts can now all be used to resolve consumer disputes, not just private mechanisms. In the case of the "one-stop" platform for the diversified resolution of international commercial disputes set up by SPC, a variety of methods can be used to resolve international commercial disputes.

As ODR has developed differently in different countries, ODR mechanisms in China have gradually formed a complex web of mutually complementary

57 Hörnle, *Cross-Border Internet Dispute Resolution*, 87.

58 Arno R. Lodder, "The Third Party and Beyond. An Analysis of the Different Parties, in Particular the Fifth, Involved in Online Dispute Resolution," *Information & Communications Technology Law* 15, no. 2 (2006): 146, https://doi.org/10.1080/13600830600676438.

59 Gunther Teubner, "Societal Constitutionalism: Alternatives to State-Centred Constitutional Theory?," in *Transnational Governance and Constitutionalism*, eds. Christian Joerges, Inger-Johanne Sand, and Gunther Teubner (Oxford: Hart Publishing, 2004), 25–26.

relationships. The concept of diversified dispute resolution is emphasized in China, with the ultimate goal of resolving disputes and enhancing social governance. This book provides a comprehensive overview of China's ODR system through institutional analyses and discussions of emerging topics. Through a rigorous presentation of the key characteristics of the Chinese system, it aims to provide an important and valuable perspective for comparative studies of ODR beyond China and contribute to the critical understanding of ODR more generally.

Chapters overview

This current introductory chapter undertakes a retrospective review of the global development of ODR. Research on ODR began with ADR and has expanded rapidly with technological advancements, now covering a wide range of theories and practices. This chapter highlights critical milestones in ODR's development and provides an overview of practical progress both in China and internationally. It focuses on recent "trends" and "new topics," including shifts in global perceptions of ODR, the advancement of public ODR, and this book's perspective on digital justice. Additionally, it highlights practices in China, presenting new topics, including platform monopoly, smart courts, and cross-border dispute resolution. Following this introductory overview, subsequent chapters will analyze the distinctive features and commonalities of various ODR types.

Chapter 2 provides a theoretical analysis of ODR, elucidating the two developmental pathways: exogenous and endogenous. It analyzes the institutional differences between these two types of mechanisms through the dimensions of incentives, agents, information, and methodology. These distinct characteristics indicate they confront different issues of social embedding. Exogenous systems, such as online arbitration, emulate traditional ADR methods, introducing uncertainties in the connection between ODR and existing legal frameworks. As a result, they sometimes struggle to operate as effectively as traditional arbitration systems and lack a competitive advantage within cyberspace's rules. This challenge explains the developmental challenges encountered by exogenous ODR systems. In contrast, endogenous systems evolve with online disputes and establish institutional connections. By analyzing dispute resolution models in major online marketplaces, such as Taobao, this chapter presents a critical evaluation of the characteristics of endogenous ODR. Additionally, ODR mechanisms are likely to experience two trends in the future, namely, the "endogenization of exogenous ODR" and the "specialization of endogenous ODR."

Chapter 3 focuses on private dispute resolution as an important practical and doctrinal advancement in the internet era. The spectrum of public regulation, private regulation, and technology-based dispute resolution adds another important dimension to theorize various ODR mechanisms. In combination with the exogenous and endogenous nature of ODR mechanisms, a more comprehensive analytical framework, known as the ODR Quadrant Diagram, is developed to demonstrate the different characteristics of ODR mechanisms as well as their intended evolutionary paths. This chapter then highlights the challenges with public regulation and enforcement in cyberspace, using the example of the implementation of EU's consumer e-commerce and ODR initiatives. A number of well-established private ODR mechanisms, such as online marketplace reputation system and escrow services, are examined to explain the operation and characteristics of private ODR. Furthermore, the realm of private ODR often responds most proactively to technological advancements, with crowdsourced ODR and decentralized dispute resolution based on blockchain technology serving as two prime examples. Crowdsourcing has altered dispute resolution by shifting some types of disputes from experts to amateur enthusiasts, transforming a closed system to an open one. Effective dispute resolution through crowdsourcing depends on refining mechanism design at both the technological and legal levels. Meanwhile, the advent of blockchain technology has introduced a shift from centralization to decentralization, highlighting the evolving relationship between technology and law. Although notable barriers and challenges exist in the wider acceptance of these ODR mechanisms, there are reasons to remain optimistic about progress in this phenomenon with new technological developments.

Chapter 4 examines online arbitration as one of the clearest online counterparts of a well-established ADR mechanism, with a particular emphasis on the status of online arbitration in China. In the early stages of ODR development, online arbitration emerged as a significant method for resolving commercial disputes and garnered considerable research attention. However, despite the theoretical advancement and institutional differences in online arbitration across various countries, its practical implementation lagged for some time. This chapter explores the reasons behind this issue as well as the impact of the COVID-19 pandemic in catalyzing online arbitration. Several important issues in the Chinese context are examined in detail, including the use of asynchronous hearings in arbitration and their legal effects, as well as the validity of arbitration clauses in consumer agreements with online platforms. To gain deeper insights, a number of original empirical studies were undertaken to more accurately ascertain the status and development of online arbitration in China, including the online capacity of all Chinese arbitration institutions, analysis of court judgments on asynchronous arbitral awards, and the content of service agreement from major online services in China.

Chapter 5 investigates the intriguing question of why China has been able to rapidly advance online courts within a short period. This chapter delineates and analyzes the digitization of the Chinese court system as a three-stage process for a structured understanding of ongoing and multi-fronted development, comprising multiple components and initiatives, including internet courts, smart courts, online courts, and one-stop diversified dispute resolution mechanisms. China's three internet courts are not only the world's first internet courts but also the first fully online courts, providing rich empirical data for the study of judicial practice in the internet era. Moreover, the positioning of all courts as service providers further enhances the Chinese legal system's long-established emphasis on mediation as a non-litigatory strategy and priority of judicial task. Should any disputes come to litigation, however, the highly digitized courts of China offer a potentially paradigm-shifting hybrid model of online courts, not only for court hearings, but also for all stages of civil and administrative litigation. Overall, the Chinese experiments and practice of online courts demonstrate a different conception of digitization of justice, underpinned by notably Chinese characteristics of the legal and political system and the contemporary society.

Chapter 6 consolidates the diverse threads explored throughout the book, offering a holistic view of ODR both in China and beyond. Building upon the detailed analyses in previous chapters – from the institutional framework and sociological implications to technological innovations and legal challenges – this chapter provides a comprehensive synthesis of China's ODR landscape. Reflecting on the journey from the inception of ODR in China to its current state, this chapter traces the evolution of digital dispute resolution mechanisms within the unique contours of China's legal and technological environment. As a concluding chapter, it not only reflects on the journey covered in earlier sections but also succinctly outlines the future outlook and potential trajectories of ODR in China and its global implications. Thus, this chapter serves as a comprehensive summary and reflective closure to the in-depth study presented in the book, offering a concise yet profound understanding of the state and future of ODR in China and beyond.

Bibliography

Arsic, Jasna. "International Commercial Arbitration on the Internet: Has the Future Come Too Early?" *Journal of International Arbitration* 14 (1997): 209–21.

Briggs, Lord Justice. "Civil Courts Structure Review: Final Report." *Judiciary of England and Wales*, July 2016. https://www.judiciary.uk/guidance-and-resources/civil-courts-structure-review-final-report/.

Chaisse, Julien, and Jamieson Kirkwood. "Smart Courts, Smart Contracts, and the Future of Online Dispute Resolution." *Stanford Journal of Blockchain Law & Policy* 5, no. 1 (2022): 62–91.

Conley Tyler, Melissa. "115 and Counting: The State of ODR 2004." In *Proceedings of the Third Annual Forum on Online Dispute Resolution*, edited by Melissa Conley Tyler, Ethan Katsh, and Daewon Choi. International Conflict Resolution Centre, 2004.

Cortés, Pablo. "Online Dispute Resolution for Consumers." In *Online Dispute Resolution: Theory and Practice*, edited by Mohamed S. Abdel Wahab, Ethan Katsh, and Daniel Rainey, 151–73. The Hague: Eleven, 2012.

Crane, Daniel A. "After Search Neutrality: Drawing a Line Between Promotion and Demotion." *I/S: A Journal of Law and Policy* 9, no. 3 (2014): 397–406.

Denvir, Catrina, and Amanda Darshini Selvarajah. "Safeguarding Access to Justice in the Age of the Online Court." *Modern Law Review* 85, no. 1 (2022): 25–68. https://doi.org/10.1111/1468-2230.12670.

Ebner, Noam, and Elayne E. Greenberg, "Strengthening Online Dispute Resolution Justice." *Washington University Journal of Law & Policy* 63, no. 1 (2020): 65–117.

Etherton, Terence. "Rule-Making for a Digital Court Process: The Civil Procedure Rules 20th Anniversary Conference, 2019." In *The Civil Procedure Rules at 20*, edited by Andrew Higgins, 57–64. Oxford: Oxford University Press, 2020. https://doi.org/10.1093/oso/9780198863182.001.0001.

Gao, Wei, and Lu Xu. "Online Courts in China: A New Hybrid Model for Access to Justice." *The China Review* 25 (2025).

Gao, Wei, and Yao Yang. "Chaining Cyber-Titans to Neutrality: An Updated Common Carrier Approach to Regulate Platform Service Providers." *Computer Law & Security Review* 31 (2015): 412–21. https://doi.org/10.1016/j.clsr.2015.03.003.

Hanriot, Maxime. "Online Dispute Resolution (ODR) As a Solution to Cross Border Consumer Disputes: The Enforcement of Outcomes." *McGill Journal of Dispute Resolution* 2 (2015): 1–22.

Hörnle, Julia. *Cross-Border Internet Dispute Resolution*. Cambridge: Cambridge University Press, 2009. https://doi.org/10.1017/CBO9780511576102.

Huiling, Jiang 蒋惠岭, Long Fei 龙飞, and Wang Li 王丽. "Studies on the Dispute Resolution Mechanism for the Belt and Road (I) '一带一路'纠纷解决机制研究(上)." *China Institute of Applied Jurisprudence*, March 2018. http://yyfx.court.gov.cn/upload/file/2018/06/27/15/36/20180627153647_46393.pdf.

Katsh, Ethan. "Online Dispute Resolution (ODR): A Look at History." In *Online Dispute Resolution: Theory and Practice*, edited by Daniel Rainey, Ethan Katsh, and Mohamed S. Abdel Wahab, 2nd ed., 1–18. The Hague: Eleven, 2021.

Katsh, Ethan, and Orna Rabinovich-Einy. *Digital Justice: Technology and the Internet of Disputes*. Oxford: Oxford University Press, 2017. https://doi.org/10.1093/acprof:oso/9780190464585.001.0001.

Katsh, Ethan, and Colin Rule. "What We Know and Need to Know About Online Dispute Resolution." *South Carolina Law Review* 67, no. 2 (2016): 329–44.

Khan, Lina M. "Amazon's Antitrust Paradox." *Yale Law Journal* 126 (2017): 710–805.

Kim, Pauline T. "Data-Driven Discrimination at Work." *William & Mary Law Review* 58, no. 3 (2017): 857–936.

Lodder, Arno R. "The Third Party and Beyond. An Analysis of the Different Parties, in Particular the Fifth, Involved in Online Dispute Resolution." *Information & Communications Technology Law* 15, no. 2 (2006): 143–55. https://doi.org/10.1080/13600830600676438.

Pasquale, Frank. "Internet Non-discrimination Principles: Commercial Ethics for Carriers and Search Engines." *University of Chicago Legal Forum* (2008): 263–99.

Pasquale, Frank. "Platform Neutrality: Enhancing Freedom of Expression in Spheres of Private Power." *Theoretical Inquiries into Law* 17 (2016): 487–513.

Pearlstein, Arthur, Bryan Hanson, and Noam Ebner. "ODR in North America." In *Online Dispute Resolution: Theory and Practice*, edited by Mohamed S. Abdel Wahab, Ethan Katsh, and Daniel Rainey, 443–64. The Hague: Eleven, 2012.

Prescott, J. J. "Using ODR Platforms to Level the Playing Field." In *Legal Tech and Future of Civil Justice*, edited by David Freeman Engstrom, 286–304. Cambridge: Cambridge University Press, 2023. https://doi.org/10.1017/9781009255301.

Prescott, J. J., and Alexander Sanchez. "Platform Procedure: Using Technology to Facilitate (Efficient) Civil Settlement." In *Selection and Decision in Judicial Process Around the World*, edited by Yun-Chien Chang, 30–72. Cambridge: Cambridge University Press, 2020.

Rahman, K. Sabeel. "The New Utilities: Private Power, Social Infrastructure, and the Revival of the Public Utility Concept." *Cardozo Law Review* 39 (2018): 1621–89.

Rainey, Daniel, and Alma Abdul-Hadi Jadallah. "ODR and Cultural Components of Dispute Engagement." In *Online Dispute Resolution: Theory and Practice*, edited by Daniel Rainey, Ethan Katsh, and Mohamed S. Abdel Wahab, 2nd ed., 229–48. The Hague: Eleven, 2021.

Spaulding, Norman W. "Online Dispute Resolution and the End of Adversarial Justice?" In *Legal Tech and Future of Civil Justice*, edited by David Freeman Engstrom, 251–85. Cambridge: Cambridge University Press, 2023. https://doi.org/10.1017/9781009255301.

Sung, Huang-Chih. "Can Online Courts Promote Access to Justice? A Case Study of the Internet Courts in China." *Computer Law & Security Review* 39 (2020): 105461. https://doi.org/10.1016/j.clsr.2020.105461.

Susskind, Richard. *Online Courts and the Future of Justice*. Oxford: Oxford University Press, 2019. https://doi.org/10.1093/oso/9780198838364.001.0001.

Teubner, Gunther. "Societal Constitutionalism: Alternatives to State-Centred Constitutional Theory?" In *Transnational Governance and Constitutionalism*, edited by Christian Joerges, Inger-Johanne Sand, and Gunther Teubner, 3–28. Oxford: Hart Publishing, 2004.

Thierer, Adam. "The Perils of Classifying Social Media Platforms as Public Utilities." *CommLaw Conspectus* 21 (2013): 249–97.
Van Arsdale, Suzanne. "User Protections in Online Dispute Resolution." *Harvard Negotiation Law Review* 21 (2015): 107–42.
Wang, Liyuan. "Application of Information Technology in Judicial Field: The Development Model of Online Litigation in China." *Computer Law & Security Review* 52 (2024): 105936. https://doi.org/10.1016/j.clsr.2024.105936.
Wing, Leah. "Mapping the Parameters of Online Dispute Resolution." *International Journal of Online Dispute Resolution* 9, no. 1 (2022): 3–16. https://doi.org/10.5553/IJODR/235250022022009001001.
Xu, Lu. *Chinese Legal Reforms: Transformations in a Decade*. Leiden: Brill, 2024. https://doi.org/10.1163/9789004537125.

2 Analytical framework

Exogenous ODR and endogenous ODR

An overview: exogenous ODR and endogenous ODR in institutional perspectives

Legal research on ODR typically centers on two primary areas: the examination of various ODR mechanisms and the analysis of the laws and regulations that govern or facilitate ODR. However, the rapid evolution of commerce and technology often outpaces the establishment of legal frameworks, particularly during the early stages of ODR development. Scholarly investigations from a jurisprudential standpoint therefore yield rather limited insights due to the disparity between practice and theory. The shortcoming is notable in the failure of these studies to recognize ODR mechanisms as institutions fundamentally integrated within the societal structure, undermining a comprehensive understanding of the ODR system's role and status within society. Moreover, most research has been confined to merely describing the mechanisms and the legal contexts in which they operate, without elucidating the evolutionary trajectories of ODR. Such an approach, therefore, falls short of providing robust explanations for the various challenges encountered during the evolution of these mechanisms.

This chapter aims to introduce a unified analytical framework to differentiate between exogenous and endogenous ODR through institutional analysis, exploring the evolutionary paths of ODR in terms of their integration within social structures. By examining the characteristics and societal integration of both exogenous and endogenous ODR mechanisms, this analysis seeks to explain why certain ODR mechanisms have faltered while others have successfully integrated into the internet's global rule system and functioned effectively. Subsequent chapters will delve deeper into the primary ODR mechanisms within this framework, including various types of private ODR, online arbitration, and online litigation, to provide a more detailed examination of their operational dynamics and societal impacts.

This chapter primarily utilizes ODR mechanisms in the field of e-commerce activities as examples to develop the analytical framework and provide illustrations. Focusing on a specific area enables a clearer and more illustrative analytical framework without compromising its explanatory power. While the field of ODR has diversified considerably, dispute resolution in the commercial sector remains

DOI: 10.4324/ 9781003594512-2

a significant part of the overall ODR landscape. Specifically, online arbitration is examined as an exogenous mechanism, while Taobao's ODR is analyzed as a representative of endogenous mechanisms.

Distinguishing exogenous ODR and endogenous ODR

Conception

Institutions can be construed as "the rules of the game in a society, or more formally, the humanly devised constraints that shape human interactions."[1] Rulemaking is often subject to the deliberate designs of legislators, political entrepreneurs, or economists; their primary concern is enforcing a pre-designed mechanism to achieve a predetermined societal objective, which may not inherently be self-enforceable.[2] Indeed, ODR has been deliberately crafted in this manner, with providers of ODR services and arbitration institutions initially aiming to resolve e-disputes through "innovative" mechanisms, such as online arbitration and mediation. These mechanisms are considered external to cyberspace since they are designed based on traditional dispute resolution frameworks and conditions, hence termed "exogenous ODR."

In contrast, endogenous ODR arises from within cyberspace, evolving through the strategic interactions of agents within the digital environment.[3] Game theorists and proponents of the evolutionary game approach view institutions as "spontaneous orders," self-organizing systems, or a self-sustaining system of shared beliefs.[4] Many legal scholars share this view regarding laws, customs, and technological standards that develop organically rather than being imposed.[5] As industry practices demonstrate, sectors motivated to enhance online transactions have developed their own dispute resolution mechanisms that naturally evolve in self-organizing network environments. Moreover, the internet's capability for private ordering has facilitated the development of various

1 Douglass C. North, *Institutions, Institutional Change and Economic Performance* (Cambridge: Cambridge University Press, 1990), 3.

2 Leonid Hurwicz, "Inventing New Institutions: The Design Perspective," *American Journal of Agricultural Economics* 69, no. 2 (1987): 395; Leonid Hurwicz, "Toward a Framework for Analyzing Institutions and Institutional Change," in *Markets and Democracy: Participation, Accountability, and Efficiency*, eds. Samuel Bowles, Herbert Gintis and Bo Gustafsson (Cambridge: Cambridge University Press, 1993).

3 Masahiko Aoki, *Toward a Comparative Institutional Analysis* (Cambridge: MIT Press, 2001), 209.

4 Carl Menger, *Investigation into the Method of the Social Sciences with Special Reference to Economics*, trans. Francis J. Nock (New York University Press, 1985); Fredrick A. Hayek, *Law, Legislation and Liberty, Volume 1: Rules and Order* (Chicago, IL: University of Chicago Press, 1978); Aoki, *Comparative Institutional Analysis*, 10.

5 I. Trotter Hardy, "The Proper Legal Regime for 'Cyberspace'," *University of Pittsburgh Law Review* 55 (1994): 993; David G. Post and David R. Johnson, "Chaos Prevailing on Every Continent: Towards a New Theory of Decentralized Decision-Making in Complex Systems," *Chicago-Kent Law Review* 73 (1998): 1055.

Table 2.1 Distinctions between exogenous ODR and endogenous ODR

	Exogenous ODR	*Endogenous ODR*
Examples	Online arbitration, online mediation, online litigation	Online reputation system, integrated ODR mechanism, domain name dispute resolution system
Agents	Outsider	Insider
Incentives	Derive financial or social benefits through dispute resolution	Eliminate transaction risk, expand trading volume
Information collection	Observable information regarding dispute resolution; verifiable information regarding online activity	Observable information regarding online activity; verifiable information regarding dispute resolution
Methodology for establishment	"Imitation" of offline eponymous	Experimental "trial and error"

dispute prevention and resolution mechanisms, including online reputation systems, third-party ODR, and online payment systems. These mechanisms, particularly those in online marketplaces, are "endogenous ODR," having emerged from within cyberspace.

Distinctions between exogenous ODR and endogenous ODR

Table 2.1 encapsulates the principal differences between exogenous and endogenous ODR. In the following sections, an in-depth explanation is provided for each column.

Agents

The agents of endogenous ODR, referred to as insiders, directly participate in online transactions and primarily comprise three groups: consumers, online retailers, and online marketplace operators. These participants are actively engaged within the online commercial sphere, employing various strategies to navigate the marketplace. In contrast, the agents of exogenous ODR, known as outsiders, include rule-makers, such as lawyers, arbitrators, and academics, who are not directly involved in online transactions. Agents on both sides are instrumental in designing ODR frameworks and serve as catalysts for institutional changes.

The distinction between insiders and outsiders not only underscores their differing roles but also highlights their varying access to resources. Insiders possess greater advantages, including more substantial capital and labor resources, which enable them to invest significantly in resolving disputes. For example, financially robust marketplaces allocate specific funds for compensating customers in cases of non-performance.[6] One notable example is eBay's money-back guarantee, which ensures that if a buyer does not receive an item, eBay refunds the full cost of the item and the original postage, provided the transaction was conducted using an approved electronic payment method like PayPal. Subsequently, eBay retains the right to recover the amount from the seller involved. Additionally, these marketplaces maintain a team of live customer support specialists, available continuously via phone, email, or integrated messaging services, to assist with any issues or disputes. Outsiders involved in exogenous ODR often lack such resources, which means that ODR activities must be facilitated and funded by other sources, such as arbitration institutions or the court.

Incentives

As stakeholders in online transactions, insiders are motivated to achieve equilibrium through the substantial profits derived from maintaining robust online activities. For instance, in the realm of e-commerce platforms, unresolved disputes can heighten risks associated with online transactions. Efficient ODR mechanisms enhance user trust and subsequently boost profits for platforms. In contrast, the designers of exogenous ODR, primarily legal practitioners, aim to replace traditional dispute resolution mechanisms with innovative online alternatives, such as online arbitration.[7] Consequently, the primary advantage of endogenous ODR lies in the potential benefits it brings to all online activities,[8] whereas the benefits of exogenous ODR are primarily realized through the cost savings achieved by replacing traditional systems.

Furthermore, the creators of exogenous ODR might view these mechanisms as supplementary to traditional offline dispute resolution practices. A failure in exogenous ODR systems does not typically impact the core interests of their designers. However, ineffective ODR can be highly detrimental to online transaction participants, providing insiders with greater incentives to refine these mechanisms. Such differences may be reflected in the ongoing modifications to dispute resolution rules. For example, the online arbitration rules of China International Economic and Trade Arbitration Commission (CIETAC) have only been revised once, in 2014, since their introduction in 2009. These rules are now marginalized by the general arbitration rules, as to be explained in Chapter 4. In contrast, the e-commerce platform Taobao frequently updates its terms and introduces new rules regarding dispute resolution and rating systems, reflecting

6 For example, Taobao created a guarantee fund of 100 million RMB in 2010 to compensate buyers in case of non-performance by sellers. CCTV, "*Xinwen Lianbo,*" March 15, 2010, at 18:44, https://tv.cctv.com/2010/03/15/VIDExFrkTWrd29QSUCbl7weE100315.shtml.

7 Mohamed S. Abdel Wahab, "ODR and E-Arbitration," in *Online Dispute Resolution: Theory and Practice*, eds. Mohamed S. Abdel Wahab, Ethan Katsh, and Daniel Rainey (The Hague: Eleven, 2012), 425.

8 Orna Rabinovich-Einy and Ethan Katsh, "Lessons from Online Dispute Resolution for Dispute System Design," in *Online Dispute Resolution: Theory and Practice*, eds. Daniel Rainey, Ethan Katsh, and Mohamed S. Abdel Wahab, 2nd ed. (The Hague: Eleven, 2021), 53.

a proactive approach to adapting to market changes and better serving its user base.[9]

It is noteworthy that online arbitration or online litigation have not substantially replaced traditional offline systems. In the context of international arbitration, the primary goal of ODR designers is to enhance service quality by offering an online alternative and attracting more cases, thereby generating more profits from dispute resolution activities. The establishment of China's online litigation system aims to achieve digitization of justice and improve litigation services, contributing to broader and better societal governance through effective dispute prevention and resolution. Although there are significant differences between online arbitration and online litigation – both representative of exogenous systems – the primary driving force behind their development remains the resolution of disputes. However, these systems can experience rapid growth, fueled by special external incentives or events, such as those seen during the COVID-19 pandemic, which often have a more pronounced effect than prolonged governmental promotion of ODR. The impact of such emergencies on exogenous systems is typically more substantial than on endogenous systems, as the operation of online platforms is often less susceptible to sudden changes in the physical world.

Information

Decision-making in ODR systems is guided by the information available to agents. The type of information accessible to exogenous and endogenous agents differs significantly. In ODR, two distinct types of knowledge are pertinent: knowledge concerning online commercial activities and knowledge regarding dispute resolution, particularly for disputes that originate offline. Hayek characterizes these types as "the knowledge of the particular circumstances of time and place."[10] This knowledge is processed and utilized solely by those who are actively engaged in and directly involved with decision-making processes. Dixit identifies two classifications of information relevant in this context: observable information and verifiable information.[11] *Observable information* is implicit and exclusively visible to the parties involved in the transaction, while *verifiable information* can be confirmed by third parties, such as courts. Li labels observable information as "local information," and verifiable information as "public information."[12]

This discourse extends these definitions in the realm of ODR to propose that observable information is accessible only to insiders within a specific domain,

9 Taobao released various rules, including its general terms of services, rules for different categories of transaction, dispute resolution, rating, etc. It reported its amendments of existing rules as well as the newly released ones every month. In the year of 2015, four to seven rules have been changed every month. And its rules for rating have been changed in October 2014, March 2015, and June 2015.

10 F. A. Hayek, "The Use of Knowledge in Society," *The American Economic Review* 35 (1945): 521.

11 Avinash Dixit, "Power of Incentives in Private versus Public Organizations," *The American Economic Review* 87 (1997): 378.

12 John Shuhe Li, "Relation-Based versus Rule-Based Governance: An Explanation of the East Asian Miracle and Asian Crisis," *Review of International Economics* 11 (2003): 657.

whereas verifiable information is publicly accessible and can be confirmed by outsiders. The manner in which participants in endogenous and exogenous ODR utilize information about online commercial activities and dispute resolution varies significantly in terms of observability and verifiability. Online business models evolve rapidly, surpassing the development of traditional dispute resolution mechanisms and necessitating expertise in both dispute resolution and online transactions. Aoki posits that the intensified competition fueled by digitalized information, owing to its widespread accessibility, might amplify the economic value of tacit and uncodifiable knowledge.[13] This type of knowledge, available solely on-site or within a community of relevant professionals, is most effectively utilized through well-functioning mechanisms tailored to the local context.

Consequently, insiders, who are deeply embedded into the online environment, are uniquely positioned to possess comprehensive knowledge related to online transactions or technology, thereby making them more adept at resolving online disputes. In contrast, outsiders, such as legal experts, despite being well-versed in dispute resolution, often lack detailed knowledge of online transactions. Hence, information pertaining to online transactions constitutes observable information for insiders and verifiable information for outsiders.

Conversely, information on dispute resolution is "observable information" for outsiders and "verifiable information" for insiders. This type of information encompasses a substantial amount of fixed data related to the drafting, interpretation, and implementation of laws by the legislative, judicial, and executive branches, respectively. However, given the distinct nature of cyberspace compared to the offline world, the information that outsiders derive from resolving offline disputes may not suffice for designing effective online dispute resolution systems. Information on online transactions is observable solely by the participating parties themselves. Outsiders can only access parts of this information, and certainly not in its entirety. Furthermore, insiders may conceal information related to online transactions to protect privacy,[14] further hindering outsiders from designing suitable online dispute resolution systems.

Methods

Economist Alchian suggests that effective results can be achieved even when the information relied upon is neither complete nor entirely accurate.[15] This can be accomplished through two forms of conscious adaptive behaviors: "imitation" and

13 Aoki, *Comparative Institutional Analysis*, 91.

14 Heins Marjorie, "The Brave New World of Social Media Censorship," *Harvard Law Review Forum* 127 (2014): 326, refers to the non-transparency of Internet companies' rules and internal procedure: "Ammori tells us that Facebook lawyers have created 'a set of rules that hundreds of employees can apply consistently without having to make judgment calls.' The details of these rules, however, we do not know. Unlike censorship decisions by government agencies, the process in the private world of social media is secret."

15 Armen A. Alchian, "Uncertainty, Evolution, and Economic Theory," *Journal of Political Economy* 58 (1950): 211.

"trial and error." Exogenous ODR primarily employs imitation, while endogenous ODR adopts the trial-and-error method.

Designers of exogenous ODR possess extensive information regarding dispute resolution, enabling them to replicate the qualities and approaches of offline processes with relatively low transaction costs. However, imitation faces two significant challenges. First, a changing environment may render initial strategies ineffective. Second, imperfect imitation often results from incomplete information and limited capacity to replicate. Therefore, if designers of exogenous ODR attempt to perfectly imitate offline dispute resolution mechanisms, they must ensure that the offline world is equivalent to the online environment. Nonetheless, the unique characteristics of online activities are not always compatible with traditional dispute resolution mechanisms.

Another type of conscious adaptive behavior is "trial and error." As Alchian asserts, "this has been used with 'profit maximization', wherein, by trial and ensuing success and failure, more appropriate actions are selected in a process presumed to converge to a limit of 'profit maximization' equilibrium."[16] Endogenous ODR evolves precisely through such a trial-and-error process. The key to this process is selecting a set of strategies as a starting point. Subsequently, these strategies are compared with the original ones to assess whether improvements have been made. If the outcome is suboptimal, the process reverts to the original strategies; if not, further adjustments are made. Incidentally, it is not surprising to observe that ODR providers continuously revise service patterns and related rules to enhance effectiveness. A salient example is eBay's feedback system, which has undergone numerous experiments to provide redress within the feedback system, evolving from SquareTrade and Mutual Feedback Withdrawal to Independent Feedback Review and the Community Court.[17]

Endogenous ODR arises from interactions among participants engaged in online activities. This development of the system is driven by two primary evolutionary forces: (1) conscious trial and error and (2) competition among different endogenous ODR systems. Combined with the advantage of acquiring detailed information about online transactions, insiders within these systems seldom resort to mimicking traditional, offline dispute resolution mechanisms. However, the application of trial and error alone cannot guarantee success. True success in these frameworks can only be gauged through what may be described as a "blanketing shotgun process," where multiple strategies are tested to identify which are most effective.[18] In the early days of ODR's development, it was unclear which individual ODR mechanism or platform would ultimately prevail. The ongoing competition between different endogenous ODR systems serves to monitor and facilitate the adaptation process, allowing

16 Alchian, "Uncertainty," 219.

17 Colin Rule and Harpreet Singh, "ODR and Online Reputation Systems – Maintaining Trust and Accuracy Through Effective Redress," in *Online Dispute Resolution: Theory and Practice*, eds. Mohamed S. Abdel Wahab, Ethan Katsh, and Daniel Rainey (The Hague: Eleven, 2012), 178–81.

18 Alchian, "Uncertainty," 219.

the most effective methods to emerge through a dynamic akin to economic natural selection.

Another critical difference between endogenous and exogenous ODR lies in their methods of evolution. Endogenous ODR mechanisms have organically developed from within the internet, such as through e-commerce platforms or virtual communities that deal with disputes that have arisen exclusively in the online environment. This origin makes endogenous ODR inherently more suited for resolving disputes entirely online. Conversely, exogenous ODR is designed to handle disputes that can originate both in the online and offline worlds, with many disputes still rooted in traditional, physical contexts. For disputes that arise offline, it is understandable that individuals might prefer to resolve them through offline means. This preference is due not only to convenience but also to factors such as the psychological comfort of the disputants; the current level of societal development, which has not yet achieved full virtualization of all human activities; and the deep-seated trust and reliance on traditional dispute resolution systems that have been in place for decades.

Thus, preserving the function of providing offline dispute resolution remains essential within the current ODR system framework. If the primary goal of dispute resolution is outcome-based, then ensuring that litigants are satisfied with the outcomes becomes paramount. However, research suggests that process-based models, which emphasize the procedural aspects of dispute resolution, more accurately capture why individuals value the opportunity to have their cases heard in court.[19] For example, the role of Chinese judges in educating parties during litigation proceedings underlines the significant value of offline hearings.[20] It is also noteworthy, as mentioned in Chapter 1, that internet courts in China, characterized by a fully online approach to resolving disputes that arise in cyberspace, represent a shift toward an all-online method of resolving online disputes, reflecting the broader trend of "endogenization of exogenous ODR," discussed later in this chapter.

The development of exogenous ODR has generally lagged behind that of endogenous ODR. This slower progression is partly due to the methodological approach of exogenous ODR, which relies heavily on imitating existing legal systems and traditional dispute resolution mechanisms, such as litigation, arbitration, and mediation. It seems that the more established legal systems have greater path dependence on the traditional mechanisms, which has hindered the rapid development of ODR equivalent. These systems have been slow to evolve and adapt to the rapid changes and needs of online interactions. Nevertheless, the development of these mechanisms can be significantly accelerated by strong external drivers. For

19 Norman W. Spaulding, "Online Dispute Resolution and the End of Adversarial Justice?," in *Legal Tech and Future of Civil Justice*, ed. David Freeman Engstrom (Cambridge: Cambridge University Press, 2023), 261.

20 "Judge Lectured Parents of Child on Parenting After Court Hearing 庭审后法官给孩子的父母上了堂'辅导课'," *Fujian Courts* 福建法院网, May 23, 2022, https://fjfy.fjcourt.gov.cn/article/detail/2022/05/id/6699134.shtml.

instance, the COVID-19 pandemic has notably pushed the development of online arbitration and litigation forward. The pace of development in online litigation varies across different countries, with some regions like the UK and Switzerland experiencing slower progress. In contrast, China employs a flexible approach, allowing litigation[21] and arbitration[22] to be conducted entirely online or offline, at the choice of the parties, or in a hybrid model combining both. This flexibility is an important advancement or necessary compromise of exogenous systems due to their inherent characteristics, as previously explained, which require balancing traditional legal reliance with the innovative possibilities of online dispute resolution.

Exogenous ODR case study: online arbitration

Embeddedness of online arbitration

Arbitration stands as the most prominent traditional out-of-court dispute resolution process, widely recognized for its binding nature, finality, global regulation, and the enforceability of arbitral awards. In line with the shift toward a paperless society, moving arbitration online involves integrating state-of-the-art technologies into proceedings that are conducted either wholly or substantially online. This adaptation is viewed as a necessary evolutionary step for arbitration, aligning with modern technological advancements.[23] Hence, online arbitration, often considered the most established form of ODR, is discussed here as a representative form of exogenous ODR.

Exogenous ODR is crafted to reflect offline dispute resolution behaviors within the online environment, amidst the considerable challenges of fully grasping the essence of ODR in its formative stages. Initially, the advent of online arbitration was perceived primarily as a technological advancement rather than a fundamental shift in institutional dispute resolution in the digital era. It was logical for early designers to utilize the internet both for resolving e-commerce disputes and for disputes that originated from offline transactions.[24] However, this approach raises potential concerns about embeddedness.

Firstly, while traditional arbitration has historically evolved in conjunction with offline markets, introducing it into an online setting may result in what is termed

21 Rules of Online Litigation of People's Courts (2021) Article 4 (3): "If some parties agree to the application of online litigation and others disagree, the corresponding litigation steps may be completed online by the parties that agree and offline by the parties that disagree."

22 Article 37 (5) of the CIETAC Arbitration Rules: "After consultation with the parties and taking into consideration of the circumstances of the case, the arbitral tribunal may, at its own discretion, decide to conduct the oral hearing in person, by remote virtual conference, or by other appropriate means of electronic communication."

23 Jasna Arsic, "International Commercial Arbitration on the Internet – Has the Future Come Too Early?," *Journal of International Arbitration* 14, no. 3 (1997): 209.

24 For example, Art 1 of the CIETAC online arbitration rules stipulates that the rules shall apply to the resolution of e-commerce disputes and may also to the resolution of other economic and trade disputes upon the agreement of the parties.

"institutional crowding out."[25] This phenomenon raises concerns about whether online arbitration might overshadow traditional arbitration methods, potentially impacting its successful integration into the offline domain. Secondly, there exists potential conflict between online arbitration and endogenous ODR systems. It is questionable whether online arbitration could displace endogenous systems that have developed in tandem with online platforms. Caught between these two alternatives, it becomes apparent that online arbitration faces significant challenges due to competition from both traditional arbitration practices and endogenous ODR systems. This struggle to outperform these established and emerging systems contributes to the slower development and adoption of online arbitration.

Proliferation of online arbitration: implications for traditional arbitration practices

Online arbitration and its offline counterpart differ only in the information technologies employed by the former. Many arbitration institutions make only the necessary adjustments to accommodate such differences, without substantively altering their practice. For instance, CIETAC Rules 2024 stipulate that arbitration proceedings can be conducted via videoconference or other electronic or computer communication methods. CIETAC has been particularly mindful of integrating these new forms with the existing legal framework, ensuring a seamless connection with traditional legal institutions. For example, in compliance with many national laws and international conventions that mandate written arbitral awards, CIETAC requires that awards specify the date and place of issuance and be signed by the arbitrators, with an official seal affixed.[26]

Despite these similarities to offline arbitration, significant differences remain. Berman pointedly notes that there is a common misconception among legal scholars and policymakers that once legal norms are established, they automatically effectuate and create a legal regime.[27] If online arbitration is to be viewed as an exogenous institution within the online environment, then its effectiveness post-integration becomes a critical concern.

Often touted as an advanced form of traditional arbitration, online arbitration is praised for being faster, more cost-effective, and more efficient. These advantages could potentially allow it to supplant traditional offline arbitration. However, the reality of achieving such a transition is complex. Traditional arbitration has developed through a bottom-up approach, initially emerging from within the community, then gaining acceptance by state entities, and eventually becoming institutionalized into law. This deep-rooted integration with offline societal structures

25 Samuel Bowles, *Microeconomics: Behavior, Institutions, and Evolution* (Princeton, NJ: Princeton University Press, 2004), 495.

26 Article 39 of the CIETAC online arbitration rules (2015); Article 52 of the CIETAC Arbitration Rules (2024).

27 Paul Schiff Berman, "From International Law to Law and Globalization," *Columbia Journal of Transnational Law* 43 (2005): 498.

has enabled traditional arbitration to establish strong connections with both the market and the existing legal framework, tailored to address high-value and complex disputes.

In contrast, the objectives of online arbitration are less clearly defined. Initially designed to address disputes arising purely from online interactions,[28] it has since been adapted to handle both online and offline disputes.[29] Proponents argue that online arbitration is versatile enough to manage both small-claims and high-value disputes.[30] However, a lack of empirical evidence supporting its effectiveness across such a broad spectrum of disputes raises substantial doubts. Moreover, the regulatory frameworks that support traditional arbitration are not fully applicable to online contexts, posing numerous legal challenges, from the drafting of arbitration agreements to the enforcement of awards.

Arbitration inherently requires strict adherence to procedural safeguards and norms, which may not seamlessly translate to an online format.[31] The early stages of online arbitration's development thus necessitate greater institutional support to mitigate the risks for its users. Without adequate adaptation, it is unlikely that online arbitration alone could handle the complex demands of large international commercial transactions that form the bulk of traditional arbitration caseloads. While information and communication technology can reduce costs, these savings do not address the fundamental challenges of integrating online arbitration into the existing legal framework. Consequently, participants in online transactions are unlikely to opt for online arbitration if it lacks a stable and recognized connection with the established legal system, regardless of its apparent technological conveniences and potential cost savings.[32]

Online arbitration, as an exogenous arrangement, faces inherent uncertainties due to its institutionalization. These uncertainties cannot be resolved solely within the framework of online arbitration but require further adaptation and an evolutionary approach for full integration into existing legal systems. This integration challenge calls for a robust enforcement mechanism to support and facilitate this institutional evolution. Two potential initiatives could serve this purpose.

First, legislators could enact new laws or amend existing regulations. However, even with these changes, enforcement challenges persist. Law traditionally lags behind market and technological developments, particularly in the rapidly evolving

28 The first ODR project, Virtual Magistrate, was launched in March 1996. However, it rendered only one decision in 1996, involving the dispute over one message posted by Email America on America Online.

29 For example, Article 1 of the CIETAC online arbitration rules stipulates that it intends to independently, impartially, efficiently, and economically resolve e-commerce disputes as well as offline disputes upon the agreements of the parties.

30 Wahab, "ODR and E-Arbitration," 391.

31 Wahab, "ODR and E-Arbitration," 424.

32 Mireze Philippe, "Where Is Everyone Going with Online Dispute Resolution," *International Business Law Journal* 2 (2002): 167. (He argued that ODR was not competent to resolving high value and complex disputes. B2B can hardly be resolved solely online, thus it seems native to let lawyers and arbitrators welcome ODR.)

domain of the internet. Consequently, newly enacted laws can quickly become outdated.[33] Second, and more importantly, legislators need to establish stable expectations among stakeholders to ensure that their intentions are legally enforceable. As Aoki points out, stable expectations are essentially shared beliefs held by agents.[34] If legislation is not viewed as reflecting the codes of behavior that individuals inherently adopt, it risks becoming irrelevant.[35]

In the context of ODR, the absence of recognized legal standards for cross-border online disputes exacerbates the challenge. According to the American Bar Association, it is currently impossible to identify "internationally recognized best practices" for e-commerce disputes.[36] This highlights the significant difficulties, perhaps even the impossibility, of crafting an adaptive legal framework for online arbitration in the short term. Such a framework would need to not only address the rapid changes in technology and e-commerce but also harmonize with international legal standards, a complex and demanding endeavor that extends beyond simple legislative actions.

Governmental intervention as a theoretical alternative should be taken into account. Several scholars have highlighted the crucial role of government in promoting ODR systems, arguing that governmental involvement can significantly enhance the effectiveness and societal recognition of ODR. This is particularly important at the initial stages, when the inherent value of ODR services may not be fully appreciated by consumers and businesses.[37] As Schultz strongly advocates, governmental intervention is essential to bridge the gap between the high potential of ODR and its limited actual utilization. He proposes that governments should initially focus on building trust in ODR systems, subsequently promoting their widespread adoption.[38]

Financing ODR services through public funding represents another form of governmental intervention. Some successful ODR providers, such as the Austrian

33 UNCITRAL has established the Working Group III in 2010 to undertake the work in the field of ODR relating to cross-border electronic commerce transactions. Since then, it has moved ahead to develop a generic set of rules applicable to both B2B and B2C transactions. But five years passed and in 2015 the "draft for procedural rules" had not come out yet and was still being discussed intensively. It is worth asking whether the final version will be a response to an actual need of market. The likelihood is that this is not a "New York Convention of 1958," which has gone through 50 years.

34 Aoki, *Comparative Institutional Analysis*, 10.

35 Robert Sugden, *The Economic of Rights, Cooperation and Welfare* (Oxford: Basil Blackwell, 1986), 5.

36 American Bar Association, "Addressing Disputes in Electronic Commerce: Final Report and Recommendations of the American Bar Association's Task Force on Electronic Commerce and Alternative Dispute Resolution," 2002, https://www.mmwr.com/wp-content/uploads/2016/02/FinalReport102802.authcheckdam-1.pdf. During the UNCITRAL Working Group's second meeting held in May 2011 in New York, the Group considered the absence of international standards on ODR in both developed and developing countries.

37 Thomas Schultz, "Does Online Dispute Resolution Need Governmental Intervention? The Case for Architectures of Control and Trust," *North Carolina Journal of Law & Technology* 6 (2004): 71.

38 Schultz, "Does Online Dispute Resolution," 97–98.

Internet Ombudsman, have benefited from public funding. However, this approach can impose a substantial burden on taxpayers and might also inhibit the growth of a private and competitive ODR sector.[39] Therefore, it has been suggested that public financing should be used to establish an ODR network with the expectation that it will become self-financing once operational.[40] Despite these intentions, achieving this self-sustaining model has proven challenging. There have been several unsuccessful attempts,[41] often because these projects did not meet market demands or were introduced in markets that were not yet ready for such innovations.

Competition between online arbitration and endogenous ODR

Online arbitration mimics traditional arbitration in many respects. However, traditional arbitration is predominantly utilized for resolving large commercial disputes, which hinders its straightforward adoption online. The crux of the issue lies in the fact that, although the aggregate value of e-commerce disputes might align with the typical environment of traditional arbitration, the value of individual transactions is considerably lower. Consequently, traditional arbitration may not be economically feasible for resolving such disputes. For instance, in 2020, the average monthly spending of user in China on online shopping was approximately RMB 1,138, and this may include shopping from different sellers and buying several different products.[42] This is substantially lower than the minimum fee for CIETAC's online arbitration, which stands at RMB 4,000 for domestic disputes and RMB 14,000 for international or foreign-related disputes.[43] Therefore, it is reasonable to anticipate that participants in online transactions are unlikely to opt for online arbitration due to these economic disparities. As of now, arbitration is often prohibitively expensive for resolving consumer disputes. Moreover, once the arbitration agreement is deemed valid and enforceable, it results in the parties being unable to submit their disputes to court, thus depriving them of their right to a fair trial as a result.

Even if online arbitration reduces its fees, it still faces significant challenges. One of the primary difficulties is the need for qualified experts in dispute resolution.

39 Jonathan Hill, *Cross-Border Consumer Contracts* (Oxford: Oxford University Press, 2008), 318, 391.

40 Pablo Cortés, "Online Dispute Resolution for Consumers," in *Online Dispute Resolution: Theory and Practice*, eds. Mohamed S. Abdel Wahab, Ethan Katsh, and Daniel Rainey (The Hague: Eleven, 2012), 145.

41 Cortés, "Online Dispute Resolution for Consumers," 146. Electronic Consumer Dispute Resolution was initially funded by the European Commission, but it did not succeed in becoming a self-financed ODR provider.

42 "2018 Industrial Report of E-commerce," December 27, 2018, https://www.cqcb.com/wealth/2018-12-27/1340807.html. In 2022, the value of total transactions on Taobao for the "Double Eleventh Festival" was RMB 3.187 billion, and the number of transactions was 49 million. The average value of a single transaction was roughly RMB 65. "Double 11 Shopping Festival: Full Data Report," November 13, 2022, https://www.jiemian.com/article/8374951.html.

43 CIETAC, "CIETAC's Fee Schedule," accessed July 31, 2024, http://www.cietac.org/index.php?m=Page&a=index&id=121.

Traditional arbitration laws often specify stringent qualifications for arbitrators.[44] This requirement increases the cost of establishing arbitral tribunals and reduces the opportunity costs for qualified experts, particularly in the field of online disputes. Traditional arbitration typically involves disputes with considerable factual or legal complexities and high value, motivating parties to hire competent experts. In contrast, online disputes are markedly different from traditional or offline disputes in terms of type, scale, and frequency. Traditional arbitration mechanisms are not well-suited for handling these online disputes.

For instance, a traditional arbitrator is not expected to be available 24/7 or to handle hundreds of small-value disputes. In contrast, many online marketplaces have implemented in-house complaint handling mechanisms (endogenous ODR) that operate around the clock. Furthermore, online disputes often involve straightforward issues, such as "delivery not on time," "the item not as described," or "the quality being subpar," which do not necessarily require highly specialized knowledge. Case handler teams at many online marketplaces are mainly composed of laypersons. Hence, online arbitration that evolves directly from traditional arbitration does not effectively fit the online world.

Another significant challenge for online arbitration pertains to enforcement. Arbitral decisions with cross-border implications also face hurdles in enforcement settings. Enforcing such decisions requires adherence to international conventions, such as the Convention on the Recognition and Enforcement of Foreign Arbitral Awards (the New York Convention). The legal costs associated with utilizing an international treaty limit its utility to high-value cases because the winner is likely to incur high costs. When dealing with high-volume, low-value disputes, which constitute the core of most successful ODR applications, it may not be worthwhile to pursue conventional court enforcement for ODR non-compliance cases.[45]

In comparison, endogenous ODR systems maintain an equilibrium created internally through strategic interactions among participants, making them self-enforcing. Examples of endogenous ODR include the dispute resolution systems established by the Internet Corporation for Assigned Names and Numbers (ICANN) and Taobao. ICANN manages all domain name registrations and transfers, and once a dispute between domain name owners and claimants is resolved, ICANN can unilaterally change domain name registrations, ensuring effective and quick enforcement.[46] Similarly, Taobao uses Alipay, an electronic payment system, for transactions occurring on its site and can freeze and reallocate funds according to a dispute resolution decision, thereby unilaterally enforcing the decision.

44 For instance, Article 13 of the Arbitration Law of the People's Republic of China; s 3 of the Arbitration Regulation of 1985 (Saudi Arabia); and Clause 12 of 1994 Act on Arbitration (Hungary).

45 Ruha Devanesan and Jeffrey Aresty, "ODR and Justice – An Evaluation of Online Dispute Resolution's Interplay with Traditional Theories of Justice," in *Online Dispute Resolution: Theory and Practice*, eds. Mohamed S. Abdel Wahab, Ethan Katsh, and Daniel Rainey (The Hague: Eleven, 2012), 270.

46 Devanesan and Aresty, "ODR and Justice," 270.

Despite the apparent appeal of online arbitration, its practical enforcement remains challenging. Mechanisms designed for self-compliance, such as trust-marks, reputation management systems, marketplace exclusions, penalties for delayed performance, escrow systems, and credit card charge-backs, offer more efficient enforcement solutions and warrant further exploration.[47] Even proponents of online arbitration acknowledge its limitations,[48] which highlight endogenous ODR as a more viable solution for the digital age.

Although the COVID-19 pandemic had substantially altered the perception and need for online operations in arbitration, the long-term post-pandemic impact requires further observation. Overall, while online arbitration has the potential to offer many advantages, its effectiveness in practice is constrained by several significant factors, making endogenous ODR a more suitable approach for handling online disputes.

Endogenous ODR: spontaneous order in online marketplace Taobao

Embeddedness issue of online marketplace

Endogenous ODR is intricately woven into the fabric of online society, emerging spontaneously from the dynamics of cyberspace. As it primarily focuses on resolving e-commerce disputes, its principal function is to harmonize with online transactions, forging what can be described as institutionalized linkages.[49] These connections effectively enable endogenous ODR systems to not only adapt to the scale of online markets but also facilitate their expansion. Within a single online marketplace, such as eBay or Taobao, various ODR mechanisms coexist, often complementing each other in ways that mutually enhance the effectiveness of one mechanism through the presence of another within the same or a related domain.[50]

In contrast to the creators of exogenous ODR, who may seem relatively indifferent to the popularity of ODR systems, stakeholders within the online economy highly value the success of ODR. This concern is especially evident in online

47 UNCITRAL Working Group III, Online Dispute Resolution for Cross-Border Electronic Commerce Transactions: Issues for Consideration in the Conception of a Global ODR Framework (A/CN.9/WG.III/WP.110, November 2011), Section 49.

48 For example, during the conference organized by the UNCITRAL in May 2013, the EU delegation raised the question whether to consider "[a]rbitration as a model for designing a global standard for ODR for low-value, high-volume electronic commerce transactions." See UNICTRAL, "Online dispute resolution for cross-border electronic commerce transactions: draft procedural rules Proposal by the European Union observer delegation," May 22, 2013, https://undocs.org/en/A/CN.9/WG.III/WP.121.

49 Aoki, *Comparative Institutional Analysis*, 209.

50 Aoki, *Comparative Institutional Analysis*, 87: "[T]heir relationships may be complementary in the following sense: the effectiveness (or the presence) of one exchange (property rights) governance mechanism can be reinforced, either directly or indirectly, by the presence (institutionalization) of a particular mechanism in the same or embedding domain."

marketplaces, which represent a critical business model for online transactions. Marketplace operators, functioning as neutral platforms, do not assume responsibility for the transactions between sellers and buyers yet prioritize creating a secure and user-friendly system. A fundamental component of achieving this is building trust among participants regarding their ODR systems.

Marketplace operators face three main challenges in this endeavor: (1) screening out dishonorable sellers to prevent disputes before they arise (*ex ante*), (2) swiftly resolving disputes after they occur (*ex post*), and (3) effectively enforcing the outcomes of dispute resolutions. These challenges correspond directly to three types of mechanisms: dispute and complaint prevention (*ex ante*), dispute resolution (*ex post*), and enforcement mechanisms. Addressing these challenges distills the broader issue of social embeddedness in endogenous ODR into two key inquiries: (1) What mechanisms have emerged in the search for the most appropriate measures? (2) What linkages have been developed between these various mechanisms during their evolution?

The subsequent discussion will use Taobao, which means "searching for treasure" in Chinese, as an illustrative example. Taobao, founded by the Alibaba Group in 2003, is China's largest consumer-to-consumer (C2C) online platform, with nearly 500 million registered users and over 60 million regular visitors per day, more than 800 million listed items on any day, and 48,000 items sold per minute on average.[51] With the expansion of Taobao and the increase in the number of users, Taobao has evolved from a single C2C online bazaar into a comprehensive retail shopping mall encompassing C2C, group-buying, distribution, auctions, and other e-commerce modes. It has now become one of the largest international e-commerce trading platforms. Taobao exemplifies how diverse ODR mechanisms can coexist within a single marketplace, highlighting the effectiveness of endogenous ODR in a highly dynamic online environment. It has been described as among the most remarkable ODR initiatives, alongside eBay's complaint handling system.[52]

Reputation system and feedback

The internet economy is characterized by asymmetric information between sellers and buyers, and by limited enforceability due to the high costs associated with public enforcement. An online reputation system serves as a preventive measure to foster trust among participants in online transactions.

Taobao's multilateral reputation system operates on a feedback and rating mechanism similar to that of eBay, where both systems are often juxtaposed together

51 Taobao, "Introduction About Taobao," accessed July 31, 2024, https://www.taobao.com/tbhome/page/about/home.

52 Pablo Cortés, Aura Esther Vilata Nicuesa, and Chittu Nagarajan, "ODR for E-Commerce: Legal Standard and Developments in Asia and Europe," in *Online Dispute Resolution: Theory and Practice*, eds. Daniel Rainey, Ethan Katsh, and Mohamed S. Abdel Wahab, 2nd ed. (The Hague: Eleven, 2021), 249.

as leading examples of building institutional trust.[53] However, unlike eBay, which has a single "feedback score" for each user, Taobao maintains separate seller and buyer reputations for each user. To address the aforementioned information asymmetry, all information is readily quantifiable and highly visible to all transaction parties.

After completing a transaction, both buyers and sellers can rate each other. Ratings are categorized into "positive," "neutral," and "negative," with each rating corresponding to a specific point. Sellers receive 1 point for each positive rating, get no point for neutral ratings, and lose 1 point for each negative rating. Such a system is typical of online marketplaces, but there are notable innovations. On eBay, for instance, a large number of users, particularly buyers, often do not leave any feedback if there is no problem in a transaction. This, in turn, means that sellers do not get the credit they deserve unless buyers proactively rate them positively. To address this issue and counteract user inertia, Taobao implements a default rating mechanism that currently activates after 15 days of inaction by users following the successful completion of a transaction. The default rating score for either buyer or seller is positive (+1), unless overridden by a neutral (+0) or negative (−1) score from the other party. The rating score is the sum of these feedback scores from all transactions and is represented by different symbols. Sellers are graded into four symbols, from lowest to highest: heart, diamond, crown, and golden crown, with each category further divided into five levels (indicated by the number of symbols). It becomes progressively more difficult to advance to higher levels; for example, achieving one golden crown requires half a million points, while five golden crowns take 10 million points.

A user's rating grade, represented by these symbols, is displayed alongside their ID on Taobao. Additionally, Taobao assigns another set of symbols, known as certificates, to sellers who participate in specific buyer protection schemes, such as "no-reason return and refund within 7 days," "guarantee of authentic commodities," "prompt delivery of virtual items," "three-time compensation for counterfeits," and "secure payment methods." These certificates offer a highly visible way for potential buyers to assess a seller's feedback and commitment to consumer protection.

Taobao also displays the rating grades that each seller has received over various time periods – the previous week, the previous month, the past six months, and more than six months before – along with the percentage of positive ratings. All this information is shown on the seller's profile and can be accessed with just a few clicks. Figure 2.1 shows a screenshot of a Taobao shop from 2015 showing all the aforementioned information.

The specific criteria for these certificates may change over time. These changes in Taobao's shop certificate criteria over time can be observed by comparing the shop profiles in Figure 2.1 with those in Figures 2.2 and 2.3.

53 Naom Ebner, "The Human Touch in ODR: Trust, Empathy, and Social Intuition in Online Negotiation and Mediation," in *Online Dispute Resolution: Theory and Practice*, eds. Daniel Rainey, Ethan Katsh, and Mohamed S. Abdel Wahab, 2nd ed. (The Hague: Eleven, 2021), 84.

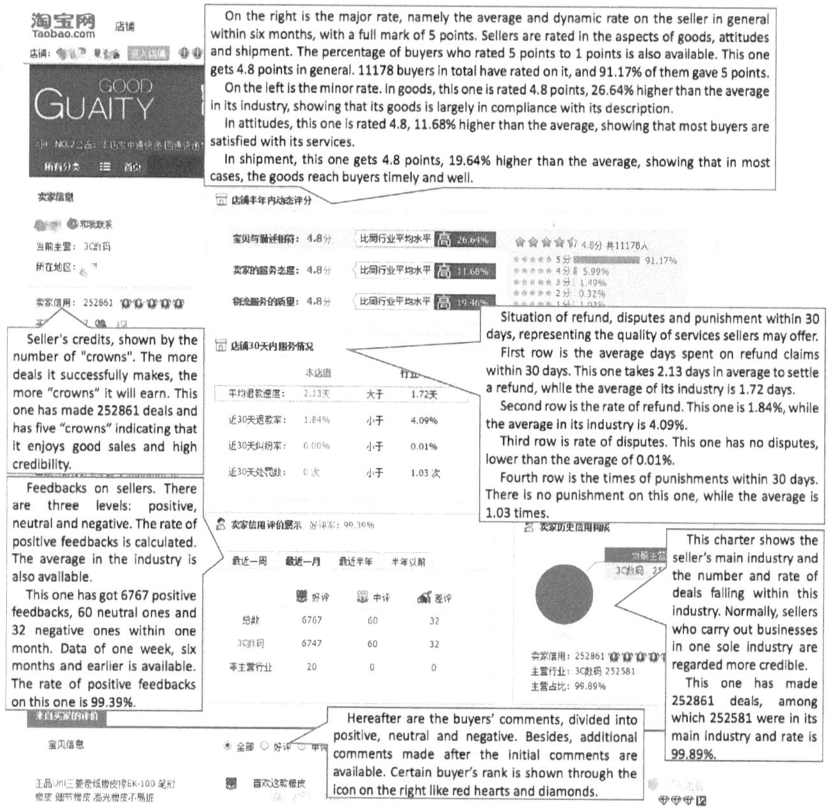

Figure 2.1 Example screenshot of Taobao's feedback profile, with explanation.

Source: Created by the author.

With the rise of mobile applications, the same shop can be accessed from both mobile and computer simultaneously. Figures 2.2 and 2.3 illustrate the shop screenshots of the same store on mobile and PC, respectively. Clicking on the shop avatar in the Taobao app reveals three certification categories: "Store Popularity," "Service Guarantee," and "Basic Information."

For example, under the "Service Guarantee" category, more specific tags, such as "average dispatch time of 15 hours" and "average customer service response time of 31 seconds," are shown. These detailed metrics provide an intuitive reflection of the shop's product sales, product quality, delivery speed, service attitude, and other aspects, contributing to a higher ranking in a list of similar shops. Additionally, users can click for Taobao's specific rules governing service guarantees next to the "Service Guarantee" section.

In summary, regardless of the specific changes to the certificates, their functionality remains consistent. Consequently, reputation on Taobao effectively reflects

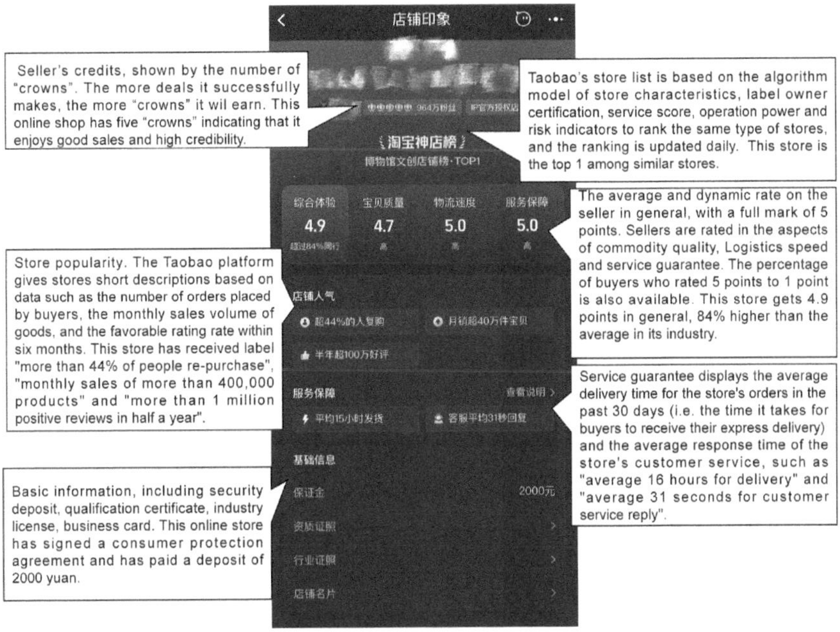

Figure 2.2 Example screenshot of store profile on Taobao app, with explanation.

Source: Created by the author.

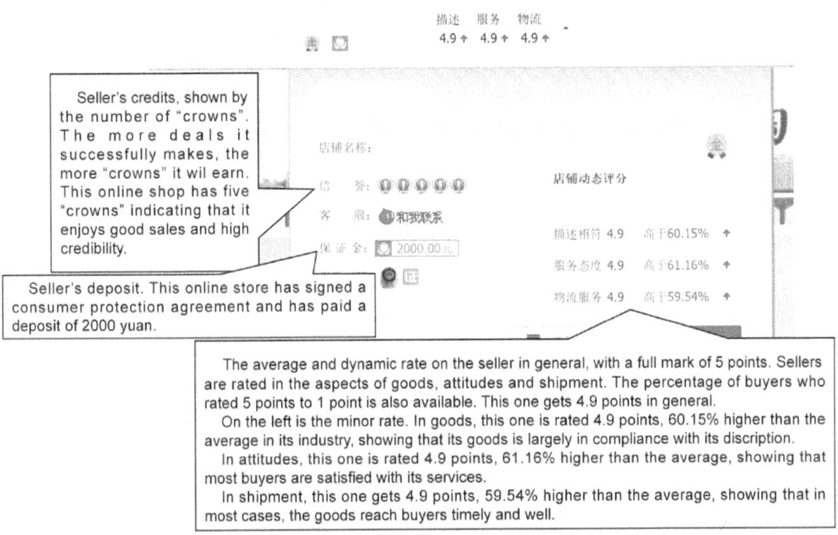

Figure 2.3 Example screenshot of Taobao's seller credit system, with explanation.

Source: Created by the author.

the quality of sellers' products and the purchasing power of buyers. This significantly reduces moral hazards and adverse selection for the many sellers and buyers involved in numerous transactions on Taobao.

Payment services and disputes resolution

Although reputation is effective in preventing disputes *ex ante*, its role becomes limited when disputes actually occur. In such cases, certain forms of dispute resolution are still needed. Taobao encourages users to negotiate with each other first. If an agreement cannot be reached, both the buyer and the seller can resort to Taobao's dispute resolution process by contacting Taobao's customer service specialists. Moreover, Taobao's dispute resolution is enhanced by its exclusive payment system, Alipay. Alipay started as a subsidiary part of Alibaba's Taobao operation in 2003 but quickly gained formalistic independence in 2004. It is now the largest mobile payment service in China, with over 50% of market share.[54]

One major reason Taobao won its competition with other websites was its reliance on Alipay as an escrow tool. Alipay serves as a trusted third party in a transaction, providing secure methods to transfer items and payments to both parties. It first receives payments from the buyer on behalf of the seller. When the payment is received, the seller is notified to ship the item. Once the item is received with no issues, Alipay releases the payment to the seller.

There are two ways to confirm the acceptance of the item: The buyer can manually confirm receipt, or if the buyer takes no action, the Taobao system will automatically determine receipt in due course to facilitate the conclusion of the transaction. For instance, if the item is shipped by tracked courier services, the system will automatically confirm receipt and release payment ten days after the seller updates the transaction status to "item shipped."

Taobao's release time for payment to sellers is a relatively complex issue that depends on numerous factors, including the seller's account type, reputation rating, and transaction history. For instance, Taobao has specific requirements for sellers' creditworthiness; the higher the creditworthiness, the faster the payment may arrive. Sellers can improve their reputation to speed up payment arrival. A seller's transaction history also affects the time it takes for the payment to arrive. If a seller has a consistently dispute-free transaction history, the system may release the payment faster. If there are frequent refunds or post-sale issues, release of the payment may be delayed, until the final status of the transaction is settled with no dispute. The speed of payment arrival also relates to the payment method. Generally speaking, using third-party, dedicated online payment methods such as Alipay and WeChat Pay can expedite payment arrival, while payment to traditional bank accounts may take longer.

54 "Do Alipay and Tenpay Misuse Their Market Power?," *The Economist*, August 6, 2020, https://www.economist.com/finance-and-economics/2020/08/06/do-alipay-and-tenpay-misuse-their-market-power.

Taobao's "Dispute Resolution Rules" distinguish between disputes arising before a transaction is concluded and those occurring afterward.[55] A transaction is not deemed concluded until the buyer instructs Alipay to transfer the payment after receiving the product. Until then, buyers can apply to get their money back through the refund process, for reasons such as non-delivery, misrepresentation of the item, or the delivery of the wrong item. Subsequently, the dispute can be resolved through direct negotiation between sellers and buyers, Taobao's dispute resolution process, or even litigation. Taobao offers the possibility of intervention by its customer services personnel, known as "Xiao'er,"[56] for scenarios such as the seller having not received the returned item, the item not matching the description, or the item having quality issues. During the dispute resolution process, Taobao freezes the payment.

After a transaction has concluded, a buyer can still submit complaints to Taobao through the "Advance Compensation" program. Taobao mandates that all sellers participating in the Consumer Protection Service sign a consumer protection agreement and deposit a guarantee in their Alipay accounts according to the type of seller and the commodities they sell. For example, private sellers offering ladies' wear or boutique items are required to deposit RMB 1,000. The amount of the deposit is displayed in the seller's public profile. When a transaction is concluded via Alipay and the buyer cannot resolve the dispute directly with the seller, they can apply to Taobao for compensation. Xiao'er then determines whether the complaint has valid grounds. If a complaint is upheld, Xiao'er has the right to instruct Alipay to deduct the corresponding amount from the seller's account to compensate the buyer. Even if a seller has made no deposit, or if the deposit is insufficient to cover the compensation, Taobao may still pay the refund or compensation from its own account. Subsequently, the seller is obliged to reimburse Taobao. If the deposit is used for compensation, Taobao requires the seller to replenish the deposit after compensation; failure to do so in a timely manner will result in the seller being unable to sell items on Taobao.

To facilitate buyer–seller communication during transactions, Taobao developed a powerful online instant messaging system where all past communications between the parties could be stored and examined by Taobao as evidence in dispute resolution. Additionally, Taobao sellers and buyers can join group chats to exchange information. All such information is again stored by Taobao for future use in dispute resolution if needed. Through these institutional arrangements, Taobao, as an insider, acquires all the information pertaining to online transactions and is thus in an advantageous position to settle disputes.

However, Taobao's ecosystem has inherent weaknesses. Its in-house dispute resolution mechanism relies on its employees, who adjudicate disputes based on

55 Taobao, "Taobao Platform Dispute Resolution Rules," May 6, 2019, https://rule.taobao.com/?type=detail&ruleId=99&cId=1154#/rule/detail?ruleId=99&cId=1154.

56 Xiao'er was an ancient term in Chinese to address waiters in restaurants and hotels. Taobao borrows it for its personnel in the customer services.

their own knowledge. The limited expertise of customer service personnel to evaluate evidence raises questions of impartiality, integrity, and accountability. Previously, corruption among Xiao'er has attracted public attention.[57] In contrast, eBay employs a better practice by utilizing a dispute resolution tool provided by SquareTrade, a third party offering assisted negotiation and mediation. eBay can discontinue cooperation with SquareTrade if corruption occurs. As mentioned earlier, the evolution of endogenous ODR occurs via a trial-and-error process. Taobao incidentally makes adjustments to address perceived problems. Most notably, Taobao has established an innovative approach, namely, crowdsourcing dispute resolution, where a dispute is adjudicated by a group of jurors who are registered members on Taobao. These members are not randomly selected and must meet certain requirements. This new approach highlights the dynamics and evolution of endogenous ODR, which will be further introduced and analyzed in Chapter 3.

Linkage between different mechanisms

Aoki observes that "one source of the diversity in overall institutional arrangements in market governance is mutually supportive, complementary relationships among constituent governance mechanisms. The presence of complementarity implies that the configuration of overall arrangements can be internally coherent and robust."[58] Applying this to the online world, various forms of ODR and individual mechanisms, as well as their networks as a whole, contribute to the overall diversity of platforms like Taobao. Complementarity is evident among these individual endogenous ODR mechanisms. Through their interactions, the effectiveness of one mechanism is reinforced, either directly or indirectly, by others, while the limitations of one mechanism can be mitigated by others.

Online transactions are characterized by asymmetric information and high enforcement costs. These challenges can be significantly mitigated in advance of transactions through the implementation of online reputation systems. One major reason eBay triumphed over its competitors was its fully integrated online reputation system,[59] primarily via user feedback. Taobao has adopted a similar approach. However, its online reputation systems still have some limitations. First, individuals with poor ratings can easily create new accounts or switch to another site, continuing dishonest practices. While this may be feasible for onetime sellers, it is too costly for professional sellers. For the latter, accumulated reputation becomes an asset, creating lock-in effects as their trade volume increases.[60]

57 "A Hangzhou e-commerce platform employee accepted bribes totaling 92 million yuan in one year, drawing attention to internal corruption issues within the e-commerce platform 杭州电商平台小二一年受贿9200万，电商平台内部腐败问题引发关注," *Sohu* 搜狐, May 15, 2024, https://www.sohu.com/a/779062808_211762.

58 Aoki, *Comparative Institutional Analysis*, 88.

59 Rule and Singh, "ODR and Online Reputation Systems," 178–81.

60 David P. Baron, "Private Ordering on the Internet: The eBay Community of Traders," *Business and Politics* 4 (2002): 253.

Second, user feedback–based reputation systems may not always be accurate and truthful, as users might abuse their privileges by manipulating feedback.[61] Third, and related to the previous point, Taobao's online reputation systems currently lack a mechanism for challenging or reviewing negative ratings, even if there is a misunderstanding or malicious intent, unlike that of eBay. The nature of online reputation systems dictates that they are stricter than their offline counterparts, leaving a permanent record against all parties, whether deservedly or not. Therefore, reputation systems alone cannot be relied upon and must be supported by other institutions.

As reputation systems fail to eliminate all incentive-related problems, dispute resolution mechanisms remain necessary. Taobao primarily uses Xiao'er to address disputes arising on its platform. In Taobao's ecosystem, Xiao'er enforces all of Taobao's rules. Additionally, crowdsourced ODR has been introduced, offering redress to users who prefer not to use Taobao's internal dispute resolution mechanisms.

Some online platforms utilize dispute resolution mechanisms not only to resolve disputes but also to remove unjustified negative feedback, as seen with SquareTrade at eBay.[62] Negative feedback can sometimes be inaccurate and caused by unjustified reasons, so mechanisms are needed for the removal of such feedback. This creates a linkage between the ODR mechanism and the feedback system. During the feedback removal process, sellers and buyers have an opportunity to recommunicate and resolve misunderstandings. This process enables sellers to correct their behavior without losing their reputation, thereby alleviating the overly stringent nature of online reputation systems. Moreover, reputation systems are only effective when based on accurate information. Thus, the ability to remove unjustified negative feedback helps maintain the integrity of the reputation system.

Another important complementary relationship exists between the payment tool Alipay and other mechanisms. While online payment systems primarily provide a convenient way to complete transactions, they also play two crucial roles in dispute resolution. First, they effectively prevent disputes from one-shot transactions by significantly reducing enforcement costs *ex post*, in combination with online reputation systems. Second, they expedite the dispute resolution process. Funds held in escrow by Alipay can be automatically used to compensate consumers promptly.

61 Sulin Ba, Andrew B. Whinston, and Han Zhang, "Building Trust in Online Auction Markets Through an Economic Incentive Mechanism," *Decision Support Systems* 35 (2003): 276.

62 SquareTrade provided mechanisms to remove negative feedback. This, in turn, strengthened merchants' incentive to comply with SquareTrade requirements. There were two options for this purpose. A merchant could send a buyer a form for mutual feedback withdrawal, and SquareTrade would remove negative feedback based on the signed form from both parties. Alternatively, if the buyer did not respond, the merchant could apply to SquareTrade with the transaction details. Upon receiving the application, SquareTrade would contact the other party. If the other party did not respond within 14 days, the applicant could automatically request the removal of feedback. If the other party responded, both would resolve the matter through a mediator. If it was ultimately decided to remove the negative feedback, eBay would do so within 14 days at SquareTrade's request.

In addition, as mentioned earlier, the release time for sellers' payments is also tied to their reputation. The higher the seller's reputation, the faster the payment may arrive. Sellers can enhance their reputation to expedite the payment process.

In summary, Taobao's dispute resolution mechanism operates as a spontaneous order by Hayek's threshold, as a network of mutually supportive and complementary relationships as described by Aoki, and as a "system" in the context of internet dispute mechanism design by Rabinovich-Einy and Katsh.[63] This feature of private ordering is consciously recognized and purposefully designed by Taobao. It remains Taobao's incentive to enforce private ordering to add value for its members and expand trade volume. In terms of methods, Taobao continually redesigns and improves its services through trial and error. This includes continuously adjusting the rules and integrating different mechanisms, such as insurance, escrow, and third-party dispute resolution. These endogenous institutions interact within the overall sophisticated arrangements of online marketplaces. The institutional linkages between these mechanisms have demonstrated their genuine value in overcoming the limitations of individual mechanisms.

Summary

This chapter presents an analytical framework that distinguishes between two forms of ODR: exogenous and endogenous. It examines the social embedding of these forms within the online environment, focusing on two central questions: (1) why exogenous ODR has not prospered, and (2) how endogenous ODR becomes self-sustaining and co-evolves with online transactions.

In the digital era, dispute resolution mechanisms can be categorized into traditional mechanisms, exogenous ODR, and endogenous ODR, all of which are employed to resolve online disputes. Traditional dispute resolution mechanisms, such as litigation and alternative dispute resolution, originated in the offline environment and continue to evolve with disputes arising from that domain. These mechanisms are unlikely to be completely replaced by ODR and thus remain the dominant method for resolving disputes in the offline world, at least for now.

Exogenous ODR might find its place in resolving both online and offline disputes by competing with traditional dispute resolution mechanisms and endogenous ODR, provided it can address issues related to social embedding. Endogenous ODR, however, holds significant potential to become the primary dispute resolution mechanism for online activities due to its intrinsic advantages.

Nevertheless, the future of both endogenous and exogenous ODR remains undetermined, leaving ample scope for governmental and legal intervention. Several international organizations have begun to reassess current ODR mechanisms. For instance, the Organisation for Economic Co-operation and Development

63 Rabinovich-Einy and Katsh, "Lessons from Online Dispute Resolution," 52.

(OECD),[64] the Asia-Pacific Economic Cooperation (APEC),[65] the International Chamber of Commerce,[66] and Consumers International[67] have issued reports and guidelines advocating for the integration of ODR into the practices of various countries and companies. Such efforts may profoundly impact the future evolution of institutional frameworks. In addition, in 2023, UNCTAD issued a report titled "Technology and the Future of Online Dispute Resolution (ODR) Platforms for Consumer Protection Agencies," focusing on improving consumer ODR through the use of electronic communications and other information and communication technology.[68]

A 2017 article by this author predicted two main trends for the future of ODR: the "endogenization of exogenous ODR" and the emergence of "specialized endogenous ODR."[69] The former trend suggests that exogenous ODR may gradually adapt to the overall institutional arrangements of both online and offline societies, driven by strong external influences. This adaptation could occur in two ways: first, by stabilizing the linkage between exogenous ODR and the law, thereby gaining firm legal recognition, and second, by potentially encoding exogenous ODR within online communities, transforming it into endogenous ODR. The latter trend envisions the development of specific endogenous ODR systems tailored to address niche online problems. Examples include the domain name dispute resolution system established by ICANN and the highly specialized ODR models used by platforms like Alipay and the Taobao Pan Center.

Looking back at the development of ODR over the past few years up to 2024, it is evident that these trends have begun to materialize. For instance, China has enacted several laws and regulations to facilitate the development of online litigation, and revisions to its arbitration law are currently in progress. Exogenous ODR systems are now being increasingly utilized to resolve both offline and online disputes.

As cyberspace becomes an increasingly vital arena for human activities, ODR – leveraging sophisticated internet-based tools – is poised to become a resource of growing value, potentially forming the core of future dispute resolution

64 OECD has consistently encouraged the promotion of ODR. Among the existing initiatives from international governmental bodies, the most influential is the OECD's guidelines and reports in the context of electronic commerce. For example, Guidelines for Consumer Protection in the Context of Electronic Commerce (December 9, 1999); Consumers in the Online Marketplace: The OECD Guidelines Three Years Later (February 3, 2003); OECD Recommendation on Consumer Dispute Resolution and Redress (July 12, 2007).

65 APEC Economic Committee, "Study on Best Practices Using ODR" (January 2023).

66 The International Chamber of Commerce, "Resolving Disputes Online: Best Practices for ODR in B2C Disputes" (November 2003).

67 Consumers International, "World Consumer Rights Day 2018 Briefing: Better Protection Online."

68 UNCTAD, "Technology and the Future of Online Dispute Resolution (ODR) Platforms for Consumer Protection Agencies," 2023, https://unctad.org/system/files/official-document/tcsditcinf2023d5_en.pdf.

69 Wei Gao, "The Success and Failure of Online Dispute Resolution," *Hong Kong Law Journal* 47 (2017): 445.

systems. These systems may evolve into diverse forms, extending well beyond traditional dispute resolution methods. As Aoki asserts, "the emergent situation is somewhat reminiscent of the one prevailing prior to the emergence of nation states when many private-order mechanisms were experimented and competed."[70] Only time will reveal the full scope of this transformation. What is certain is that we are currently witnessing a significant phase of institutional evolution.

Bibliography

Alchian, Armen A. "Uncertainty, Evolution, and Economic Theory." *Journal of Political Economy* 58, no. 3 (1950): 211–21.

Aoki, Masahiko. *Toward a Comparative Institutional Analysis*. Cambridge: MIT Press, 2001.

Arsic, Jasna. "International Commercial Arbitration on the Internet: Has the Future Come Too Early?" *Journal of International Arbitration* 14, no. 3 (1997): 209–21.

Ba, Sulin, Andrew B. Whinston, and Han Zhang. "Building Trust in Online Auction Markets Through an Economic Incentive Mechanism." *Decision Support System* 35, no. 3 (2003): 273–86. https://doi.org/10.1016/S0167-9236(02)0074-X.

Baron, David P. "Private Ordering on the Internet: The eBay Community of Traders." *Business and Politics* 4, no. 3 (2002): 24584. https://doi.org/10.2202/1469-3569.1041.

Berman, Paul Schiff. "From International Law to Law and Globalization." *Columbia Journal of Transnational Law* 43 (2005): 485–556.

Bowles, Samuel. *Microeconomics: Behavior, Institutions, and Evolution*. Princeton, NJ: Princeton University Press, 2004.

Cortés, Pablo. "Online Dispute Resolution for Consumers." In *Online Dispute Resolution: Theory and Practice*, edited by Mohamed S. Abdel Wahab, Ethan Katsh, and Daniel Rainey, 151–73. The Hague: Eleven, 2012.

Cortés, Pablo, Aura Esther Vilata Nicuesa, and Chittu Nagarajan. "ODR for E-Commerce: Legal Standard and Developments in Asia and Europe." In *Online Dispute Resolution: Theory and Practice*, edited by Daniel Rainey, Ethan Katsh, and Mohamed S. Abdel Wahab, 2nd ed., 249–74. The Hague: Eleven, 2021.

Devanesan, Ruha, and Jeffrey Aresty. "ODR and Justice – An Evaluation of Online Dispute Resolution's Interplay with Traditional Theories of Justice." In *Online Dispute Resolution: Theory and Practice*, edited by Mohamed S. Abdel Wahab, Ethan Katsh, and Daniel Rainey, 263–305. The Hague: Eleven, 2012.

Dixit, Avinash. "Power of Incentives in Private versus Public Organizations." *The American Economic Review* 87, no. 2 (1997): 378–82.

Ebner, Naom. "The Human Touch in ODR: Trust, Empathy, and Social Intuition in Online Negotiation and Mediation." In *Online Dispute Resolution: Theory and Practice*, edited by Daniel Rainey, Ethan Katsh, and Mohamed S. Abdel Wahab, 2nd ed., 73–136. The Hague: Eleven, 2021.

Gao, Wei. "The Success and Failure of Online Dispute Resolution." *Hong Kong Law Journal* 47, no. 2 (2017): 445–74.

Hardy, I. Trotter. "The Proper Legal Regime for 'Cyberspace'." *University of Pittsburgh Law Review* 55 (1994): 993–1055.

Hayek, Fredrick A. "The Use of Knowledge in Society." *The American Economic Review* 35 (1945): 519–30.

Hayek, Fredrick A. *Law, Legislation and Liberty, Volume 1: Rules and Order*. Chicago, IL: University of Chicago Press, 1978.

Hill, Jonathan. *Cross-Border Consumer Contracts*. Oxford: Oxford University Press, 2008.

70 Aoki, *Comparative Institutional Analysis*, 91.

Hurwicz, Leonid. "Inventing New Institutions: The Design Perspective." *American Journal of Agricultural Economics* 69, no. 2 (1987): 395–402.
Hurwicz, Leonid. "Toward a Framework for Analyzing Institutions and Institutional Change." In *Markets and Democracy: Participation, Accountability, and Efficiency*, edited by Samuel Bowles, Herbert Gintis, and B. O. Gustafsson, 51–67. Cambridge: Cambridge University Press, 1993.
Li, John Shuhe. "Relation-Based versus Rule-Based Governance: An Explanation of the East Asian Miracle and Asian Crisis." *Review of International Economics* 11, no. 4 (2003): 651–73. https://doi.org/10/1111/1467-9396.00409.
Marjorie, Heins. "The Brave New World of Social Media Censorship." *Harvard Law Review Forum* 127 (2014): 325–30.
Menger, Carl. *Investigation into the Method of the Social Sciences with Special Reference to Economics*. Translated by Francis J. Nock. New York: New York University Press, 1985.
North, Douglass C. *Institutions, Institutional Change and Economic Performance*. Cambridge: Cambridge University Press, 1990.
Orna, Rabinovich-Einy, and Ethan Katsh. "Lessons from Online Dispute Resolution for Dispute System Design." In *Online Dispute Resolution: Theory and Practice*, edited by Daniel Rainey, Ethan Katsh, and Mohamed S. Abdel Wahab, 2nd ed., 49–72. The Hague: Eleven, 2021.
Philippe, Mireze Philippe. "Where Is Everyone Going with Online Dispute Resolution." *International Business Law Journal* 2 (2002): 167–211.
Post, David G., and David R. Johnson. "Chaos Prevailing on Every Continent: Towards a New Theory of Decentralized Decision-Making in Complex Systems." *Chicago-Kent Law Review* 73, no. 4 (1998): 1055–99.
Rule, Colin, and Harpreet Singh. "ODR and Online Reputation Systems – Maintaining Trust and Accuracy Through Effective Redress." In *Online Dispute Resolution: Theory and Practice*, edited by Mohamed S. Abdel Wahab, Ethan Katsh, and Daniel Rainey, 175–96. The Hague: Eleven, 2012.
Schultz, Thomas. "Does Online Dispute Resolution Need Governmental Intervention? The Case for Architectures of Control and Trust." *North Carolina Journal of Law & Technology* 6, no. 1 (2004): 71–106.
Spaulding, Norman W. "Online Dispute Resolution and the End of Adversarial Justice?" In *Legal Tech and Future of Civil Justice*, edited by David Freeman Engstrom, 251–85. Cambridge: Cambridge University Press, 2023. https://doi.org/10.1017/9781009255301.
Sugden, Robert. *The Economic of Rights, Cooperation and Welfare*. Oxford: Basil Blackwell, 1986.
Wahab, Mohamed S. Abdel. "ODR and E-Arbitration." In *Online Dispute Resolution: Theory and Practice*, edited by Mohamed S. Abdel Wahab, Ethan Katsh, and Daniel Rainey, 399–441. The Hague: Eleven, 2012.

3 Private online dispute resolution

Overview of private ODR

Any transaction carries potential risks, and e-commerce is no exception. Its distinguishing characteristics include anonymity, virtuality, and the cross-regional nature of transactions. Specifically, in e-commerce transactions, all information is transmitted via digital signals, with both agreements and payments executed as electronic data files through computer networks. Often, it is challenging to ascertain the identity of the transaction participants and the locales of these transactions. Additionally, transaction information, when existing solely as electronic data, is prone to alteration and loss. These novel circumstances not only exert significant impacts on the extant legal system, which is anchored in physical space and territoriality, but also present formidable challenges in jurisdiction determination, law application, and judgment enforcement in the resolution of commercial disputes in cyberspace, increasing the risk for individuals seeking public relief.

In cyberspace, the cost of enforcing contracts and resolving disputes through legal channels is relatively high, and judicial interventions, even when feasible, are often inefficient. It is indisputable that cyberspace necessitates a corresponding legal system; however, the development of cyberlaw has been sluggish, and the rapid pace of technological advancements has rendered the legal framework unable to address new circumstances promptly. The swift evolution of business models is hampered by outdated laws, and the legal system awaits adequate experiential feedback from these new business models, creating a vicious cycle that impedes the development of an innovative online economy. The lack of timely laws, the high cost of legal enforcement, and the slow pace of the legislative process make the legal system, as a public regulatory means, clearly inadequate for governing online business activities.

Even in modern countries with well-developed legal norms, when commercial or non-commercial disputes arise, both parties often first resort to various private methods to resolve them. The challenges faced by the legal system in resolving disputes in cyberspace have underscored the importance of private mechanisms in facilitating cooperation in online transactions and resolving online disputes.

Private ordering is a mode of self-organization through private rulemaking, private jurisdiction, and private enforcement. Even though modern states regulate

DOI: 10.4324/ 9781003594512-3

economic behaviors by enacting and enforcing laws, it is challenging for laws to cover all the intricacies of transactions. Many commercial transactions are sustained by customs, practices, and ongoing relationships. When a dispute arises, the parties to a transaction first try to resolve it through informal arrangements, such as negotiation. When attempts at private resolution fail, the law is often the last resort. The discussion of private order can be found in the literature of many disciplines, including law, economics, sociology, and anthropology.[1] From the Middle Ages to the information society, there are numerous examples of private organizations and economic activities utilizing "private law." The characteristics of the internet have vast potential for generating private order. Consequently, the industry has created a spontaneous incentive to establish governance mechanisms for e-commerce in cyberspace, with a wide range of private governance mechanisms emerging.

The importance of private regulation in the field of internet governance has been widely recognized. Johnson and Post are strong advocates of private governance. They point out that cyberspace significantly decreases the association between legally significant online phenomena and physical locations. However, many of the jurisdictional and substantive issues arising from border-crossing electronic communications can be resolved by a simple principle: recognizing that there is a legally significant boundary between cyberspace and the "real world", and treating the internet as a separate space. Following this line of thought, the governance of cyberspace should aim to find the most appropriate rules, set by those who understand and participate in cyberspace, and make enforcement possible and effective through new globalized forms of communication.[2] Other scholars favor a hybrid system that combines public and private governance and agree that *lex electronica* plays a significant role in regulating commercial activities on the internet.[3] Due to the transnational nature of digital communication, it is often difficult for individual national regulation to succeed. Similarly, internet regulation by international lawmaking risks failure due to the difficulty of reaching consensus among different countries. Self-regulation of the internet has thus become an important concern for internet administrators.

Private self-regulation has significant advantages in cyberspace, as evidenced by the various endogenous ODR mechanisms discussed in Chapter 2. Private rules are set by internal members of the organization based on their particular skills and preferences, rather than being imposed by external entities unfamiliar with the rules. The norms developed within the organization, and the written behavioral norms

1 Choon-Piew Pow, "Constructing a New Private Order: Gated Communities and the Privatization of Urban Life in Post-Reform Shanghai," *Social & Cultural Geography* 8, no. 6 (2007): 813; Tehila Sagy, "What's So Private About Private Ordering?," *Law & Society Review* 45, no. 4 (2011): 923; Jean-Phiilippe Platteau, "Behind the Market Stage Where Real Societies Exist-Part I: The Role of Public and Private Order Institutions," *The Journal of Development Studies* 30, no. 3 (1994): 533.

2 David R. Johnson and David Post, "Law and Borders – The Rise of Law in Cyberspace," *Stanford Law Review* 48 (1996): 1378–79; David G. Post, "What Larry Doesn't Get: Code, Law, and Liberty in Cyberspace," *Stanford Law Review* 52 (2000): 1440.

3 Henry H. Perritt, "Towards a Hybrid Regulatory Scheme for the Internet," *University of Chicago Legal Forum* (2001): 252.

based on them, stem from a set of common values shared by the internal members. As such, the use of self-developed standards reinforces the collective consciousness of the participants, and internal members are often sufficiently motivated to adhere to the internal rules. In addition, rules developed within an organization are more concrete than laws and can be corrected or changed more quickly in response to specific forms of environmental change. In short, private regulation is more effective and flexible than public regulation. Another immediate advantage of private regulation is that it circumvents the jurisdictional and choice-of-law dilemmas inherent in managing internet disputes, since there is no reliance on the formal legal system.

In addition, public agents and private organizations participate in the economy in distinct ways, exhibiting different behaviors and pursuing varied objectives. Public agents may prioritize justice and equity for society as a whole. However, lacking competitive pressure, they have less incentive to enhance their services. Enterprises, on the other hand, focus on maximizing profits and are driven by a strong profit motive. Under competitive pressure, they are incentivized to improve their practices. Consequently, private regulation benefits from stronger internal incentives.

Another significant advantage of relying on private ordering to resolve disputes is its greater cost-effectiveness compared to the formal legal system. The actual costs, particularly in terms of time, are frequently higher within the formal legal framework than those incurred under alternative private ordering systems. Consequently, the anticipated outcome of a court judgment serves more effectively as a deterrent, prompting parties to seek amicable compromises in private. This benefit of private dispute resolution is especially pronounced in the context of cyberspace.

However, private regulation is not without its drawbacks. For instance, the rules can be amended at any time, lacking the stability associated with legal provisions; it may confer advantages on certain individuals, potentially disadvantaging other participants; and private dispute resolution mechanisms may lack the enforceability that judicial systems provide. Nonetheless, the unique nature of cyberspace often renders traditional legal regulations ineffective without the support of private regulatory frameworks. Particularly in the early stages of e-commerce development, the choice is not between a "second-best" and a "better" solution but between having a regulatory mechanism and none at all. The viability of private regulation as a dispute resolution method depends solely on the needs of its potential users. It will be adopted to the extent that it fulfills the widely recognized need for a flexible, cost-effective, and relatively just dispute resolution mechanism. In the online business environment, private regulation becomes the predominant governance model in cyberspace if the legal system proves inadequate or ineffective.

Analysis of types of private ODR

Types of private regulation in cyberspace

This section categorizes ODR regimes by examining the interconnections between private ODR systems and formal legal frameworks, thus providing a foundational understanding of private regulatory regimes. It is now evident that the internet, contrary to the early cyber-anarchist vision of being a domain governed solely by customary rules lacking enforcement and policymaking mechanisms, requires greater governance structure. The governance of internet society often necessitates a multifaceted approach involving various mechanisms and institutions supporting and complementing each other, including private mechanisms, administrative regulations, and legal frameworks. These elements collectively delineate the boundaries of online commercial activities.

Scholars have proposed various models to explain the public–private interaction of rulemaking, enforcement, and dispute resolution. Schwarcz posits that there are four classes in the relationship between private regulation and public regulation: (1) rules formulated and enforced by sovereign governments, (2) rules originated by private actors but put into force by sovereign governments, (3) rules originated and enforced by private actors under governmental delegation, and (4) rules adopted by private actors without government sanction or enforcement. Among these four types, the last three pertain to private regulation.[4] Meanwhile, Perritt postulates that private regulation, including private rulemaking and dispute resolution, occurs in four basic scenarios: (1) Public institutions delegate some of their rulemaking and adjudication authority to private institutions or defer to private decisions after the fact; (2) those subject to private regulation consent in advance to the private regulatory regime; (3) private decisions are sufficiently acceptable to those affected that they acquiesce after the fact rather than pursuing their disputes before public institutions; or (4) persons or entities in control of valuable resources issue rules and enforce them by threatening denial of access to the valuable right.[5] Similarly, Abramson believes that the models of private regulation include (1) formal governmental deputizing of private regulators, (2) formal connection between government and private regulators, and (3) no formal connection between government and private regulators.[6]

These categorizations of private orders have been developed to address various issues within the field. Schwartz focuses on scenarios where rules are privately formulated yet enforced by the state. Using the Internet Corporation for Assigned Names and Numbers (ICANN) as an exemplar, he questions the legitimacy of private regulation, critiquing its singular focus on economic efficiency. Perritt, however, explores hybrid network governance, advocating that public law should scaffold the overarching regulatory framework, while private regulation refines operational details. Abramson's research centers on the constitutionality of private regulation. There is observable overlap in the frameworks proposed by these scholars, with all three addressing government-authorized private regulation, specifically citing ICANN as a prominent example of state-delegated private regulation. Additionally, a shared category across all three frameworks is private regulation

4 Steven L. Schwarcz, "Private Ordering," *Northwestern University Law Review* 97, no. 1 (2002): 324–29.

5 Perritt, "Hybrid Regulatory Scheme," 226–27.

6 Harold I. Abramson, "A Fifth Branch of Government: The Private Regulators and Their Constitutionality," *Hastings Constitutional Law Quarterly* 16 (1989): 169–74.

independent of any public regulatory linkage. Moreover, Perrett's fourth situation, involving denial of access to a valuable right, holds particular significance for internet regulation.[7]

Building on these theoretical foundations, and recognizing the distinctions between private regulation in cyberspace and offline environments, the private order of dispute resolution in cyberspace can be categorized into three distinct types: (1) private regulation connected to public regulation, (2) private regulation independent of public regulation, and (3) technology-based regulation and enforcement.

The fundamental difference between cyberspace and physical space lies in the utilization of cyber resources and codes. Codes facilitate the development of unique private mechanisms in cyberspace that are infeasible in physical realms, such as constitutional code-based digital private governance mechanisms. These mechanisms lack institutional equivalents in the physical world and are therefore classified separately. Additionally, in offline contexts, transactional governance mechanisms vary significantly, with some areas governed by legal systems and others by non-legal systems or social norms. This diversity persists in cyberspace. Thus, private regulation in cyberspace can be further divided based on its interaction with formal legal systems into "private regulation connected to public regulation" and "private regulation independent of public regulation." Unlike digital private regulation, many mechanisms within these two categories have analogies in offline contexts, although technology imparts new characteristics to them. The focus of scholarly research in this area tends to be on institutional differences and the novel attributes introduced by the internet. Notably, in any taxonomic approach, certain cases may exhibit traits of multiple types simultaneously; for example, ICANN could be perceived as a private mechanism independent of public regulation due to its unique enforcement mechanism, but also as a private, code-based governance structure. These three types of private order in cyberspace will now be examined in turn.

Private regulation connected to public regulation

A prime example of private regulation connected to public regulation is the system of international commercial arbitration. Originating in the customary law of medieval European merchants, international commercial arbitration in its contemporary form – particularly as managed by international arbitration institutions – developed in the late 19th and early 20th centuries. The cornerstone of international commercial arbitration is the principle of party autonomy. This principle allows parties to submit existing or potential future disputes to arbitration through an arbitration agreement. By recognizing the validity of this arbitration agreement and endowing the arbitral tribunal with the authority to settle disputes, the state effectively transfers a portion of its dispute resolution authority to private arbitrators chosen

7 Perritt, "Hybrid Regulatory Scheme," 237.

by the parties. Furthermore, it ensures the enforcement of arbitral awards through state coercion. Arbitration thereby establishes a formal linkage between private and public regulation, embodied in a legally sanctioned institutional arrangement.

Online arbitration serves as the digital adaptation of traditional arbitration within the context of the internet society. It retains the structural framework of traditional arbitration, operating based on an arbitration agreement and having decisions rendered by a third-party arbitrator who evaluates the relevant evidence and claims. Additionally, online arbitration utilizes network technology to conduct proceedings within a virtual space, thereby enhancing traditional arbitration's capabilities in terms of information dissemination and interaction.

The evolution of the traditional commercial arbitration system demonstrates that arbitration originated as a private order and gradually established itself as an effective method of dispute resolution in commercial practices. It was eventually recognized by legislative action, transitioning into a form of public regulation. This represents a prolonged process of institutional evolution from a private dispute resolution mechanism to a state-sanctioned system which transitioned from being tightly restricted by the state to gradually receiving state support. International commercial arbitration epitomizes an endogenous dispute resolution system that evolved from offline environments to achieve an institutional equilibrium.

Nevertheless, both traditional and online arbitrations are exogenous systems to cyberspace, facing the challenge of institutional integration in this new setting, as explained in Chapter 2. In this process, they contend with private mechanisms that have spontaneously emerged in cyberspace, which are inherently better suited to the unique characteristics of online transactions. Consequently, there is considerable uncertainty regarding whether online arbitration can be self-enforcing. A private dispute resolution system that lacks self-sustainability will eventually become obsolete.

To ensure that online arbitration becomes an effective ODR mechanism, it is imperative to actively seek integration with the existing legal system to garner its support. Since traditional arbitration is predicated on physical jurisdiction, the institutional design of online arbitration must meet the mandatory requirements stipulated by current arbitration law to effectively connect with the prevailing legal framework.

For instance, initially, there were significant concerns regarding the ability of online arbitration to address the issue of the seat of arbitration in cyberspace. The China International Economic and Trade Arbitration Commission (CIETAC), for example, explicitly allows parties to choose the place of the arbitration.[8] Should there be no agreement, the place of the arbitration defaults to CIETAC's location. By definitively anchoring online arbitration to a physical location, a direct link is established between online arbitration and the prevailing international arbitration legal framework through the determination of the arbitration venue. Additionally, current rules require that awards be made in written form and signed by the arbitrators,

8 CIETAC, online arbitration rules (2015), Article 8.

with CIETAC's official seal affixed.[9] Although arbitral awards can now be created and delivered electronically, a physical copy of the award is still mandated. These provisions comply with Chinese law, ensuring that the award will not be nullified or deemed unenforceable in China, and facilitate the global enforcement of awards.

As a form of private dispute resolution, international arbitration, including its online variants, typically does not depend heavily on judicial enforcement. This independence largely stems from the highly autonomous nature of arbitration itself. It is widely acknowledged that, in most cases, arbitral awards are voluntarily executed by the parties involved. For example, it has been reported that over 90% of International Chamber of Commerce (ICC) arbitral awards are voluntarily complied with by the parties. The primary reason for this compliance is that business entities generally avoid damaging their reputations by refusing to adhere to the decisions of arbitral tribunals to which they have voluntarily agreed.[10] Therefore, international arbitration, as typified in this discussion, retains its autonomy while establishing a direct, albeit predominantly symbolic, connection with the formal legal system, which typically functions more as a final deterrent than as an active enforcement mechanism.

Private regulation independent of public regulation

Private regulation, as an alternative to public regulation, inherently presupposes self-enforcement. Classical studies, such as Greif's examination of the historical trade regime among Maghribi merchants, demonstrate the viability of private regulation operating under the auspices of the law but independent of legal enforcement mechanisms.[11] While the deterrent effect of legal sanctions may have historically prevented misconduct, evidence shows that many, if not most, agency relationships were not predicated on legal contracts. Moreover, there is little literature suggesting that disputes between traders and agents were adjudicated through courts; instead, it indicates that such legal proceedings were both time-consuming and costly.

Courts historically faced challenges in apprehending agents who had relocated and struggled to handle cases that required gathering information from events occurring months earlier and at distant locations. Bernstein's study of the private legal order within the cotton industry illustrates that, although arbitration awards could technically be enforced through the courts, this was seldom done in practice.[12] Non-compliance with arbitration decisions typically resulted in exclusion

9 CIETAC, Online Arbitration Rules (2015), Article 39; CIETAC, Arbitration Rules (2024), Articles 52.4 and 52.10.

10 United Nations Conference on Trade and Development, "5.7 Recognition and Enforcement of Arbitral Awards: The New York Convention"(UNCTAD/EDM/Misc.232/Add.37), 2003, https://unctad.org/system/files/official-document/edmmisc232add37_en.pdf, 4.

11 Avner Greif, "Reputation and Coalitions in Medieval Trade: Evidence on the Maghribi Traders," *The Journal of Economic History* 49 (1989): 864.

12 Lisa Bernstein, "Private Commercial Law in the Cotton Industry: Creating Cooperation Through Rules, Norms, and Institutions," *Michigan Law Review* 99 (2001): 1737–38.

from commercial organizations, a penalty publicly disclosed and highly effective, given the importance of membership for participating in the international cotton trade. This measure, combined with other social and reputational penalties, often sufficed to ensure timely enforcement of arbitral awards by the traders themselves.[13] Ellickson, in his research on Sacramento County, observed that ranchers often resolved disputes without legal recourse, sometimes in ways that contravened statutory law.[14] However, such private regulation effectively maximized group welfare without governmental oversight. These studies have demonstrated that, when private regulation is highly self-enforcing, insiders are content with internal mechanisms, and disputes rarely escalate beyond the realm of private regulation, thereby indicating a lack of substantial (*de facto*) connection between private and public regulation.

In cyberspace, this type of private regulation is exemplified by various endogenous ODR tools. The absence of specific legal regulations complicates judicial intervention in online disputes, and the costs associated with litigation or ADR are disproportionately high relative to the transaction value. As discussed in Chapter 2, online platforms like eBay and Taobao have developed sophisticated reputation systems that effectively promote cooperation between transaction parties. For dispute resolution, Taobao primarily relies on its own mechanisms, including customer service (Xiao'er), negotiations between buyers and sellers, and crowdsourcing mechanisms.

In contrast, eBay delegates dispute resolution to SquareTrade, a third-party mediation platform, in addition to its own Resolution Centre. Private third-party dispute resolution plays a crucial role in cyberspace, complementing the reputational mechanisms of online platforms. Despite originating from traditional mediation practices, SquareTrade's ability to enforce dispute resolution outcomes is pivotal, enhancing the governance mechanisms of the online platforms. A seller's commitment to resolving disputes through a third-party mechanism not only builds trust among potential buyers but also earns them a SquareTrade seal. This seal serves a similar function as the medieval records of judgment fulfillment by merchants' courts, whereby the enforcement records are monitored and merchants with declining reputations face sanctions from the merchant community.

This exemplifies a third-party mechanism that complements other governance structures on online platforms. As a third-party mechanism, it facilitates the dissemination of information regarding deceptive behaviors. Given the potential anonymity of traders and the rapid exchange of information online, news of defaults and non-compliance can spread swiftly. This dynamic enables third-party private adjudication mechanisms to scale to unprecedented levels. Furthermore, online dispute resolution mechanisms assist traders in rectifying unjust negative evaluations, enhancing the fairness and integrity of the trading environment. As Katsh

13 Bernstein, "Private Commercial Law," 1738–39.

14 Robert C. Ellickson, *Orders without Law: How Neighbors Settle Disputes* (Cambridge, MA: Harvard University Press, 1991), 3–4.

puts it, these mechanisms operate in the shadow of eBay law and are empowered by users agreeing to the terms and conditions for participation that eBay presents to them. They exhibit weak connectivity to the legal system yet possess robust autonomy and a de facto strong capacity for self-enforcement.[15]

Technology-based regulation and enforcement

Cyber governance is prominently characterized by code-based regulation. Unlike traditional regulatory methods in physical spaces, technology occupies a unique and crucial position in the regulation of cyberspace. Here, the rules of cyberspace can be enforced purely through code, without the need for legal or even social sanctions. In this context, code effectively becomes the law in cyberspace. In other words, ODR manifests as technology disguised as dispute resolution, rather than merely dispute resolution enhanced by technology.

From the early development of ODR, numerous applications have utilized automated, specialized computer systems to aid in resolving disputes. Notable examples include Cybersettle.com, Clicknsettle.com, and OneAccordinc.com, although several of these have since ceased operation.

Additionally, third-party preservation services, such as escrow services, serve as a guarantee measure in online transactions. The common practice in online transactions often requires the buyer to make payment in advance, posing a significant risk that the goods may not be received post-payment. Employing a third-party custodian as a trustee to collect and disburse payment on behalf of the seller significantly reduces the likelihood of fraud.

The domain name dispute resolution mechanism also exemplifies the intricate governance of cyberspace. Domain names, originally designed to facilitate the networking of computers and communication links on the internet, have been recognized by commercial organizations for their enormous potential in e-commerce. Merchants use trademarks, trade names, and other commercial symbols as domain names for their websites to attract consumers and enhance their visibility in the online marketplace, thereby assigning substantial commercial value to domain names. Under the Uniform Domain-Name Dispute-Resolution Policy (UDRP), ICANN and domain name registries regulate domain names according to the provisions of the UDRP framework.

The dispute resolution process managed by ICANN differs significantly from traditional arbitration in several key aspects: The outcomes of the UDRP dispute resolution process are not final, and courts are not bound by them. Participants in the process may initiate legal action either during the process or after its conclusion. Moreover, a domain name registrant must accept the domain name dispute resolution mechanism on a take-it-or-leave-it basis as part of the terms and conditions of the domain name registration agreement, forfeiting the opportunity to negotiate on equal footing as parties in traditional arbitration would.

15 Ethan Katsh, Janet Rifkin, and Alan Gaitenby, "E-commerce, E-disputes, and E-Dispute Resolution: In the Shadow of eBay Law," *Ohio State Journal on Dispute Resolution* 15, no. 3 (1999): 731.

One of the critical values of ICANN's UDRP lies in its self-enforcing nature, as UDRP decisions do not require judicial recognition or enforcement. Instead, they are implemented – upheld, revoked, or transferred – by ICANN-authorized domain name registrars following the expert's decision. The speed and efficiency of ICANN's domain name dispute resolution mechanism are crucial to the domain name community. The most valuable aspect of holding a domain name lies in its use, and a lengthy litigation process would severely hinder a trademark owner's ability to capitalize on the value of their trademark on the internet. Thus, while domain name dispute resolution mechanisms do not prohibit a party's right to bring a lawsuit, such actions are rare. The process requirements set in the UDRP remains the most significant domain name dispute resolution process to date and is considered one of the most successful online dispute resolution mechanisms.

Another of the latest developments in code-based digital private regulation, namely, blockchain-based digital enforcement and dispute resolution mechanisms, will be discussed later. Meanwhile, examining the public–private nature of ODR mechanisms facilitates a more comprehensive theoretical framework for the analysis and comparison of various ODR mechanisms, which will be explained next.

ODR Quadrant Diagram

Building on the differentiation between exogenous and endogenous ODR expounded in Chapter 2, the addition of the public–private spectrum of ODR mechanisms allows for a more nuanced theoretical analysis. By combining these two sets of factors, it becomes possible to create a two-dimensional diagram, labelled the "ODR Quadrant Diagram," as shown in Figure 3.1.

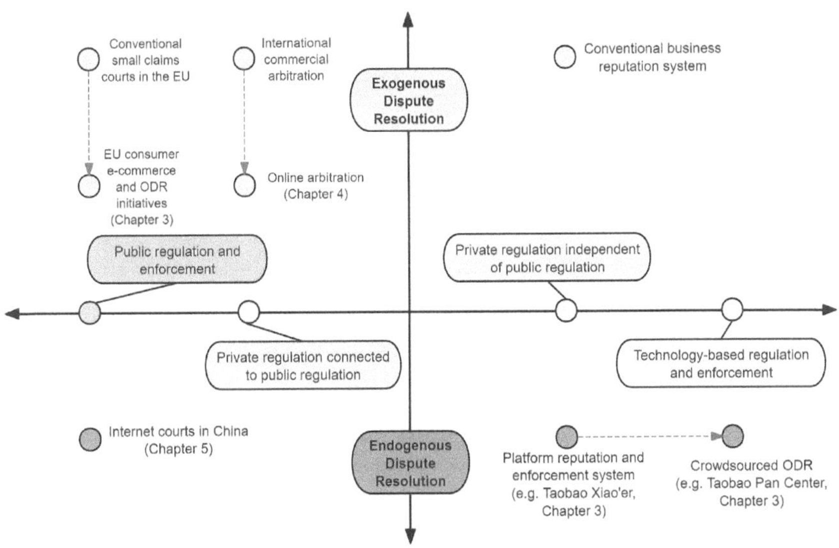

Figure 3.1 ODR Quadrant Diagram.

The horizontal X-axis represents the different levels of public or private regulation and enforcement of dispute resolution mechanisms. Starting from the most public institutions, such as courts of law, on the left, these mechanisms become increasingly less dependent on public authorities and endorsement, culminating on the right, where dispute resolution and enforcement are ensured by computer and internet technologies.

The vertical Y-axis represents the spectrum between exogenous and endogenous dispute resolution mechanisms in relation to cyberspace. As explained previously, some mechanisms gradually adapt and transform alongside technological and social changes and may move downward on the diagram. These movements can be representable on the ODR Quadrant Diagram, offering valuable insight into the intention and impact of various initiatives and reforms.

For example, international commercial arbitration, discussed in Chapter 4, is a private dispute resolution mechanism with public endorsement. It moves downward on the ODR Quadrant Diagram as it endeavors to become online arbitration and more endogenous to cyberspace. Nevertheless, endogenous and exogenous ODR often harbor very different values, with the former more focused on efficiency. This means that the compromise of the formality of international commercial arbitration by engaging with online operations may not necessarily be the most productive approach, which could potentially explain the rather limited popularity of online arbitration.

Some ODR mechanisms may also move horizontally on the ODR Quadrant Diagram. For example, Taobao's reputation system, to be examined later in this chapter, begins as a private ODR mechanism. However, it has since made notable efforts to integrate technology-based ODR mechanisms, including crowdsourced ODR. Despite this, its crowdsourced Taobao Pan Center has encountered major difficulties and has effectively been halted in its operation, demonstrating the challenges that ODR mechanisms face when they strive to alter their inherent nature.

The European Union's (EU) consumer ODR initiatives provide another important example, as they tried to leverage the power of the supranational infrastructure to transform the conventional court systems of different countries into a system more suited to cross-border e-commerce. However, this bid to become more endogenous to cyberspace met with little success, which will be examined next.

Achievements and deficiencies of judicial enforcement: an EU-based examination

The EU as a supranational case study

Internet activities frequently transcend national borders, and traditional enforcement mechanisms, confined by physical boundaries, may struggle to address cross-border enforcement challenges, particularly concerning the availability of legal resources and the high costs associated with enforcement. A significant advantage of private ODR mechanisms over public dispute resolution methods lies in their superior ability to facilitate effective enforcement. This section will delve into the EU's recent achievements and challenges within its judicial system regarding cross-border enforcement. By highlighting the obstacles encountered in public enforcement, this, in turn, emphasizes the importance and value of private enforcement in resolving cross-border disputes.

There are principally two approaches for judicial intervention in the resolution and enforcement of cross-border e-commerce disputes. The first approach involves developing litigation procedures tailored to cross-border consumer claims and ensuring the enforcement of judicial decisions across borders. The second approach provides judicial enforcement as a safeguard when disputing parties choose to resolve their issues through ADR. In recent years, EU has implemented numerous legislative initiatives aimed at resolving consumer disputes arising from cross-border e-commerce. These efforts have fostered a significant harmonization of substantive and procedural laws across the region, reducing barriers to cross-border enforcement among institutions and serving as an exemplary model for evaluating the effectiveness of a cross-border enforcement regime.

Another critical aspect of examining the EU's ODR system is its establishment of an ODR platform. To enhance the resolution of disputes stemming from business-to-consumer (B2C) transactions, the EU enacted Directive 2013/11/EU of the European Parliament and of the Council of May 21, 2013, on alternative dispute resolution for consumer disputes (Consumer ADR Directive) and amended Regulation (EC) No. 2006/2004 and Directive 2009/22/EC. Simultaneously, Regulation (EU) No. 524/2013 of the European Parliament and of the Council of May 21, 2013, on online dispute resolution for consumer disputes (ODR Regulation) was also adopted, amending Regulation (EC) No. 2006/2004 and Directive 2009/22/EC. The Consumer ODR Regulation aims to resolve contractual debt disputes between consumers residing in the EU and EU traders arising from online sales and service contracts through the use of the ODR platform and associated ADR entities.

The Consumer ADR Directive and the ODR Regulation are interrelated and complementary legislative instruments.[16] The ODR Regulation mandates the establishment of an ODR platform which serves as a single point of entry for consumers and traders seeking out-of-court resolution of online disputes through ADR entities connected to the platform which offer ADR procedures of verified quality. The presence of qualified ADR entities across the EU is crucial for the effective functioning of the ODR platform. Operational since 2016, the ODR platform functions as a comprehensive multilingual digital infrastructure where consumers can request online traders to resolve disputes using an ADR entity. The platform itself does not directly resolve disputes; instead, it consolidates ADR resources within the EU, facilitating the selection of an ADR organization by consumers to handle their disputes. The EU's efforts in consolidating ADR resources and promoting ODR through this approach warrant close observation and analysis.

16 Consumer ADR Directive, Recital Para.12.

Judicial remedies and enforcement of judicial decisions

Since the 1980s, the EU has enacted a series of substantive laws aimed at e-commerce to protect the rights and interests of consumers, including the right to safety and physical health, the right to be informed, and the right to redress. However, the protection provided by these laws is often difficult to realize, particularly in the cumbersome procedural landscape of cross-border transactions. Traditional mechanisms for protecting rights struggle to meet the demands of the internet era. Consequently, the EU has intensified its efforts to refine its legal framework, specifically focusing on adapting procedural laws to better address the resolution of disputes arising from internet commerce.

There is a pronounced emphasis on reducing litigation costs, addressing the need to resolve small-claims disputes, and establishing appropriate mechanisms for cross-border enforcement. To facilitate the resolution of small claims, most EU member states have established specific small-claims procedures.[17] Moreover, some member states have even eliminated the requirement for compulsory mediation before litigation in these procedures as part of their judicial reforms, arguing that such requirements were either unconstitutional or unduly restrictive of individuals' right to access the courts.[18] To "simplify and speed up litigation concerning small claims in cross-border cases, whilst reducing costs," the EU introduced Regulation (EC) No. 861/2007 of the European Parliament and of the Council of July 11, 2007, establishing the European small-claims procedure (small-claims regulation). This regulation, which covers litigation involving amounts up to €2,000, is founded on the principles of simplicity, speed, and proportionality.[19]

According to the provisions of the small-claims regulation, a judgment issued in one member state under such procedures is automatically recognized and enforced in another member state. Furthermore, EU countries have also adopted the small-claims procedure as an entry point for the development of electronic litigation, thereby improving litigation efficiency and strengthening consumer protection. Indeed, the trend toward electronic litigation has become global, driven by the pervasive influence of technology on the judicial system in the internet era, which has catalyzed efforts to better adapt the judicial system to the demands of the information society.

17 Horst Eidenmüller and Martin Engel, "Against False Settlement: Designing Efficient Consumer Rights Enforcement System in Europe," *Ohio State Journal on Dispute Resolution* 29, no. 2 (2014): 267.

18 For example, in Germany, most states have cut back the statutory requirement for small claims (amount in dispute lower than €750) to be conciliated or mediated before they can be brought to court. Eidenmüller and Engel, "Against False Settlement: Designing Efficient Consumer Rights Enforcement System in Europe," 29.

19 Since July 14, 2017, the EU amended the small-claims regulation to include "proceedings with a subject matter not exceeding EUR 5,000." Regulation (EU) 2015/2421 of the European Parliament and of the Council of December 16, 2015, amending Regulation (EC) No. 861/2007 establishing a European small-claims procedure and Regulation (EC) No. 1896/2006 creating a European order for payment procedure, Art. 2, 2015 O.J. (L 341) pp. 2, 5.

Cross-border consumer disputes typically involve multiple countries, adding layers of complexity to the application of law. To mitigate uncertainties surrounding the application of law, Regulation (EC) No. 593/2008 on the law applicable to contractual obligations (Rome I) establishes uniform choice of law rules for contracts across all EU member states (except Denmark), supporting the expansion of cross-border consumption and, in particular, cross-border business-to-consumer electronic transactions. Additionally, for the enforcement of judgments in civil and commercial matters, Regulation (EU) No. 1215/2012 of the European Parliament and of the Council of December 12, 2012, on jurisdiction and the recognition and enforcement of judgments in civil and commercial matters has streamlined the circulation of civil and commercial judgments among member states.

Despite these notable legislative efforts at the EU and member state levels to make both the legal framework and court jurisdiction more consumer-friendly, many individuals still hesitate to seek judicial remedies. The reasons are clear: They consider cost–benefit factors and question the efficacy of cross-border enforcement mechanisms.[20] Notably, the European small-claims procedure is underused due to the requirements for both parties to navigate foreign laws and judicial procedures, alongside practical barriers, such as rising translation costs and the need for parties to attend oral hearings in person across borders.[21] Moreover, the caseload in small-claims courts across EU member states has been steadily declining. In Germany, for example, the number of local small-claims cases has decreased by approximately 2% each year for several consecutive years, with other EU member states experiencing similar trends.[22] One of the main reasons for this decline is that the cost of dispute resolution often exceeds the amount in dispute itself. For many cases, consumers end up spending several hundred euros on litigation. According to a study by the EU Consumer Law Study Group, the average cost of cross-border litigation in the EU is €2,500 for a €2,000 case. Additionally, depending on the country, a litigation case takes between 12 and 64 months on average. Further EU statistics released in 2011 showed that as high as 21% of EU residents encounter issues resulting from their purchases of goods or services in a single year, but only 2% of them resort to litigation for dispute resolution.[23]

20 *Green Paper from the Commission – Legal Aid in Civil Matters: the Problems Confronting the Cross-border Litigant*, COM/2000/0051 final (Feb. 9, 2000).

21 See Regulation (EC) No. 861/2007 of the European Parliament and of the Council of July 11, 2007, establishing a European small-claims procedure, 2007, O. J. (L 199) pp. 1–22. See also Regulation (EU) No. 2015/2421 of the European Parliament and of the Council of December 16, 2015, amending Regulation (EC) No. 861/2007 establishing a European small-claims procedure and Regulation (EC) No. 1896/2006 creating a European order for payment procedure, 2015, O. J. (L 341) pp. 1–13.

22 Eidenmüller and Engel, "Against False Settlement," 268 fn23.

23 *Commission Staff Working Paper, Impact Assessment, Accompanying the Document Proposal for a Directive of the European Parliament and of the Council on Alternative Dispute Resolution for consumer disputes (Directive on consumer ADR) and Proposal for a Regulation of the European Parliament and of the Council on Online Dispute Resolution for consumer disputes (Regulation on consumer ODR)*, at 13, 81, SEC (2011) 1408 final (November 29, 2011).

Research and experience within the EU show that cost remains the most significant hurdle for consumers in the e-commerce dispute resolution process. Even with mechanisms such as the small-claims procedure, electronic litigation, and international conventions in place, judicial enforcement – especially cross-border enforcement – remains largely infeasible in practice.

Judicial enforcement of alternative dispute resolution

Various obstacles to enforcing judicial remedies have prompted individuals to seek out-of-court dispute resolution alternatives. As discussed in Chapter 1, ADR has been integrated with internet technology to form ODR, which is seen as having the potential to replace traditional judicial remedies that are often cumbersome, time-consuming, and costly. Currently, almost all traditional ADR mechanisms have a counterpart in cyberspace. In theory, the online development of ADR does not necessarily undermine the original legal framework for ADR, nor does it require the formulation of new legal rules. Therefore, the enforcement of ODR outcomes discussed generally aligns with the enforcement of ADR outcomes within an online environment.

In practice, there are many forms of ADR/ODR, which differ significantly from country to country, but a distinction can still be drawn between the binding and non-binding nature of the outcomes. Only binding outcomes can be enforced and guaranteed by the state's coercive power. Otherwise, parties to disputes will have to initiate a new claim, reverting to litigation, or seek private remedies. Such a distinction often determines the scope and feasibility of judicial enforcement for ADR.

In fact, the Consumer ADR Directive, the ODR Regulation, and the United Nations Commission on International Trade Law (UNCITRAL) Technical Notes on Online Dispute Resolution (UNCITRAL Technical Notes) have all drawn this distinction. The goal of the EU legislation is to provide consumers with efficient, swift, and cost-effective resolutions to disputes outside of traditional litigation. However, since Article 47 of the Charter of Fundamental Rights of the European Union guarantees that everyone has the right to an effective remedy and a fair trial, the recitals of the Consumer ADR Directive stipulate that ADR/ODR "should not be designed to replace court procedures and should not deprive consumers or traders of their rights to seek redress before the courts." As a result, Article 10 of the Consumer ADR Directive clarifies that agreements made before a dispute – where the consumer and the trader decide to submit a complaint to an ADR entity – will not be binding if the agreement has the effect of depriving the consumer of the right to bring an action before the courts. Furthermore, the Consumer ADR Directive maintains the non-binding nature of the outcomes of ADR upon consumers when the consumer had not been informed in advance and did not previously agree to be bound.

Nevertheless, the non-binding approach poses certain practical challenges. First, this non-binding arrangement may not guarantee that ADR outcomes will be enforced. It may even disincentivize consumers from complying with such outcomes due to the availability of an enforcement mechanism in litigation. In essence, consumers are aware that they can always bring an action before the court if they are unsatisfied with ADR outcomes. Second, the fact that litigation is not precluded does not mean it is feasible. Since litigation is too costly, too slow, and impractical for consumers, their right of access to justice may be, in effect, denied. Such an outcome would contradict the original design of the system. Therefore, a unilaterally binding ADR process could be considered.[24] Some scholars have also suggested the introduction of mandatory ADR.[25]

A legally binding ADR outcome is judicially enforceable, and the formality of online arbitration itself has not hindered its enforcement. The United Nations Convention on the Recognition and Enforcement of Foreign Arbitral Awards (the New York Convention), which facilitates the global enforcement of arbitral awards, was not specifically designed for online arbitration. However, the fact that an arbitration agreement is reached and an arbitral award is rendered through electronic means does not necessarily exclude online arbitration from the scope of application of the New York Convention. In fact, UNCITRAL has already recognized the validity of electronic arbitration agreements in the newly revised text of the New York Convention. Moreover, there is a trend toward recognizing the validity of electronic documents and electronic evidence in national legislation in many countries.

The obstacles to enforcement are more often encountered when consumers are involved in arbitration. The provisions of the New York Convention do not necessarily apply to consumer dispute resolution. Contracting states to the New York Convention may exclude its application in consumer disputes arbitration through commercial reservation. Additionally, the validity of pre-dispute arbitration agreements remains controversial. Furthermore, the cost of enforcing arbitral awards through the New York Convention presents a practical obstacle. In light of these issues, some scholars have proposed the idea of an international convention dedicated to foreign online arbitral awards, similar to the New York Convention.[26] However, no such international opportunity exists yet. UNCITRAL has acknowledged that an enforcement scheme based on an international convention may not be ideal, and its Working Group III has suggested relying on private enforcement mechanisms rather than judicial enforcement.[27] Thus, arbitration is not suitable for resolving consumer disputes.

Another notable advancement in facilitating the cross-border enforcement of ADR is Directive 2008/52/EC of the European Parliament and of the Council of May 21, 2008, on certain aspects of mediation in civil and commercial matters

24 Maxime Hanriot, "Online Dispute Resolution as Solution to Cross Border Consumer Disputes: The Enforcement of Outcomes," *McGill Journal of Dispute Resolution* 2 (2015–2016): 9.

25 Pablo Cortés, "What Should the Ideal ODR System E-commerce Look Like? The Hidden World Consumer ADR: Redress and Behavior," *CSLS Oxford*, October 8, 2011, at 2, https://www.law.ox.ac.uk/sites/files/oxlaw/dr_pablo_cortes.pdf.

26 Hanriot, "Online Dispute Resolution," 12.

27 United Nations Commission on Trade Law: "Online Dispute Resolution for Cross-border E-commerce Transactions: An Overview of the Current Private Enforcement System," A/CN.9/WG.III/WP.124.

(Mediation Directive). Unlike judicial and arbitral proceedings, outcomes from mediation are not inherently enforceable and rely on parties' autonomy to implement their agreements. To address this limitation, the Mediation Directive enhances the enforceability of mediated agreements through several legislative techniques. Specifically, Article 6 of the Mediation Directive allows the parties involved in a dispute to request that the content of a written agreement resulting from mediation be made enforceable by a court or another competent authority. This is achieved through a judgment, decision, or authentic instrument, in accordance with the law of the EU member state where the request is made. These provisions also extend to online mediation.[28]

Generally, parties to mediation and other non-adjudicative ADR processes tend to honor the terms resolved by the mediator voluntarily and do not seek judicial enforcement afterward.[29] However, as with the challenges of judicial enforcement of arbitral awards, once courts become involved in enforcing mediated agreements, even the simplest procedures may lead to increased costs.

The analysis of judicial enforcement is not merely a critique of how dispute resolution mechanisms that center on the judicial system may falter in the information society. Instead, it highlights the recent international efforts to enforce cross-border dispute resolution outcomes. Guided by the principles of consumer protection and access to justice, the EU has progressively established unified legal rules internally. The UNCITRAL Technical Notes possess a "soft law" character and can be incorporated into dispute resolution arrangements by agreement between the parties, similarly to the application of the ICC Incoterms. Unfortunately, the application of EU legislation is confined to EU member states, while the UNCITRAL Technical Notes are non-binding. Thus, a global uniform judicial enforcement mechanism is still lacking.[30] Furthermore, even with a well-established legal framework, there might still be a mismatch between the supply and demand of such rules in practice. Evidently, legal systems may not function optimally immediately upon establishment, and ODR requires more robust enforcement mechanisms to realize its full potential.

Lessons from the EU model

While the EU has enacted relevant legislation for small-claims, mediation, and cross-border enforcement and is highly concerned about the successful operation of the ODR platform, the practical implementation of several EU regimes has fallen short of expectations.

28 Hanriot, "Online Dispute Resolution," 13.

29 Hanriot, "Online Dispute Resolution," 13.

30 The "United Nations Convention on International Settlement Agreements Resulting from Mediation" (Singapore Convention on Mediation) was adopted in 2018 to facilitate the enforcement of mediation agreements across borders. However, not all countries have ratified the convention, leading to a situation where there is no global enforcement mechanism akin to the New York Convention for arbitration. This highlights a significant gap in the mediation field, where an international framework for the enforcement of mediation agreements is still lacking.

According to a 2013 survey, 75% of EU citizens were unaware that a small-claims procedure existed, and many were deterred from pursuing valid claims due to cumbersome procedures and long delays. Although Greece had established a dedicated small-claims court, 92% of the Greek respondents had not heard of it.[31] Statistics from 2011 to 2019 show that in Portugal only 220 small claims were judged in total.[32] A 2019 report by the European Consumer Centres Network (ECC-Net) highlights that awareness and engagement with small-claims procedures across the EU remained consistently low. Various obstacles, such as language barriers, costs, and lack of information about jurisdiction and enforcement procedures, continue to hinder the widespread use of these mechanisms. "Awareness of the European Small Claims procedure seems to be very low, both among consumers and the judiciary," the report states.[33]

The implementation of the Consumer ODR Regulation has exposed inconsistencies across countries in terms of consumer awareness and the practical effectiveness of dispute resolution in practice. Additionally, cross-border enforcement mechanisms have proven inadequate. Despite the EU's ODR platform receiving significant traffic, its function has not been fully realized. A 2019 EU report noted that, one year after implementing the consumer ADR system and three and a half years after the launch of the ODR platform, the ADR/ODR framework remained underused and had not reached its full potential. Notably, 50% of the complaints on the ODR platform are cross-border complaints. Of the complaints formally submitted to the ODR platform, 89% were automatically closed after the 30-day period because the trader did not agree to continue the ADR process, 6% were rejected by the trader, and 4% were withdrawn by consumers. Only 1% of complaints reached an ADR entity.[34] The report concluded that this level of performance does not justify the costs incurred by the Commission to maintain the tool or the cost borne by public administrations and online businesses to comply with their obligations under the ODR Regulation.

Therefore, in October 2023, the European Commission submitted a proposal to revise the Consumer ADR Directive,[35] accompanied by a report assessing the

31 World Bank Group, "Fast-Tracking the Resolution of Minor Disputes: Experience from EU Member States," 9–10, accessed July 31, 2024, https://documents1.worldbank.org/curated/pt/670181487131729316/pdf/Fast-tracking-the-resolution-of-minor-disputes-experience-from-EU-Member-States.pdf.

32 Lurdes Varregoso Mesquita and Catia Marques Cebola, "European Small Claims Procedure: An Effective Process? A Proposal for an Online Platform," *Access to Justice in Eastern Europe* 14 (2022): 9–10, https://doi.org/10.33327/AJEE-18-5.2-a000206.

33 *European Consumer Centres Network, Position Paper: European Small Claims Procedure*, at 2, (July 2019), https://www.eccnet.eu/sites/default/files/2021-11/ECC%20Network%20-%20position%20paper%20-%20ESCP.pdf.

34 *European Commission Statistical Report on the Functioning of the European ODR Platform*, at 1–4, (December 2021), https://commission.europa.eu/system/files/2021-12/2021-report-final.pdf.

35 *Proposal for a DIRECTIVE OF THE EUROPEAN PARLIAMENT AND OF THE COUNCIL amending Directive 2013/11/EU on alternative dispute resolution for consumer disputes, as well as Directives (EU) 2015/2302, (EU) 2019/2161 and (EU) 2020/1828*, COM (2023) 649 final (October 17, 2023).

past application of the Consumer Directive. The report highlights issues with the application of several consumer directives, and the proposal recommends specific improvements to address these issues.[36] On the same day, the European Commission also put forward a proposal to repeal the EU Consumer ODR Regulation, discontinuing the ODR platform and removing the requirement on online businesses to provide a link to the ODR platform and manage an email for communication.[37]

The attached report examined the continued relevance of the ADR Directive in light of the rapid and unregulated digitalization of ADR processes and the increasing dominance of private online dispute resolution (PODR) systems imposed by large online marketplaces. According to data from 2020, 12% of EU consumers who experienced a problem with a trader attempted to resolve it directly through a PODR, while only 5% opted for an ADR procedure and 2% pursued legal action in a national court. Considering that, in the same year, 9% of EU consumers experienced issues with online purchases, it was estimated that at least 3.2 million consumers used a PODR mechanism. PODR services are designed to offer a streamlined and user-friendly solution to consumers, removing the need for them to search for suitable dispute resolution mechanisms elsewhere. These systems should facilitate a quick resolution with minimal transaction costs, as most of the necessary data on the parties and the transactions is already integrated within the system.

However, unlike ADR, PODR is not subject to any specific legal requirements. Consequently, several concerns arise regarding (1) the qualification and independence of the natural persons in charge of PODR, (2) the clarity and accessibility of the information provided to consumers before they decide to engage in a PODR procedure, and (c) the fairness of the PODR process and the enforceability of the final outcome on third-party traders or other consumers. To assess the quality standards of the PODR systems, a screening of nine major online platforms operating within the EU was conducted, using the ADR Directive's requirements as a benchmark. The screening was performed based on a structured checklist aimed at assessing various elements, such as the transparency of the PODR systems (e.g., if the dispute resolution rules are clearly disclosed), their accessibility (e.g., if consumers can submit complaints in any language, at any time, or if there are restrictions), and their fairness (e.g., if the natural persons in charge are impartial; if consumers can be represented). The findings revealed that compliance with the ADR Directive quality criteria ranged from 42% for the system with the least amount of information provided to consumers to 88% for the system with the most complete information. Thus, despite the widespread reliance on

36 *Commission Staff Working Document, Impact Assessment Report Accompanying the document Proposal for a DIRECTIVE OF THE EUROPEAN PARLIAMENT AND OF THE COUNCIL amending Directive 2013/11/EU on alternative dispute resolution for consumer disputes, as well as Directives (EU) 2015/2302, (EU) 2019/2161 and (EU) 2020/1828*, SWD (2023) 335 final, Part 2/2 (Oct. 17, 2023).

37 *Proposal for a REGULATION OF THE EUROPEAN PARLIAMENT AND OF THE COUNCIL repealing Regulation (EU) No 524/2013 and amending Regulations (EU) 2017/2394 and (EU) 2018/1724 with regards to the discontinuation of the European ODR Platform*, at 1, COM (2023) 647 final (October 17, 2023).

PODR offered by online marketplaces, none of these systems meet the full quality standards required by ADR Directives for the benefit of consumers.[38]

In particular, the Commission report proposes to "[p]romote a self-regulatory approach for PODR services provided by online marketplaces." Under this approach, platforms offering dispute resolution services to their customers would be encouraged to adhere to common guidelines established at the EU level, aimed at increasing transparency and providing consumer-friendly PODR procedures.[39]

A decade after its adoption, the EU Mediation Directive remains far from achieving its stated objectives of promoting the use of mediation and establishing a "balanced relationship between mediation and judicial proceedings," as outlined in Article 1. The paradox of mediation – widely endorsed yet utilized in less than 1% of civil and commercial litigation cases within the EU – continues to widen. This discrepancy is especially alarming, as official data and multiple studies have consistently demonstrated that the most effective way to significantly increase the number of mediated disputes is to mandate that litigants engage sincerely and reasonably in initial mediation efforts. In 2017, the European Parliament chose to leave the directive unchanged, failing to offer guidance for national legislators on how to accomplish the directive's ultimate goals and leaving EU citizens and businesses without the financial and other benefits that greater use of mediation could provide.[40]

As previously mentioned, the enforceability of private ODR offered by platforms stands out as a significant advantage. One conclusion from the discussion is that, currently, ODR and the enforcement mechanisms provided by platforms remain among the most effective methods for resolving cross-border disputes. In contrast, relying on the judicial system for cross-border enforcement continues to face numerous obstacles. The inherent nature of disputes in cyberspace, being better suited for endogenous ODR, distinguishes dispute resolution in the internet society. This reliance on private dispute resolution necessitates increased regulatory attention to how platforms are governed and the imposition of standards on private dispute resolution mechanisms, particularly regarding fairness and transparency.

Another takeaway from the EU model is that, given the diversity of legal systems across countries, this approach highlights the challenges faced in harmonizing legal systems regionally or globally when adopting a platform-based model.

38 *Commission Staff Working Document, Impact Assessment Report Accompanying the document Proposal for a DIRECTIVE OF THE EUROPEAN PARLIAMENT AND OF THE COUNCIL amending Directive 2013/11/EU on alternative dispute resolution for consumer disputes, as well as Directives (EU) 2015/2302, (EU) 2019/2161 and (EU) 2020/1828*, at 16, 17, SWD (2023) 335 final, Part 1/2 (October 17, 2023).

39 *Commission Staff Working Document, Impact Assessment Report Accompanying the document Proposal for a DIRECTIVE OF THE EUROPEAN PARLIAMENT AND OF THE COUNCIL amending Directive 2013/11/EU on alternative dispute resolution for consumer disputes, as well as Directives (EU) 2015/2302, (EU) 2019/2161 and (EU) 2020/1828*, at 30, SWD (2023) 335 final, Part 1/2 (October 17, 2023).

40 European Parliament, "A Ten-Year-Long 'EU Mediation Paradox' When an EU Directive Needs to Be More Directive," November 1, 2018, accessed September 5, 2024, https://www.europarl.europa.eu/RegData/etudes/BRIE/2018/608847/IPOL_BRI(2018)608847_EN.pdf.

Conversely, China has embraced a similar approach to the EU in its establishment of a one-stop diversified dispute resolution process, by creating a platform that connects approved mediation organizations to the court's platform. However, unlike the EU, China, as a unitary country, has promoted the court-led construction of the "one-stop, diversified dispute resolution" system through a unified top-down model. Furthermore, as Chinese society has long been accustomed to using mediation to resolve civil and commercial disputes, the People's Court online mediation rules released by the SPC provide for a direct interface between online mediation and online litigation. This integration of the two principal ODR methods into one online platform potentially positions the Chinese approach as an example of effective integration of ADR and litigation resources, discussed in Chapter 5.

Effective alternatives to judicial enforcement: private enforcement

Shift from public enforcement to private enforcement

As discussed earlier, when it comes to resolving disputes arising from online activities, particularly those involving a large number of low-value consumer disputes, the current judicial system struggles to balance justice, efficiency, and cost. This disparity challenges the notion of access to justice as guaranteed by law, especially when enforcement through state coercion is not feasible. Consequently, industry practitioners have spontaneously established governance mechanisms suited to commercial activities in cyberspace. The evolution of ODR has been driven by such spontaneous private orders, characterized by self-organizing models motivated by private rulemaking, private jurisdiction, and private enforcement. Since these private orders originate organically within the inherently borderless cyberspace, private enforcement naturally overcomes the hurdles of "cross-border" enforcement, enabling expansion beyond the traditional confines of judicial enforcement.

Private enforcement offers significant advantages over public enforcement in terms of professionalism, costs, and incentives. The success of online dispute resolution on the internet currently depends heavily on private enforcement. However, as power shifts from state entities to private parties, concerns arise about the implications of private enforcement. These include issues such as the lack of legal stability in rules formulated by private organizations, the emergence of individuals in powerful positions that may negatively impact other participants, and potential defects in procedural fairness within private enforcement. Nonetheless, the decision to adopt ODR represents a binary choice, rather than a selection between better options.[41] This paradigm shift has led to a transition from public bodies to private third parties as the primary enforcers. Although there is no precise definition of a "private enforcement mechanism," a description by the UNCITRAL Working Group III as "an alternative to a court-enforced arbitration award or settlement

41 Orna Rabinovich-Einy and Ethan Katsch, "A New Relationship Between Public and Private Dispute Resolution: Lessons from Online Dispute Resolution", *Ohio State Journal on Dispute Resolution* 32 (2017): 719.

agreement" offers valuable insights into this concept.[42] Additionally, " 'enforcement' implies that a decision of some kind has been issued and that a mechanism exists to provide enforcement thereof."[43]

The resolution mechanisms currently discussed in the ODR field include both private mechanisms that encourage compliance with decisions (such as rating systems and trustmarks) and mechanisms for enforcing decisions that may be enforceable in national courts (such as settlement agreements and non-binding awards).[44] The former aids in building consumer confidence in e-commerce and motivates the enforcement of dispute resolution outcomes, while the latter facilitates direct enforcement of such outcomes. In the broader landscape of online dispute resolution, two additional forms can be observed: tools and systems.[45] "Enforcement tools" refer to specific enforcement mechanisms, such as reputation mechanisms, refunds, and escrow services. The "enforcement system" is exemplified by third-party trading platforms and domain name dispute resolution systems which operate autonomously and integrate the generation, resolution, and enforcement of disputes as a cohesive whole.

Enforcement tools: reputation, refunds, and escrow

Reputation or credit has always played a pivotal role in commercial societies. In ancient Mesopotamia, traders developed a reputation system by engraving lists of cross-border transactions and their prices on stone monuments.[46] Similarly, Maghribi traders involved in Mediterranean commerce during the 11th century established a long-distance trade agency mechanism grounded in honesty and reputation.[47] The advent of the internet has significantly enhanced these reputation mechanisms, offering greater speed and broader dissemination of information compared to offline methods. Currently, rating systems and trustmarks serve as commonly employed private enforcement mechanisms designed to incentivize disputing parties to comply with rulings or adhere to specific standards.[48] Both rating systems and trustmarks operate as indicators of credit that rely on

42 United Nations Commission on Trade Law, "Online Dispute Resolution for Cross-border E-commerce Transactions: An Overview of the Current Private Enforcement System" (A/CN.9/WG.III/WP.124), para. 4.

43 UNCITRAL, "Online Dispute Resolution," para. 5.

44 Schultz summarized seven self-enforcement mechanisms; see Thomas Schultz, "Online Arbitration: Binding or Non-Binding?," *ADR Online Monthly*, November 2002.

45 Rabinovich-Einy and Katsch, "New Relationship," 712.

46 Colin Rule and Harpreet Singh, "ODR and Online Reputation Systems – Maintaining Trust and Accuracy Through Effective Redress," in *Online Dispute Resolution: Theory and Practice*, eds. Mohamed S. Abdel Wahab, Ethan Katsh, and Daniel Rainey (The Hague: Eleven, 2012), 176.

47 Avner Greif, *Institutions and the Path to the Modern Economy: Lessons from Medieval Trade* (Cambridge: Cambridge University Press, 2006), 58.

48 In addition to these two mechanisms, other mechanisms that rely on reputation, such as "blacklists" have been implemented. See Maxime Hanriot, "Online Dispute Resolution as Solution to Cross Border Consumer Disputes: The Enforcement of Outcomes," *McGill Journal of Dispute Resolution* 2 (2015–2016): 18.

reputation to promote enforcement. The primary difference is that rating systems are generated by users, while trustmarks are issued by third-party institutions.

Some online business platforms, like eBay or Taobao, effectively utilize feedback and rating mechanisms. Upon the completion of an online transaction, both traders and consumers have the opportunity to provide feedback, which is then incorporated into the trader's online profile. This ongoing record of feedback helps screen out dishonest traders before future transactions. Such mechanisms not only significantly enhance the platform's commercial scale and profitability but also serve as effective means of dispute prevention. However, these systems have shortcomings. The feedback mechanism is prone to the subjective perceptions of evaluators, not all parties may leave feedback after each transaction, and the potential for feedback manipulation can lead to the dissemination of inaccurate information. These flaws undermine the credibility of the feedback mechanism, as discussed in Chapter 2.

Consequently, neutral and independent third-party mechanisms, such as trustmarks, have emerged in practice. A *trustmark* is a quality label created by the issuing organization as part of an industry code of conduct and awarded to merchants meeting specific eligibility criteria. Merchants display the trustmark on their websites, allowing consumers to view it and access linked content to learn more about the merchant's credibility. In business-to-consumer ODR, trustmarks typically appear in two forms: a seal or logo provided by an ADR or ODR provider to an online merchant, indicating to buyers that the merchant is a trustworthy transaction partner certified by a third party, or a seal or logo awarded to an ODR provider by an independent third party as a form of accreditation.[49]

A notable example of a company offering trustmark services is SquareTrade, which previously offered online mediation services for eBay and awarded its SquareTrade seal to sellers engaging in online mediation. Sellers bearing the SquareTrade seal must provide clear product descriptions, participate in the mediation process, address complaints promptly, and enforce dispute resolution outcomes within a reasonable time frame.[50] Nevertheless, the implementation of trustmarks encounters several challenges. In the e-commerce marketplace, the lack of uniform regulation has resulted in a large number of trustmark providers, each with its own code of conduct and delegation of authority. For consumers, the lack of awareness and the difficulty in evaluating trustmarks often cause confusion. Additionally, if merchants and ODR providers can simply purchase trustmarks, this undermines the neutrality and credibility of these marks.

Therefore, for these mechanisms to be effective in cross-border transactions, a global verification system and the regulation of third-party verifiers are essential. A notable proposal was the EU's plan to create a pan-European trustmark as part of its digital agenda, which, regrettably, was not incorporated into either the Consumer ADR Directive or the Consumer ODR Regulation.[51] Currently, EU member

49 UNCITRAL, "Online Dispute Resolution," para.20.
50 Hanriot, "Online Dispute Resolution," 16.
51 Hanriot, "Online Dispute Resolution," 17.

states are only required to regulate ADR entities and traders, falling short of the original proposal for a centralized, unified trustmark system within the EU.

In addition to leveraging commercial reputation and recognition, other common third-party enforcement mechanisms, such as credit card charge-backs and third-party escrow services, achieve dispute resolution outcomes or enforcement by controlling the flow of funds. Credit card charge-backs allow buyers to raise objections under certain conditions, enabling them to request a refund from the merchant through the credit card company if the purchase price has already been paid. In this process, the credit card company acts as a de facto arbitrator, often supported by an arbitration committee. The company solicits information from the buyer regarding the basis for the charge-back and determines whether to approve it. During this proceeding, the burden of proof rests with the merchant. The credit card company typically evaluates the request on a prima facie basis and usually rules in favor of the consumer.[52] The criteria for justifying a charge-back vary by state, but common reasons include credit card fraud, non-delivery of goods, and delivery of non-compliant goods.[53]

Refunds have long served as a potent enforcement mechanism in traditional cross-border transactions and remain effective in cross-border e-commerce. For instance, if a buyer on Amazon believes they have not received the goods, have received incorrect goods, or were double-charged, they can initiate a charge-back claim with their credit card issuer. The bank then contacts Amazon to gather transaction details. Amazon, in turn, reaches out to the seller to obtain transaction information. If the seller fails to respond to Amazon's query in time, Amazon will directly deduct the disputed amount from the transaction. Additionally, refunds can be coordinated with a dispute resolution entity to enforce the dispute resolution outcome; an ODR provider might adjudicate and instruct the enforcement intermediary to return the money to the consumer's account.

For consumers initiating claims in good faith, the charge-back mechanism can be an efficient remedy as it circumvents further disputes between them and merchants. However, in terms of procedural justice, the charge-back mechanism may disadvantage merchants as it tends to favor consumers. This is because merchants bear the costs when a claim is initiated by consumers, which could negatively impact their credit score. Consequently, malicious refunds could harm merchants. Another limitation of the charge-back system is its restricted scope, as it is available only to buyers using a credit card and predominantly utilized in the UK and the USA.[54] Moreover, since credit card issuers are not dispute resolution providers, they do not adhere to the norms and standards established for such providers.[55]

52 Hanriot, "Online Dispute Resolution," 19.

53 Julia Hörnle, *Cross-Border Internet Dispute Resolution* (Cambridge: Cambridge University Press, 2009), 38–39, https://doi.org/10.1017/CBO9780511576102.

54 See Riikka Koulu, "Blockchains and Online Dispute Resolution: Smart Contracts as an Alternative to Enforcement," *Scripted* 13 (2016): 45.

55 Hanriot, "Online Dispute Resolution," 19.

Another widely used enforcement mechanism in some regions is the third-party escrow service. As it is not confined to credit card transactions, it has broader applicability than charge-backs. Under this mechanism, the buyer makes payments to a third-party escrow account. The third-party escrow company holds the funds until any complaints are resolved or it is confirmed that the buyer has received the goods as expected. After a specified period, the escrow company releases the funds to the seller. These companies are usually required to comply with national laws and licensing regulations. In this setup, the escrow company serves as both a third-party guarantor and a dispute resolution entity. It receives claims from the parties, reviews these claims, and decides whether a refund is warranted. An example of this service is Alipay, which has significantly enhanced transaction security and contributed to Taobao's success, discussed in Chapter 2. Similar to the charge-back mechanism, third-party escrow agencies are not professional dispute resolution entities, raising concerns about their credibility and adherence to ethical codes of conduct.

Enforcement system: third-party trading platforms as an enforcement intermediary

With the development of internet business models toward platformization, the most successful private governance models have emerged on third-party trading platforms. Disputes significantly affect a platform's attractiveness to users, negatively impacting transaction volume and the platform's competitive standing against rivals. Due to these concerns, third-party trading platforms are incentivized to spontaneously establish effective dispute resolution mechanisms.

Dispute resolution organized by a platform consists of a system of interconnected mechanisms capable of compensating for the shortcomings of any individual component. Reputation mechanisms, as discussed earlier, can regulate regular sellers and deter malicious opportunistic behavior. Third-party dispute resolution services not only resolve lingering disputes but also correct overly stringent reputation mechanisms. Third-party payments, which are highly enforceable and effective in preventing malicious behavior from onetime deals, complement reputation mechanisms for repeated transactions. Moreover, the presence of a third-party platform provides guarantees for dispute resolution. In line with such understanding, Chinese law now imposes joint liability on third-party platforms under various circumstances.[56] Some platforms have also established consumer deposits and early compensation rules, which is encouraged but not required by law.[57]

The primary challenge of platform-managed dispute resolution is the platform itself. Under this model, trading platforms act as both rule-makers and enforcers: They set the rules for transactions and dispute resolution through their terms of service and enforce the outcomes of dispute resolution. This dual role may cast doubt on the platform's legitimacy and neutrality. Internet companies in near

56 Civil Code of the People's Republic of China, Article 1204; Law of the People's Republic of China on the Protection of Consumer Rights and Interests, Article 36; E-Commerce Law of the People's Republic of China, Article 38.

57 E-Commerce Law of the People's Republic of China, Article 58.

monopolistic positions carry considerable risks of commercial corruption. Specifically, because of their monopoly power, when such companies discriminate against users and abuse their power, industry self-governance and market competition may not effectively resolve the problem. One solution to mitigate the negative effects of the dual role of private companies is crowdsourcing, discussed in the next section. In the past, examples of crowdsourcing have emerged in many internet industries, from reviews and sharing (such as reviews of books and movies) to Wikipedia to complex systems, such as Amazon's "Mechanical Turk" and the massive dispute resolution systems of eBay and Taobao.[58] This development foreshadows a more democratic approach to dispute resolution on the internet, which is set to advance further with the development of blockchain applications.

The commonality of successful current ODR enforcement mechanisms is that the third party controls a resource of significant value to the parties involved. This resource can be money, reputation, or a domain name. The organization controlling the resource thus gains the ability to issue orders and enforce compliance from those who fear losing access to it. This approach establishes a form of self-enforcing rule, regardless of whether the outcome of the dispute resolution is legally binding or non-binding, as enforcement no longer relies on traditional judicial processes. The UNCITRAL also emphasizes the importance of private enforcement and expects ODR to effectively engage entities with market power, including internet intermediaries, payment companies, and banks, to create incentives for merchants.[59]

Despite its various advantages and achievements in ODR, private third-party enforcement has its drawbacks. Key concerns include the independence, impartiality, and compliance of the third party, similar to those of platform-managed dispute resolution. Moreover, there are issues related to the costs associated with relying on third parties for private enforcement. For instance, refunds require sellers to pay fees, and platforms like Taobao require sellers or the platform itself to compensate in advance. Although the seller or third-party organization may appear to bear the cost of dispute resolution, ultimately, consumers will incur the increased costs. While the community continues to grapple with how to mitigate the drawbacks caused by third-party intermediaries, a new technological revolution has emerged. Blockchain technology, with its core feature of decentralization, provides a new solution to the current dilemmas and will be discussed later in this chapter.

Moving from closed system to open ODR: crowdsourced ODR

Crowdsourced online dispute resolution

Referring to it as the "wisdom of crowds," New Yorker columnist James Surowiecki explores the intriguing phenomenon where a large group of people often proves smarter than a small group of elites. Regardless of the elites' intelligence, a group

58 Anhai Doan, Raghu Ramakrishnan, and Alon Y Halevy, "Crowdsourcing Systems on the World-Wide Web," *Communications of the ACM* 54, no. 4 (2011): 87.

59 UNITRAL, "Online Dispute Resolution," para. 45.

is superior at solving problems, fostering innovations, making wise decisions, and even predicting the future accurately.[60] Jeff Howe first introduced the concept of crowdsourcing, describing it as a new form of business organization facilitated by the internet, where companies leverage online platforms to publicly distribute work, uncover ideas, or address technical challenges.[61]

The amalgamation of crowdsourcing with ODR has given rise to a novel concept within the realm of dispute resolution: "crowdsourced online dispute resolution" (cODR).[62] The use of crowdsourcing to resolve disputes can be traced back to iCourt house, an online dispute resolution platform launched in 1999 by a US company. On that platform, anyone could submit a dispute and act as a "juror" in a case, with the authority to issue a "verdict" to assist the parties in reaching an agreement.

Prominent examples of online platforms employing crowdsourcing for dispute resolution include eBay in the United States; marktplaats.nl, the largest e-commerce platform in the Netherlands; and Taobao, the largest e-commerce platform in China. These platforms have, to some extent, successfully achieved the goal of resolving internet disputes swiftly, inexpensively, and efficiently by tapping into the collective intelligence of a diverse online populace. The eBay Community Court, however, has been suspended due to changes in the business model, while Taobao's Pan Center has also suffered setback following judicial scrutiny.

Among the current applications of crowdsourcing in online dispute resolution, there are two distinct types: open and closed crowdsourcing. Open crowdsourcing does not require participants to meet any specific conditions and is not affiliated with any online community, akin to online opinion polls.[63] Conversely, closed crowdsourcing involves a specific group of participants who possess the necessary knowledge to address particular problems, as exemplified by the cODR systems implemented by eBay and Taobao. While this might seem to contradict the popular notion that crowdsourcing leverages the wisdom of the general populace, research indicates that closed crowdsourcing ODR programs can effectively filter participant information to identify qualified dispute resolvers from the crowd.

A study examining nearly 250 "collective intelligence systems" identified four foundational elements common to all crowdsourcing systems: system goals, organizational structures and processes, the composition of the population, and

60 James Surowiecki, *The Wisdom of Crowds: Why the Many Are Smarter Than the Few and How Collective Wisdom Shapes Business, Economies, Societies and Nations* (London: Little, Brown, 2004), xiv.

61 Jeff Howe, "The Rise of Crowdsourcing," *Wired* 14 (6): 176.

62 The term "cODR" was first coined by the Berkman Center for Internet and Society at Harvard University during a 2009 conference. Law Lab, "Theoretical Aspects of Crowd Sourced ODR," accessed July 31, 2024, http://lawlab.org/events/workshops-archive/theoretical-aspects-of-crowd-sourced-odr.

63 Jaap van den Herik and Daniel Dimov, "Towards Crowdsourced Online Dispute Resolution," *Journal of International Commercial Law and Technology* 7, no. 2 (2012): 106.

incentives.[64] This analytical framework suggests that crowdsourcing is not merely a spontaneous phenomenon but can be strategically tailored to meet the specific needs of an organization. Utilizing this framework, the operational mechanism of Taobao's crowdsourcing ODR will be further deconstructed to elucidate how it effectively meets the dispute resolution needs of its vast user base.

Case study: Taobao Pan Center

In 2012, Taobao launched the Taobao Pan Center (*dazhong pingshen*, Pan Center) to involve ordinary Taobao users in the governance of the Taobao community. This initiative empowers users to resolve disputes by enabling collective voting through public reviewers within the center. The Pan Center is designed to address a large volume of small-scale, homogeneous, cross-border disputes on the Taobao platform. These typically involve relatively simple consumer issues, such as mismatches between the received product and its description, quality concerns, and instances where buyers have not received their goods. For such disputes, a swift resolution is prioritized over the meticulous application of law. Consequently, public reviewers base their assessments primarily on the Taobao rules and their personal experiences as users of the platform.

The procedures of the Pan Center are generally straightforward and intuitive. Taobao allocates specific disputes to the center based on their nature. The system then assigns cases to reviewers on a first-come, first-served basis. Decisions are made by a simple majority of reviewers who voted within the designated time period. Between 2012 and 2015, Taobao implemented several adjustments to the details of its Public Review Convention on issues such as the minimum number of reviewers and the maximum review time for each case. If there are insufficient number of reviewers, or if no collective decision was made within the time period, Taobao intervenes and makes the decision through other means. The Pan Center's decision is final, with no mechanism for appeal. Taobao enforces these decisions according to its rules, such as by compensating consumers or holding sellers accountable for breaches of contract.

One of the advantages of endogenous ODR, such as the Pan Center, is that the dispute resolution process can be made easily grasped for lay participants through the use of diagrams, symbols, process descriptions, and other technical elements. The Pan Center utilizes terms such as "reviewers," "tasks," "rookies," and "experienced users" which align with the contemporary Chinese online lexicon and culture. These terms reflect Taobao's commercial characteristics rather than depending on traditional legal jargon, such as "courts," "jurors," and "judges."

As one of the few successful crowdsourcing dispute resolution mechanisms, the Taobao Pan Center has demonstrated the effectiveness of crowdsourcing and has deepened the understanding of crowdsourcing as a viable method of dispute

64 Thomas W. Malone, Robert Laubacher, and Chrysanthos Dellarocas, "The Collective Intelligence Genome," *IEEE Engineering Management Review* 38, no. 3 (2010): 38.

resolution. In 2013, the public review mechanisms monitored the implementation of 640 Taobao rules and optimized 22 disputed rules.[65] In 2016, 10% of all transaction disputes were resolved through public evaluation.[66] By 2018, there were 4.31 million registered reviewers, with 172,000 participants in the review process, completing over 100 million dispute adjudications.[67]

It is noteworthy that Taobao has evolved over recent years to the extent that some of its market mechanisms can substitute state governance in regulating online business activities. Its role has expanded beyond merely being an e-commerce platform; it has also become instrumental in shaping and promoting the development of China's cyber law and related regulations, leveraging its significant influence. The institutional value of Taobao crowdsourcing is particularly evident in its relationship with the Taobao platform. On the one hand, Taobao crowdsourcing is not merely a dispute resolution service provided by a third party but is deeply "embedded" within the overall structure of Taobao. The platform-organized dispute resolution is a system comprising multiple mechanisms, with institutional links between these mechanisms to address for the shortcomings of individual components. This integration effectively overcomes the typical recruitment and execution challenges associated with crowdsourcing. On the other hand, crowdsourcing functions as a dispute resolution mechanism that operates independently of the online platform. By delegating dispute resolution to the public, the power wielded by the private company is effectively balanced. Users engage in public review to alleviate concerns about potential unfairness and corruption among Taobao's junior staff. Additionally, the public plays an active role in the company's rulemaking process.

When a rule is found to be impractical in its application, reviewers have the right to challenge it on the platform. Taobao analyzes and summarizes cases handled through these reviews, proactively verifying and refining the existing dispute resolution rules on the platform. This approach of relying on public participation for both dispute resolution and rulemaking reflects a more democratic mode of operation and thought characteristic of the internet. When companies outsource certain operational aspects to online users, they not only transfer risk but also shield themselves from perceptions of arbitrariness.

Nevertheless, Taobao's public reviews face certain challenges. As a private platform, Taobao's ODR mechanism and various platform rules undergo periodic changes, such as modifications to the operational processes. These provisions are core elements of dispute resolution, and any changes should be clearly explained and prominently posted on the website alongside all rules, in accordance with the

65 Alibaba Group, "Alibaba Ecosystem Internet Volunteers Research Report 2016," accessed July 31, 2024, https://www.docin.com/p-1954069131.html.

66 Shen Xinwang申欣旺, "Taobao hulianwang Zhengyi jiejue jizhi de qishi 淘宝互联网争议解决机制的启示," *Minzhu yu fazhi* 民主与法制 754, no. 5 (2016): 26, http://e.mzyfz.org.cn/mag/paper_8871_5537.html.

67 Fu Weigang傅蔚冈, "Wanggou pingtai de ziying shenhua 网购平台的自营神话," *Dushi Kuaibao* 都市快报, November 9, 2018, https://baijiahao.baidu.com/s?id=1616627270190715540.

transparency requirements of Chinese law, including the E-Commerce Law that came into force in 2019. Unlike other public regulations, these rules are designed without undergoing rigorous internal and external scrutiny, which could prove problematic if they are later relied upon in legal proceedings. This has turned out to be highly detrimental for the Pan Center.

In 2020, a first-instance judgment from the Hangzhou Internet Court led to the indefinite suspension the Pan Center's operation by Taobao.[68] The dispute involved an alleged trademark violation by the plaintiff merchant who operated on Tmall, a branch of Taobao. The allegation was that the plaintiff's Chinese brand bore a resemblance to a more established Japanese brand, which could potentially cause confusion for consumers. Taobao sent the case to the Pan Center, asking reviewers whether they believed there was connection or confusion between the two brands concerned. Of the 185 reviewers consulted, 123 (66.49%) believed that confusion was possible, and based on this result, Taobao determined that the Chinese brand violated its trademark protection terms and terminated the contract. The merchant subsequently filed a lawsuit in the Hangzhou Internet Court, arguing that Taobao's standard terms and decision mechanism were flawed.

The court upheld the plaintiff's claim in part, criticizing several aspects of the operational design of this particular Pan Center review, including the fact that Taobao asked only one pertinent question of the reviewers, without adequately addressing the potential biasing effect of this single query. Although the court only awarded about 10% of the original sum claimed by the plaintiff, the judicial critique of the Pan Center's operation seemed to have delivered a significant blow to Taobao. Following the judgment, the Pan Center was effectively shut down, with no expectation of resuming operation in the foreseeable future.

Lessons and incentives for crowdsourcing dispute resolution

From cases such as the Taobao Pan Center, it may be observed that crowdsourcing dispute resolution displays many different characteristics from traditional, exogenous ODR. As discussed in Chapter 2, there are two types of knowledge or information critical to dispute resolution: information about online transactions and information about the dispute resolution process itself. The public reviewers at the Pan Center are registered Taobao users who actively participate in transaction activities, many of whom are highly experienced. They possess substantive knowledge about the transaction process, the rules governing transactions, and various practical scenarios that may arise during transactions. This type of information is vital for effective dispute resolution and cannot be acquired without personal experience, making it a form of private information. Although legal experts are typically adept at resolving disputes due to their specialized skills and knowledge, they are not necessarily more effective than internet users at resolving disputes

68 上海毓华商贸有限公司诉浙江天猫网络有限公司一审民事判决书, (2019)浙0192民初375号, Hangzhou Internet Court (May 25, 2020).

specific to Taobao. This is primarily because dispute resolution on Taobao relies less on legal expertise and more on an intimate understanding of Taobao's rules and transaction details, which regular users of Taobao are likely to be more familiar with.

Regarding incentives and motivations for public participation, research by Göritz shows that material incentives can enhance the average return on crowdsourcing applications by 19%.[69] Maniaci and Rogge have also demonstrated that while material incentives do increase participation in crowdsourcing applications, the magnitude of the monetary reward does not positively correlate with the rate of return and may even lead to diminishing returns with larger monetary incentives.[70] Research in other fields has similarly indicated that people do not necessarily participate solely based on profit motives, and the introduction of financial incentives can sometimes undermine the inherent value and purpose of the endeavor.[71]

The key to successful crowdsourcing lies in satisfying the participants' spiritual needs and fostering some form of meaningful engagement. While there may be material gain, it must be secondary to other, more significant motivations.[72] If monetary incentives become the primary motivation, the crowdsourcing initiative is unlikely to succeed. Most current cODR mechanisms, if they involve fees at all, are relatively inexpensive. The Taobao Pan Center is a free service that does not require significant time commitments from reviewers, which is likely a major reason that people are willing to engage with it. To encourage active participation in the review of disputes, Taobao rewards each successful reviewer with a certain amount of experience and "points," regardless of the accuracy of the decision. However, this system harbors the risk of moral hazard, as some reviewers may not carefully review the evidence from both parties involved in a transaction before voting, simply to quickly obtain a reward. This can result in incorrect judgments of transaction disputes. Therefore, Taobao must implement effective measures to deter such behavior and establish suitable penalties for malfeasance among reviewers.

A critical incentive to encourage user participation is the dual approach of "naming and shaming," coupled with recognizing credit for task completion. Taobao, in this context, employs several strategies to build and measure the reputation of its reviewers. Reviewers earn experience points for each task they adjudicate, which

69 Anja S. Göritz, "Incentives in Web Studies: Methodological Issues and a Review," *International Journal of Internet Science* 1, no. 1 (2006): 65.

70 Michael R. Maniaci and Ronald D. Rogge, "Conducting Research on the Internet," in *Handbook of Research Methods in Social and Personality Psychology*, eds. Harry T. Reis and Charles M. Judd, 2nd ed. (Cambridge: Cambridge University Press, 2014), 464, https://doi.org/10.1017/CBO9780511996481.

71 Uri Gneezy and Aldo Rustichini, "A Fine Is a Price," *Journal of Legal Studies* 29, no. 1 (2000): 1, https://doi.org/10.1086/468061; Steven D. Levitt and Stephen J. Dubner, *Freakonomics* (New York: HarperCollins, 2005), 21–23.

72 Jeff Howe, *Crowdsourcing: How the Power of Crowd Is Driving the Future of Business* (London: Random House, 2008), 149.

can be accumulated to earn various virtual "medals" and physical souvenirs, such as mugs, sun umbrellas, commemorative albums, and notebooks. Conversely, Taobao also periodically penalizes and removes reviewers who commit serious misjudgments or other violations during the review process. Research highlights that receiving feedback on the outcomes of one's decisions – such as learning whether their views align with the majority or remain in the minority – is a highly effective incentive for crowd members. In line with this, Taobao allows reviewers to see the results of their votes after the decisions are finalized, addressing this critical need for feedback.

In Taobao's public review system, participants, who are sellers and buyers themselves, find a compelling reason to engage actively – this dual role is both a requirement for becoming a reviewer and a significant incentive. As community members, users have a vested interest in fostering a fair and equitable trading environment on the platform. This motivation is often heightened by empathy, as users seek to assist others facing similar challenges through the review process. Additionally, the review process offers a chance for buyers and sellers to observe the behaviors of others, allowing them to adjust their own behaviors and judgement accordingly. Regardless of the specific motivations for participation, the presence of active, capable, and enthusiastic individuals within the crowd is crucial for the success of crowdsourcing initiatives.

Moreover, recreation or the simple desire to pass time also serves as a motivation for people to participate in crowdsourcing projects. Studies of the Amazon Mechanical Turk revealed that many participants engaged in tasks for fun or to kill time.[73] The instinctive pleasure derived from participating in crowdsourced work and the opportunity for social interaction significantly contribute to their motivation. This dimension of crowdsourcing is theoretically applicable to Taobao's model as well.

In addition to the aforementioned incentives, Taobao also encourages reviewer participation by appealing to their sense of charity. The notion of "charity" resonates deeply across various cultural contexts both in China and the West, embodying a common spiritual aspiration and a celebrated human virtue. Engaging in acts of charity offers spiritual satisfaction and personal growth. On Taobao, reviewers earn experience points for each review they complete, which can be allocated toward public welfare donations, such as providing meals to impoverished children or donating funds to rural clinics. These contributions are documented and published on the website, enhancing transparency and reinforcing a sense of community and shared purpose among participants. This blend of personal, communal, and altruistic incentives not only drives the active participation of reviewers in Taobao's crowdsourcing efforts but also highlights the platform's innovative approach

73 Gilles Adda, Joseph J. Mariani, Laurent Besacier, and Hadrien Gelas, "Economical and Ethical Background of Crowdsourcing for Speech," in *Crowdsourcing for Speech Processing: Applications to Data Collection, Transcription and Assessment*, eds. Maxine Eskénazi, Gina-Anne Levow, Helen Meng, Gabriel Parent, and David Suendermann (Chichester: Wiley, 2013), 303, https://doi.org/10.1002/9781118541241.

to integrating social values with business operations, thereby fostering a robust and dynamic online community.

Despite these intentions or visions, the rather abrupt suspension of Taobao Pan Center marks yet another instance of important crowdsourcing ODR systems not fulfilling their potential as originally envisaged. While technology has provided new opportunities and sources of inspirations, significant challenges remain in the practical design of functional ODR models that can both harness these new capabilities and complement the existing structures of cyberspace and society. These difficulties are repeatedly observed in the implementation of new technologies, such as blockchain technology, which will be addressed in the next section.

Blockchain technology and decentralized ODR

The evolution of online business models and their governing rules is intrinsically linked to the architecture of the internet and its modes of production. The transactional rules governing network markets can be categorized into three distinct temporal stages: past, present, and future. The past stage is characterized by a hub-and-spoke model. Historically, the market was dominated by this model, where large internet companies provided goods directly to consumers. Within this framework, the consumption rules were established by these large entities. Dispute resolution in this model was managed directly by the sellers, who wielded considerable influence over the outcomes.

Later on, the predominant model has shifted toward the sharing economy, where individual consumers engage in transactions with goods providers – typically micro, small, and medium-sized enterprises – via intermediary platforms. These platforms facilitate transactions and set the governing rules. In this model, the platforms themselves predominantly handle dispute resolution, acting as mediators between consumers and providers.

Looking forward, the anticipated model is a blockchain-based peer-to-peer system, where the rules of consumption are directly established by the parties involved in the transaction, without intermediary oversight. This stage promises a decentralized approach to dispute resolution, radically differing from previous models.[74] This forthcoming shift, described as "distributed jurisdiction," proposes a fundamentally different framework for resolving disputes, leveraging blockchain technology to ensure transparency and fairness autonomously.[75]

Overall, these three stages reflect a transition in control and authority from centralized corporate entities to a more dispersed and democratized system, where individuals and small businesses possess greater autonomy and influence over transactions and dispute resolution.

74 Koji Takahashi, "Block Chain and Online Dispute Resolution," Asia-Pacific Economic Cooperation, Workshop on the Use of Modern Technology for Dispute Resolution and Electronic Agreement Management Particularly Online Dispute Resolution, Port Moresby, Papua New Guinea, March 3–4, 2018.

75 Wulf A. Kaal and Craig Calcaterra, "Crypto Transaction Resolution," *The Business Lawyer* 73 (2017–2018): 142.

The rise of blockchain technology

Blockchain is a tamperproof distributed ledger technology that operates independently of intermediaries or regulatory authorities for its verification. It ensures that transactions are verified, executed, and recorded in a chronologically ordered database, where only new data (blocks) can be added and existing data cannot be altered. These blocks are "time-stamped," making all data publicly accessible for review and verification. Initially applied in the financial sector, blockchain has led to the emergence of various cryptocurrencies, which have challenged both global financial markets and their regulatory frameworks. However, the potential applications of blockchain extend well beyond financial transactions. Blockchain ledgers can record any type of data structure, encompassing proof of ownership, identity and authentication information, contracts, and more.

Emerging as a sophisticated second-generation, blockchain-based innovation are smart contracts. These are contracts, expressed in computer code, that automatically execute when specified conditions are met, with a set of instructions stipulating that a transaction will complete only when those conditions are fulfilled. One of the pivotal features of smart contracts is their self-enforcing nature, relying solely on the terms and conditions digitally inscribed within the contract, thus eliminating the need for any third-party oversight to enforce contractual obligations. The economic objectives of smart contracts include reducing losses associated with fraud, as well as arbitration, enforcement, and other transaction costs.[76]

While judicial intervention is theoretically feasible in traditional internet transactions, it faces numerous practical obstacles. Adapting to blockchain technology will encounter even greater challenges in applying traditional judicial mechanisms.

Firstly, blockchain technology is characterized by an enhanced level of anonymity. Unlike traditional internet transactions, where the identities and property details of the parties are typically known, blockchain-based smart contracting uses cryptography to maintain the anonymity of transaction parties and obscure users' IP addresses. Additionally, payment details, like credit card information or the location of property, may remain unknown in blockchain transactions, especially if parties opt to use decentralized, autonomously operating cryptocurrencies. Consequently, traditional jurisdictional approaches, such as territorial jurisdiction and personal jurisdiction, have limited applicability in the context of blockchain technology.

Secondly, while traditional internet transactions utilize established contracting mechanisms, including traditional legal tools, in electronic form, blockchain smart contracts are founded on computer code. Traditional contracting mechanisms and their legal formalities are typically not involved.

76 Nick Szabo, "Smart Contracts: Building Blocks for Digital Markets," 1996, https://fon.hum.uva.nl/rob/Courses/InformationInSpeech/CDROM/Literature/LOTwinterschool2006/szabo.best.vwh.net/smart_contracts_2.html; Zibin Zheng, Shaoan Xie, Hong-Ning Dai, Weili Chen, Xiangping Chen, Jian Weng, and Muhammad Imran, "An Overview on Smart Contracts: Challenges, Advances and Platforms," *Future Generation Computer Systems* 105 (April 2020): 476, https://doi.org/10.1016/j.future.2019.12.019.

Finally, traditional internet transactions are facilitated by centralized server networks, whereas blockchain operates through a decentralized network of computers. Blockchain represents merely a consensus of computation, embodying pure information, defined solely by the mathematical rules set at its inception and the aggregate of computational outputs. The blockchain network is maintained and owned by a distributed group of anonymous users globally who are unlikely to recognize or comply with any legal authority.[77]

Thus, blockchain represents an autonomous system based on code, necessitating an internal governance scheme. This autonomy also diverges from the private autonomy observed in traditional e-commerce, where effective private enforcement still relies on a third-party intermediary. Proponents of blockchain technology suggest that innovations like Bitcoin and smart contracts could transcend traditional ODR mechanisms by establishing a more radical self-enforcing ODR system. Due to its radical decentralization and reliance on user enforcement, a stateless currency system under blockchain technology would offer a completely different self-enforcing mechanism compared to all previous models.[78] Blockchain technology is thus posited to resolve the enduring enforcement challenges identified by UNCITRAL.

Moreover, alongside changes in dispute resolution mechanisms, the objectives of dispute resolution have also evolved. One of the core aims of current ODR system design is consumer protection. Initially, UNCITRAL focused on cross-border consumer dispute resolution. However, due to significantly divergent understandings of consumer protection across various national legal systems and the challenges of achieving harmonization, UNCITRAL has somewhat avoided addressing consumer protection in its final Technical Notes. The ODR procedural rules are applicable to both business-to-business and business-to-consumer transactions. Efforts to globally unify standards of consumer protection may encounter obstacles similar to those UNCITRAL faced initially. Additionally, the democratization of the online marketplace and the reduced vulnerability of consumers have diminished the urgency for consumer protection as a primary legislative goal. In peer-to-peer, trustless environments, such as those facilitated by Bitcoin, the specific protection of consumer interests or any particular party becomes less critical. Enforcement under blockchain technology emphasizes "decentralization," "digital enforcement," and "autonomy," thereby obviating previous dilemmas related to "cross-border enforcement" and "consumer protection."

Bitcoin escrow

In the realm of Bitcoin 1.0, transactions are irreversible; once an order of transfer is initiated, the transfer of funds is executed automatically. This level of automation introduces certain risks, highlighting the need for a security mechanism for Bitcoin transactions. Akin to a traditional escrow agreement, Bitcoin escrow ensures that

77 Kaal and Calcaterra, "Crypto Transaction Resolution," 134.

78 Pietro Ortolani, "Self-Enforcing Online Dispute Resolution: Lessons from Bitcoin," *Oxford Journal of Legal Studies* 36 (2016): 610–16.

the funds sent by the sender do not flow directly to the receiver but are instead temporarily stored in a service provider's wallet. Should disputes arise, the service provider can act as an adjudicator and return the funds to the entitled party. However, this mechanism has a clear drawback: It necessitates a trust relationship between the service provider and the parties involved. This requirement is fundamentally at odds with the "trustless" nature of the Bitcoin system, which operates without a central authority. It seems unreasonable for the sender to place more trust in the service provider than in the recipient. Moreover, the mechanism is relatively primitive; in the event of a dispute requiring the service provider's intervention, both the applicable procedural and substantive rules in resolving the dispute remain unclear. More critically, this approach mirrors the current reliance on third-party payment intermediaries, such as Alipay, which fails to eliminate the potential for misconduct by third-party escrow companies.

These issues can be addressed through technological innovations, such as a Bitcoin adjudication system based on a multi-signature address system. Traditionally, each Bitcoin address is linked to a single private key, which could be held by the escrow service provider, leading to the aforementioned trust issues. In contrast, a multi-signature address involves three associated private keys, and the successful transfer of payment requires the authorization of two keys. Each party, including the adjudicator, holds a key, and the transaction can only be completed when two out of the three keys are used simultaneously. When no dispute arises, the two parties involved can agree to release the payment to the recipient's wallet without the adjudicator's involvement. In the event of a dispute, however, the adjudicator can determine the direction of the Bitcoin transfer, logically with the consent of the recipient party. The adjudicator alone can never unlock the Bitcoins sent to the multi-signature address, virtually eliminating concerns about trust. This capability to create a multi-signature address indicates that Bitcoin technology can support a more sophisticated model of private autonomy and enforcement.[79]

This approach to dispute resolution is exemplified by OpenBazaar, an e-commerce platform akin to Taobao but fundamentally different as a peer-to-peer decentralized trading platform.[80] In OpenBazaar, vendors and customers conduct transactions using Bitcoin, with no third party overseeing the transactions. Users have complete control over the disclosure of their personal information. When a dispute arises between a vendor and a buyer, a third-party notary from the OpenBazaar network can intervene. This notary, trusted by both the vendor and the buyer, verifies the contract and sets up a multi-signature Bitcoin account. Bitcoins are only transferred from this account when two of the three keys are presented. The third-party notary, controlling the third private key, ensures that the Bitcoins remain secure until the vendor and buyer reach a settlement or the notary makes a judgment.

To safeguard user privacy, OpenBazaar employs a mechanism to select trustworthy third-party notaries through a pseudonymous web of trust, enabling all

79 Ortolani, "Self-Enforcing Online Dispute Resolution," 610.
80 Kaal and Calcaterra, "Crypto Transaction Resolution," 145.

users to submit feedback on others. This feedback system helps manage the reputation of users; those who commit fraud or fail to adjudicate disputes fairly face reputation damage. When selecting a third-party notary, vendors and buyers can view potential notaries' reputation scores, allowing them to choose or agree on a notary pool based on reputation. This system ensures the professionalism of the notaries while preserving the anonymity integral to the entire system.[81]

Decentralized justice

Apart from Bitcoin, which stands as the most successful application of blockchain technology to date, smart contracts also introduce new possibilities in dispute resolution. Smart contracts enable the pre-coding of contractual terms, which are immutable once set, effectively minimizing disputes. Nevertheless, there remain terms that cannot be explicitly coded, and issues such as incomplete information stemming from the bounded rationality of both coders and contracting parties, unpredictability, incomplete foresight, and opportunistic behavior make it nearly impossible to eliminate disputes entirely within smart contracts. In response to disputes that arise ex post facto, an intra-blockchain distributed jurisdiction system has been developed, integrating concepts of dispute resolution, crowdsourcing, online citizen participation, and transparency. This approach is exemplified by the Aragon Network,[82] which primarily utilizes crowdsourcing mechanisms to address disputes and employs tokens to incentivize participation and enforce decisions.

Within the Aragon framework, when users encounter disputes regarding the execution of a contract, they can initiate a litigation process by posting a bond. If the outcome of the dispute is favorable to the claimant, this bond is returned. The claimant may then randomly select five individuals from a pool of bonded users and appoint them as judges for the dispute. Should any selected judge decline participation, they incur a minor penalty, allowing the claimant to select another individual to fill the vacancy. These judges render decisions based on the foundational rules of the Aragon Network Jurisdiction and the encrypted materials provided by the disputing parties.

After making their decision, judges must privately generate a random number and submit a decision summary to the court. Once the submission period concludes, judges are required to disclose their random number and decision, which can then be verified publicly. Failure to disclose these details results in the forfeiture of their bond as a penalty. The resolution of the dispute is determined by a majority vote, with judges who align with the majority receiving a non-transferable reputation token as a reward, while those who do not are subjected to significant penalties.

The system allows for two rounds of appeals. The appellant must post additional bonds to initiate a prediction market, wherein any member of Aragon can post a

81 Kaal and Calcaterra, "Crypto Transaction Resolution," 146.

82 This is a decentralized autonomous organization management application running on Ethereum, which is an underlying system capable of actual smart contracts on the blockchain. Aragon is controlled by tokens, and the software executes code written using smart contracts.

bond to act as a judge. If the outcome of the second round differs from that of the first, all judges who incorrectly voted in the initial round are heavily penalized, whereas those who voted correctly are rewarded. If the appellant remains dissatisfied after two rounds, they can escalate the dispute to the ultimate level – the "supreme court" of the Aragon Network Jurisdiction, composed of nine users with the highest reputation scores.

This system is designed to discourage frivolous arbitration while protecting honest parties who may be exploited.[83] Unlike OpenBazaar, Aragon does not promote professional development in dispute resolution. Randomly selected judges, who may lack expertise in specific subject areas, might not provide fair and effective outcomes. Furthermore, Aragon's dispute resolution mechanisms are limited to its user base and do not permit opting into other resolution frameworks, making it a closed system.[84] Addressing these issues will be critical for the future development and refinement of dispute resolution models similar to that of Aragon's.

Blockchain, as a burgeoning technological revolution, has ushered in profound impacts on internet dispute resolution, introducing new dynamics to trading platforms, escrow mechanisms, and dispute resolution frameworks. Particularly, the advent of blockchain technology and the deployment of smart contracts have realized a more robust self-executing and digitized enforcement mechanism. From one perspective, this development significantly complicates judicial intervention. From another viewpoint, however, it signifies a heightened sense of autonomy compared to existing private mechanisms for internet dispute resolution. The decentralized essence of blockchain expands the dispute resolution process, challenges the centralized authority of judicial institutions, and facilitates the resolution of disputes in a more democratic manner.

Although still in its nascent stages, blockchain technology promises significant contributions to the establishment of new regulatory frameworks as it matures and its applications become more pervasive. The notion of "code is law," summarized by American cyber law scholar Lawrence Lessig, gains renewed vigor in this context.[85] The legal framework within the internet sector is indeed evolving from *Lex Informatica* to *Lex Cryptographia*, marking a significant transition toward integrating cryptographic principles into the fabric of internet governance and legal structures.[86]

Conclusion

The UNCITRAL Working Group III on online dispute resolution concluded its efforts in 2017. The technical guidelines it produced, while serving as a model rule, do not tackle the challenge of global cross-border enforcement of e-commerce

83 Kaal and Calcaterra, "Crypto Transaction Resolution," 144–45.
84 Kaal and Calcaterra, "Crypto Transaction Resolution," 147.
85 Lawrence Lessig, *Code: Version 2.0* (New York: Basic Books, 2006), 5.
86 Michael Anderson Schillig, "'Lex Cryptographi(c)a', 'Cloud Crypto Land' or What? – Blockchain Technology on the Legal Hype Cycle," *Modern Law Review* 86 (2023): 36.

disputes.[87] Conversely, EU has been gradually establishing a harmonized set of legal rules aimed at significantly facilitating the cross-border enforcement of e-commerce dispute resolutions. Notably, the pandemic led to an overall increase of 15% in ADR disputes across the EU, which were effectively managed by ADR entities equipped with the appropriate infrastructure, despite initial hurdles, such as disruptions in mail delivery, challenges in transitioning to digital platforms for virtual hearings, and reduced workforce availability at the peak of the pandemic due to increased sick leave. As with other online mechanisms impacted by the COVID-19 crisis, it underscored the importance and facilitated the growth of ODR in EU, as the theoretical and practical applications of ADR were proven to be effective in an online setting.[88] However, the EU's experience has revealed a discrepancy between the institutional supply of legal solutions and the actual needs of the business community. The pandemic did not fundamentally change that. The EU's approach has faced challenges, leading to a reliance on private autonomy, a conclusion mirroring the stance previously reached by UN initiatives. This reflects a broader recognition of the value of private autonomy and private enforcement by rule-makers, including entities like the UN and the EU.

From the inception of the first generation of internet architecture to the advent of blockchain, private dispute resolution and private enforcement have consistently held significant value. They contribute to both efficiency and justice and can act as complements, or even substitutes, to public order in cyberspace. Endogenous ODR mechanisms, along with internet autonomy, continue to be more viable. Meanwhile, the traditional legal system, though exogenous to the internet system, has persistently adapted to societal developments, as evidenced by the surge in e-justice initiatives and the increasing acknowledgment of online dispute resolution by judicial systems, alongside the development of relevant laws and regulations. For instance, the E-Commerce Law that China first enacted in 2018 highlights the importance of private ODR on e-commerce platforms from the outset, with a dedicated chapter on "e-commerce dispute resolution."[89] This recognition ensures that the private ODR system can continue to thrive under the protection of the law. Consequently, the mode of internet governance – encompassing both dispute resolution and rule enforcement – will invariably be hybrid, embodying a mixture of public regulation and private autonomy and a "combination of the rule of technology and the rule of law."

In the context of this "combination of the rule of technology and the rule of law," governance rules at the technological level comprise elements such as software,

87 UNCITRAL, "Technical Notes on Online Dispute Resolution", 2017, https://uncitral.un.org/sites/uncitral.un.org/files/media-documents/uncitral/en/v1700382_english_technical_notes_on_odr.pdf

88 *Commission Staff Working Document, Impact Assessment Report Accompanying the document Proposal for a DIRECTIVE OF THE EUROPEAN PARLIAMENT AND OF THE COUNCIL amending Directive 2013/11/EU on alternative dispute resolution for consumer disputes, as well as Directives (EU) 2015/2302, (EU) 2019/2161 and (EU) 2020/1828*, at 28, 29, SWD (2023) 335 final, Part 2/2 (October 17, 2023).

89 E-Commerce Law of the People's Republic of China, Articles 58–63.

algorithms, and supporting infrastructure, while governance rules at the regulatory and legal levels consist of regulatory frameworks, legal provisions, and industry policies (best practices). This hybrid governance is more conducive to protecting the interests of all stakeholders and enhancing societal welfare as a whole, ultimately fostering a robust business ecosystem with active participation from regulators, business organizations, and consumers.

Furthermore, an analysis of the progress and limitations of both judicial and private enforcement reveals several drawbacks inherent in the existing mechanisms for online dispute resolution. These issues are significantly linked to the reliance on third-party intermediaries. Blockchain is recognized for its potential to revolutionize existing dispute resolution mechanisms by fostering a decentralized justice system that operates independently of third-party entities. This transition from "centralized to decentralized" and the emergence of new digital enforcement mechanisms represent another profound impact of technology on the legal system and a testament to technological change's contribution to social development. Although blockchain-based dispute resolution is still in its emerging stage and some applications are underdeveloped, these initial endeavors should still spark the imagination about the future of dispute resolution on the internet.

The transformative shift from centralized to decentralized systems, driven by blockchain technology, has prominently highlighted the intricate relationship between technology and law. The high level of mathematical certainty inherent in systems built on technical specifications, such as blockchain and smart contracts, is unprecedented in human history. These systems ensure that transactions are immutable, and contracts irrevocable, enhancing efficiency and virtually eliminating the risk of default, as participants cannot opt to default without consequence. However, this raises a critical question: Is the elimination of legal recourse, along with the flexibility traditionally afforded by the legal system in interpreting and enforcing contracts, unequivocally beneficial? Looking ahead, if laws could be encoded, then the only method to violate the law would be to break the code. The relationship between the rule of law and the rule of code, and the potential integration of technology's preemptive nature with the retrospective enforcement characteristic of law, merits profound consideration and exploration.

Moreover, crowdsourcing has revolutionized dispute resolution, shifting some types of disputes from a cadre of experts to amateurs, and from a closed system to an open one. The key to effectively utilizing crowdsourcing for dispute resolution lies in the elaborate design of the mechanism, both technically and legally. This involves setting clear objectives, selecting appropriate participants, and refining the process to extract intelligent solutions. Crowdsourcing transcends being merely a buzzword in the internet society; it represents a significant shift in social behavior that challenges our traditional perceptions of professionalism, business models, and the value of intellectual labor. As an emergent form of dispute resolution, it will require time to mature. Nonetheless, it represents a promising avenue that is likely to expand further as traditional mindsets are continually reshaped by technological advancements.

Bibliography

Abramson, Harold I. "A Fifth Branch of Government: The Private Regulators and Their Constitutionality." *Hastings Constitutional Law Quarterly* 16, no. 2 (1989): 165–220.

Adda, Gilles, Joseph J. Mariani, Laurent Besacier, and Hadrien Gelas. "Economic and Ethical Background of Crowdsourcing for Speech." In *Crowdsourcing for Speech Processing: Applications to Data Collection, Transcription and Assessment*, edited by Maxine Eskénazi, Gina-Anne Levow, Helen Meng, Gabriel Parent, and David Suendermann. Chichester: Wiley, 2013. http://doi.org/10.1002/9781118541241.

Aoki, Masahiko. *Toward a Comparative Institutional Analysis*. Cambridge: MIT Press, 2001.

Bernstein, Lisa. "Private Commercial Law in the Cotton Industry: Creating Cooperation through Rules, Norms and Institutions." *Michigan Law Review* 99 (2001): 1724–90.

Cortés, Pablo. "What Should the Ideal ODR System E-commerce Look Like? The Hidden World Consumer ADR: Redress and Behavior." *CSLS Oxford*, October 8, 2011. https://www.law.ox.ac.uk/sites/files/oxlaw/dr_pablo_cortes.pdf.

Doan, Anhai, Raghu Ramakrishnan, and Alon Y. Halevy. "Crowdsourcing Systems on the World-Wide Web." *Communications of the ACM* 54, no. 4 (2011): 86–96.

Eidenmüller, Horst, and Martin Engel. "Against False Settlement: Designing Efficient Consumer Rights Enforcement System in Europe." *Ohio State Journal on Dispute Resolution* 29, no. 2 (2014): 261–98.

Ellickson, Robert C. *Orders without Law: How Neighbors Settle Disputes*. Cambridge: Harvard University Press, 1991.

Fu, Weigang傅蔚冈. "Wanggou pingtai de ziying shenhua 网购平台的自营神话." *Dushi Kuaibao* 都市快报, November 9, 2018. https://baijiahao.baidu.com/s?id=1616627270190715540.

Gneezy, Uri, and Aldo Rustichini. "A Fine Is a Price." *Journal of Legal Studies* 29, no. 1 (2000): 1–17. https://doi.org/10.1086/468061.

Göritz, Anja S. "Incentives in Web Studies: Methodological Issues and a Review." *International Journal of Internet Science* 1, no. 1 (2006): 58–70.

Greif, Avner. "Reputation and Coalitions in Medieval Trade: Evidence on the Maghribi Traders." *The Journal of Economic History* 49, no. 4 (1989): 857–82. https://doi.org/10.1017/S0022050700009475.

Greif, Avner. *Institutions and the Path to the Modern Economy*. Cambridge: Cambridge University Press, 2006. https://doi.org/10.1017/CBO9780511791307.

Hanriot, Maxime. "Online Dispute Resolution as Solution to Cross Border Consumer Disputes: The Enforcement of Outcomes." *McGill Journal of Dispute Resolution* 2 (2015–2016): 1–22.

Hörnle, Julia. *Cross-Border Internet Dispute Resolution*. Cambridge: Cambridge University Press, 2009. https://doi.org/10.1017/CBO9780511576102.

Howe, Jeff. "The Rise of Crowdsourcing." *Wired* 14, no. 6 (2006): 176–83.

Howe, Jeff. *Crowdsourcing: How the Power of Crowd Is Driving the Future of Business*. London: Random House, 2008.

James Surowiecki. *The Wisdom of Crowds: Why the Many Are Smarter Than the Few and How Collective Wisdom Shapes Business, Economies, Societies and Nations*. London: Little, Brown, 2004.

Johnson, David R., and David Post. "Law and Borders: The Rise of Law in Cyberspace." *Stanford Law Review* 48, no. 5 (1996): 1367–402, https://doi.org/10.2307/1229390.

Kaal, Wulf A., and Craig Calcaterra. "Crypto Transaction Dispute Resolution." *The Business Lawyer* 73, no. 1 (2017–2018): 109–52.

Katsh, Ethan, Janet Rifkin, and Alan Gaitenby. "E-commerce, E-disputes, and E-dispute Resolution: In the Shadow of eBay Law." *Ohio State Journal on Dispute Resolution* 15, no. 3 (1999): 705–34.

Koulu, Riikka. "Blockchains and Online Dispute Resolution: Smart Contracts as an Alternative to Enforcement." *Scripted* 13, no. 1 (2016): 40–69. https://doi.org/10.2966/script.130116.40.

Lessig, Lawrence. *Code: Version 2.0*. New York: Basic Books, 2006.
Levitt, Steven D., and Stephen J. Dubner. *Freakonomics*. New York: HarperCollins, 2005.
Malone, Thomas W., Robert Laubacher, and Chrysanthos Dellarocas. "The Collective Intelligence Genome." *IEEE Engineering Management Review* 38, no. 3 (2010): 38–52. https://doi.org/10.1109/EMR.2010.5559142.
Maniaci, Michael R., and Ronald D. Rogge. "Conducting Research on the Internet." In *Handbook of Research Methods in Social and Personality Psychology*, edited by Harry T. Reis and Charles M. Judd, 2nd ed., 443–70. Cambridge: Cambridge University Press, 2014. https://doi.org/10.1017/CBO9780511996481.
Mesquita, Lurdes Varregoso, and Catia Marques Cebola. "European Small Claims Procedure: An Effective Process? A Proposal for an Online Platform." *Access to Justice in Eastern Europe* 14 (2022): 7–21. https://doi.org/10.33327/AJEE-18-5.2-a000206.
Ortolani, Pietro. "Self-Enforcing Online Dispute Resolution: Lessons from Bitcoin." *Oxford Journal of Legal Studies* 36, no. 3 (2016): 595–629.
Perritt, Henry H. "Towards a Hybrid Regulatory Scheme for the Internet." *University of Chicago Legal Forum* 2001 (2001): 215–322.
Platteau, Jean-Phiilippe. "Behind the Market Stage Where Real Societies Exist-Part I: The Role of Public and Private Order Institutions." *The Journal of Development Studies* 30, no. 3 (1994): 533–77. https://doi.org/10.1080/00220389408422328.
Post, David G. "What Larry Doesn't Get: Code, Law and Liberty in Cyberspace." *Stanford Law Review* 52, no. 5 (2000): 1439–59. https://doi.org/10.2307/1229518.
Pow, Choon-Piew. "Constructing a New Private Order: Gated Communities and the Privatization of Urban Life in Post-Reform Shanghai." *Social & Cultural Geography* 8, no. 6 (2007): 813–33. https://doi.org/10.1080/14649360701712511.
Rabinovich-Einy, Orna, and Ethan Katsh. "A New Relationship between Public and Private Dispute Resolution: Lessons from Online Dispute Resolution." *Ohio State Journal of Dispute Resolution* 32, no. 4 (2017): 695–724.
Rule, Colin, and Harpreet Singh. "ODR and Online Reputation Systems – Maintaining Trust and Accuracy Through Effective Redress." In *Online Dispute Resolution: Theory and Practice*, edited by Mohamed S. Abdel Wahab, Ethan Katsh, and Daniel Rainey, 175–96. The Hague: Eleven, 2012.
Sagy, Tehila. "What's So Private About Private Ordering?" *Law & Society Review* 45, no. 4 (2011): 923–54. https://doi.org/10.1111/j.1540-5893.2011.00461.x.
Schillig, Michael Anderson. "'Lex Cryptographi(c)a', 'Cloud Crypto Land' or What? – Blockchain Technology on the Legal Hype Cycle." *Modern Law Review* 86, no. 1 (2023): 31–66. https://doi.org/10.1111/1468-2230.12748.
Schultz, Thomas. "Online Arbitration: Binding or Non-Binding?" *ADR Online Monthly*, November 2002. http://www.ombuds.org/center/adr2002-11-schultz.html.
Schwarcz, Steven L. "Private Ordering." *Northwestern University Law Review* 97, no. 1 (2002): 319–50.
Shen, Xinwang申欣旺. "Taobao hulianwang Zhengyi jiejue jizhi de qishi 淘宝互联网争议解决机制的启示." *Minzhu yu fazhi* 民主与法制 754, no. 5 (2016): 23–26. http://e.mzyfz.org.cn/mag/paper_8871_5537.html.
van den Herik, Jaap, and Daniel Dimov. "Towards Crowdsourced Online Dispute Resolution." *Journal of International Commercial Law and Technology* 7, no. 2 (2012).
Zheng, Zibin, Shaoan Xie, Hong-Ning Dai, Weili Chen, Xiangping Chen, Jian Weng, and Muhammad Imran. "An Overview on Smart Contracts: Challenges, Advances and Platforms." *Future Generation Computer Systems* 105 (April 2020): 475–91. https://doi.org/10.1016/j.future.2019.12.019.

4 Online arbitration

Obstacles and developments

Online arbitration and its recent development

Online arbitration generally refers to the process in which all stages of arbitration – including the filing of claims, submission of evidence, communication between the involved parties and the arbitral tribunal, as well as hearings, examinations, and the issuance of awards – are conducted through an online platform or via online meetings, thus constituting a fully online arbitration system.[1] Alternatively, it is also posited that online arbitration may adopt a hybrid model, integrating aspects of both online and traditional arbitration. In this model, only portions of the arbitration process are executed online.[2] There has always been divergence in the concept itself.

In this context, it is understandable to hold the position that processes do not qualify as online arbitration, if only the initial filing or reception of cases is online while the primary proceedings are offline. Conversely, it is untenable to doctrinally assert that arbitrations are not online if the core of proceedings transpires online, such as submission and examination of evidence and hearings, with merely isolated components occurring offline. Traditional arbitration and online arbitration essentially show little difference in terms of methods.[3]

1 Vincent Bonnet, Karima Boudaoud, Michael Gagnebin, Jürgen Harms, and Thomas Schultz, "Online Dispute Resolution Systems as Web Services," *ICFAI Journal of Alternative Dispute Resolution* 3 (2004): 58.

2 Thomas Schultz, "Online Arbitration: Binding or Non-Binding?," *ADR Online Monthly* (November 2002); Julia Hörnle, "Online Dispute Resolution: The Emperor's New Clothes?," *International Review of Law, Computers and Technology* 17, no. 1 (2003): 27–30, https://doi.org/10.1080/1360086032000063093.

3 It is also being concluded that online arbitration does not entail online hearings but rather proceeds through written deliberations, a form which has transitioned from traditional paper-based to digital submissions. This delineates the primary distinction. See Shi Hai 石海, "Internet Arbitration Requires Institutional Support and Regulation 互联网仲裁需制度支撑和规范," *Legal Daily* 法制日报, May 11, 2021, https://www.moj.gov.cn/pub/sfbgw/fzgz/fzgzggflfwx/fzgzggflfw/202105/t20210511_391799.html. In addition, according to the Shenzhen Court of International Arbitration (SCIA), *online arbitration* is defined as a dispute resolution mechanism that utilizes electronic communication along with other information and communication technologies. See Article 2 of SCIA Online Arbitration Rules (2022), https://www.scia.com.cn/index.php/Home/index/rule/id/814.html.

DOI: 10.4324/ 9781003594512-4

Despite its early inception, online arbitration has not rapidly evolved into an effective alternative to traditional dispute resolution models as initially envisioned. Long after its emergence, it struggled to realize this ambition. In 2001, the American Arbitration Association (AAA) launched its "Online Dispute Resolution" initiative, which involved filing documents through the AAA WebFile, an online case management system.[4] Similarly, the China International Economic and Trade Arbitration Commission (CIETAC), one of the busiest and the most prominent international arbitration institutions in the world, introduced its online arbitration rules in 2009. Yet for a considerable period thereafter, there were rather few cases that employed online arbitration. Over time, while an increasing number of parties opted to submit their claims, pay fees, and select arbitrators online, there was still a reluctance to conduct all proceedings through virtual means. In 1997, a seminal paper, titled "International Commercial Arbitration on the Internet – Is the Future Too Early?,"[5] highlighted various legal challenges that could arise with online arbitration, including issues related to the arbitration agreement, procedural dynamics, and the enforcement of arbitral awards.

Currently, online arbitration services are predominantly offered through two mediums: institutional arbitration services and those provided by privately established entities, such as Rapid Ruling.[6] A notable concern for private arbitration is that even well-established services could go out of business. NovaForum, for example, used to contract arbitrators around the world since the 1990s but has now disappeared.[7]

Institutional arbitration services are more stable in comparison and have reliably provided online arbitration services for many years. A prime example of institutional arbitration services is the International Chamber of Commerce (ICC) Online Arbitration Service, which currently operates via the ICC Case Connect system,[8] launched in October 2022. The AAA's system encompasses several components, including the AAA File Online application page, the party's user interface WebFile system, and the arbitrator's and mediator's client portal, the Panelist eCenter. In China, CIETAC's system includes the "File Online" section on its official website and the comprehensive "CIETAC Intelligent Hearing Platform." Despite such advancements, these institutions have not yet implemented a unified system or platform to manage all procedural aspects in a "one-stop" manner. Instead, they utilize various systems for arbitration applications, case management, and online hearings, providing parties with choices at different procedural stages. However, all three organizations possess the capability to conduct proceedings entirely online.

4 Debi Miller-Moore, "ODR at the AAA: Online Dispute Resolution in Practice," *University of Toledo Law Review* 38 (2006): 396.

5 Jasna Arsic, "International Commercial Arbitration on the Internet: Has the Future Come Too Early?," *Journal of International Arbitration* 14, no. 3 (1997): 209.

6 Rapid Ruling, accessed July 31, 2024, https://rapidruling.com/about-us/.

7 Rachel I. Turner, "Alternative Dispute Resolution in Cyberspace: There Is More on the Line, Than Just Getting 'Online'," *ILSA Journal of International & Comparative Law* 7 (2000): 142.

8 International Chamber of Commerce, "File Your Request for Arbitration," accessed July 31, 2024, https://iccwbo.org/dispute-resolution/dispute-resolution-services/arbitration/file-a-request/.

AAA and ICC require third-party platforms for online hearings, whereas CIETAC leverages its proprietary platform. The extent to which cases are conducted online varies based on the preferences of the parties, the specifics of the case, and the discretion of the arbitral tribunal.

By its very nature, online arbitration retains the core structure and legal characteristics of traditional arbitration. It continues to adhere to the legal framework of traditional arbitration, where a neutral third party adjudicates based on the arbitration agreement after evaluating the relevant evidence and claims, albeit now integrated with technological elements in its procedural structure.

The procedural framework for online arbitration facilitated by international arbitration institutions typically encompasses several key components:

1. *Pre-trial conference*. This preliminary phase involves agreeing on the detailed schedule of the hearing, the sequencing and timing for the cross-examination of witnesses and experts, connection locations for witnesses and experts, the submission deadlines for the hearing case file, and selection procedures for third-party service providers, including online hearing platforms, electronic case files, hearing transcripts, and interpreters, among other procedural matters.
2. *Selection of third-party institutions*. Arbitration services often utilize videoconferencing platforms and other online services for e-filing, transcription, and interpretation. Industry associations and international arbitration bodies frequently publish lists of approved third-party service providers on their websites, assisting parties in selecting appropriate platforms and services tailored to their specific needs and budget constraints.
3. *Agreeing on online hearing cyber-protocol*. The agreed protocols typically cover technical specifications, requirements, support personnel arrangements, confidentiality, security of online hearings, online etiquette, procedures for witness and expert cross-examination, and evidence presentation.
4. *Preparation of electronic case files*. While traditional trials require printing and binding of trial files after verification by attorneys, the preparation for online hearings differs mainly in the absence of physical printing and binding.
5. *Pre-hearing testing*. To ensure the quality of the online hearing, all participants, including parties, attorneys, witnesses, experts, interpreters, and technical support staff, must undergo testing prior to the commencement of hearings.
6. *Formal hearings*. These are conducted in accordance with the previously agreed-upon steps and the online hearing cyber-protocol.

The COVID-19 pandemic has significantly accelerated the adoption of online arbitration, leaving a lasting impact on the international legal and arbitration sectors. For example, CIETAC reported that online filings in 2023 surged by 34.63% year-on-year, representing more than a third of total case filings, with 1,631 hearings conducted online, nearly a third of the total.[9] This marks a considerable

9 CIETAC, "2023 Work Report of CIETAC," accessed July 31, 2024, http://cietac.org.cn/index.php?m=Article&a=show&id=20067.

shift from the nascent stages of online arbitration, with more defined rules now established across various international arbitration forums. Several legislative adaptations are being contemplated in different countries, including the draft revision of China's arbitration law[10] and proposed amendments to the arbitration section of the German Code of Civil Procedure.[11]

At the international level, significant legal frameworks include the UNCITRAL Model Law on Electronic Commerce (1996), which introduced the "functional equivalence approach" to affirm the legal validity of data messages.[12] This approach analogizes the legal effects of data messages with traditional written forms, thus liberating them from the constraints of a single medium and addressing the recognition of future forms of technologically enabled arbitration agreements. Further, the integration of electronic authentication and electronic signatures has been widely adopted in various international trade agreements, such as multiple free trade and digital trade agreements signed by the United States with South Korea, Canada, Mexico, and Japan.[13]

In general, the fundamental legal framework at the international level, embodied by instruments such as the Convention on the Recognition and Enforcement of Foreign Arbitral Awards (1958) and the UNCITRAL Model Law on International Commercial Arbitration (1985, with amendments as adopted in 2006), remains unchanged. However, there is an emerging trend internationally toward the recognition of electronically conducted arbitration. It is undeniable that legal frameworks evolve more slowly than industry practices, resulting in persistent uncertainties concerning the interface between existing laws and the online arbitration regime.

Revisiting the definition of *online arbitration*, it becomes apparent that the concept has been contentious for several reasons. Initially, the emergence of a novel concept necessitates a clear definition to serve as a foundation for both

10 The State Council stated its intention to submit a draft revision to the arbitration law to the Standing Committee of the National People's Congress as part of the legislative work planned for 2024. See State Council, "2024 Annual Plan of Legislative Work" (*Guo Ban Fa* 2024/no. 23), May 6, 2024, https://www.gov.cn/zhengce/content/202405/content_6950093.htm.

11 On February 1, 2024, the German Ministry of Justice released a report themed on the revision of the arbitration law. The draft amendment to Section 1047(2) of the German Code of Civil Procedure states that the arbitral tribunal may, at its discretion, decide whether to conduct hearings via videoconference instead of traditional in-person hearings, unless the parties have explicitly agreed otherwise. See the Federal Ministry of Justice, "Draft Bill for the Modernisation of Arbitration Law," February 1, 2024, https://www.bmj.de/SharedDocs/Downloads/DE/Gesetzgebung/RefE/RefE_Modernisierung_Schiedsverfahrensrecht_2024_EN.pdf

12 UNCITRAL Model Law on Electronic Commerce (1996), Articles 5–10. As of 2024, 87 countries, totaling 170 jurisdictions, have enacted laws and regulations based on the UNCITRAL Model Law on Electronic Commerce. See United Nations Commission on International Trade Law, "Status: UNCITRAL Model Law on Electronic Commerce (1996)," accessed July 31, 2024, https://uncitral.un.org/en/texts/ecommerce/modellaw/electronic_commerce/status.

13 "Free Trade Agreement between the United States of America and the Republic of Korea" (as of January 1, 2019), Chapter 15 "Electronic Commerce," Article 15.4; "Agreement between the United States of America, the United Mexican States, and Canada" (as of July 1, 2020), Chapter 19 "Digital Trade," Article 19.6; "Agreement between the United States of America and Japan Concerning Digital Trade," Article 10.

institutionalization and scholarly discourse. However, particularly post-pandemic, major arbitration institutions have demonstrated capabilities to manage processes entirely online or through a hybrid of online and offline modalities, rendering the original conceptual distinctions less significant. In essence, the understanding of what is meant by "online arbitration" has come to be defined by practice instead of doctrines. The more pertinent inquiry, as will be explored in this chapter, revolves around whether the integration of technology with arbitration procedures is capable of safeguarding the rights and interests of the parties involved, ensuring the enforceability of awards, and fulfilling the foundational objectives of arbitration.

Online arbitration in China

Status of online arbitration in China: an empirical study

Clarifying the ongoing developments and challenges within the field of online arbitration emphasizes the shift in focus from defining the concept to addressing its practical implications and effectiveness. This makes China's experience with online arbitration particularly valuable, as it provides an important case study for understanding what is truly happening in the practice of online arbitration.

China's arbitration law exclusively mandates institutional arbitration and does not permit *ad hoc* arbitration or arbitration organized by private entities. Consequently, all disputes must be submitted to a Chinese or foreign arbitration institution for settlement in order to be recognized by Chinese law. One of the legal requirements for the validity of an arbitration agreement is the choice of a recognized arbitration commission.[14] Consequently, only registered arbitration commissions in China are authorized to offer arbitration services, whether online or traditional. Moreover, all arbitration commissions must be registered with the justice departments of municipalities, provinces, and autonomous regions.[15] It is therefore feasible to obtain an exhaustive record of all operational arbitration institutions in China, by searching all municipalities and capital cities of all provinces and autonomous regions one by one for arbitration institutions according to China's 2020 Administrative Region Plan.

As of July 2024, an investigation undertaken by this author identified 282 arbitration institutions listed in China across all provincial and prefectural units, with 135 of these (48%) offering online services to some extent. These institutions can be categorized, based on their adoption of online arbitration rules and the establishment of dedicated platforms or systems, as follows:

1. *Institutions with specific online arbitration rules*. For instance, CIETAC and the Shenzhen Court of International Arbitration (SCIA) are among the 46 institutions that have established distinct online arbitration rules, constituting about

14 Arbitration Law of the People's Republic of China, Article 16.
15 Arbitration Law of the People's Republic of China, Article 10.

one-third of the total. Notably, 44 of these institutions have developed dedicated online arbitration platforms.

2. *Institutions with general but relevant arbitration rules*. Institutions, such as the Beijing Arbitration Commission (BAC), which, while lacking specific online arbitration rules, incorporate online arbitration provisions within their general arbitration rules. This group includes 42 institutions, about one-third of the total, with 31 having established online arbitration platforms and 11 lacking publicly accessible online systems.
3. *Institutions with guidelines on online arbitration*. A smaller group consisting of only two institutions, such as the Shanghai Arbitration Commission (SHAC), provides guidelines for online hearings without formal rules. Both institutions in this category have online platforms.
4. *Institutions with online platforms but no formal rules or guidelines*. This group includes 45 institutions, one-third of the total, which offer online arbitration platforms without formal rules or guidelines.

The other 147 arbitration commission had not established any platform or rules for online arbitration as of July 2024, when this study was conducted. However, it is important to note that more and more institutions have been launching online services in recent years. Apart from CIETAC's online arbitration rules, first implemented in 2009, rules and provisions regarding online arbitration in other institutions primarily came into effect after 2018.

Table 4.1 shows the number of arbitration commissions by provinces, municipalities, and autonomous regions in Mainland China, excluding Hong Kong, Macau, and Taiwan, categorized into the four groups explained earlier. The first three categories are further divided based on the presence of dedicated online arbitration platforms, regardless of how basic these platforms are, such as a single webpage for the submission of materials.

Critical analysis of online arbitration in China

Despite the proliferation of online arbitration services, the current arbitration law does not recognize online arbitration, creating potential complications during judicial review and enforcement of arbitral awards. The latest draft revisions to the Arbitration Law of the People's Republic of China, published by the Ministry of Justice in 2021, addresses online arbitration, but it remains somewhat generic and lacks specific guidance on critical issues, such as determining the venue of arbitration and remote hearings. The existing legislative framework does not adequately address the practical requirements of online arbitration, resulting in a lack of legal recognition and systematic guidance for online arbitration procedures.

However, the absence of specific arbitration law provisions has not precluded the inclusion of aspects of online arbitration in other legal frameworks. For example, electronic evidence and electronic service are accommodated under different statutes. Electronic data, as recognized in online arbitration rules by institutions such as CIETAC, Guangzhou Arbitration Commission, and SCIA, is acknowledged

Table 4.1 Online arbitration functions of arbitration commissions in China by province

	Total number of arbitration commissions	*Category 1*		*Category 2*		*Category 3*		*Category 4*	*Total number with online services*	*Total number without online services*	*Percentage with online services*
		With platform	*Without platform*	*With platform*	*Without platform*	*With platform*	*Without platform*				
Anhui	16	1		1	3			3	8	8	50%
Beijing	3	2		1					3	0	100%
Chongqing	1	1							1	0	100%
Fujian	8	2		1					3	5	38%
Gansu	8	1						1	2	6	25%
Guangdong	18	4		4	2			3	13	5	72%
Guangxi	14	4							4	10	29%
Guizhou	3	1						1	2	1	67%
Hainan	1							1	1	0	100%
Hebei	11	3		3				3	9	2	82%
Heilongjiang	12	3		1				2	6	6	50%
Henan	17	2		3	1			2	8	9	47%
Hubei	13	3		1				2	6	7	46%
Hunan	13	1		1					2	11	15%
Jiangsu	13	2		2				7	11	2	85%
Jiangxi	11		2	2	3				7	4	64%
Jilin	8							1	1	7	13%
Liaoning	14			1		1		1	3	11	21%
Neimenggu	9				1			3	4	5	44%
Ningxia	5	1		1					2	3	40%
Qinghai	1								0	1	0%
Shandong	16	4		4				7	15	1	94%
Shanxi	11	1		1				1	3	8	27%
Shaanxi	10			1				1	2	8	20%
Shanghai	2	1				1			2	0	100%
Sichuan	18	1		1	1			2	5	13	28%
Tianjin	1							1	1	0	100%
Xinjiang	5								0	5	0%
Xizang	2								0	2	0%
Yunnan	7							1	1	6	14%
Zhejiang	11	6		2				2	10	1	91%
National Total	282	44	2	31	11	2	0	45	135	147	48%

as one of the eight types of evidence under Chinese law.[16] Furthermore, electronic signatures have the same legal effect as handwritten signatures, and data messages are treated as if they were in written form.[17] Therefore, an arbitration clause in the form of a data message that fulfills these conditions complies with the formal requirements of the law for an arbitration agreement. Moreover, the 2023 amendments to the Civil Procedure Law permit electronic service of judicial documents, unless the recipient explicitly requests a paper copy. This provision aligns with the broader acceptance of electronic service within Chinese legal practice.[18] Chinese arbitration institutions have correspondingly established numerous regulations for electronic service of documents.

Regarding cross-border service, China ratified accession to the Convention of November 15, 1965, on the service abroad of judicial and extrajudicial documents in civil or commercial matters (the Hague Service Convention) in 1991.[19] The application of the Hague Service Convention to arbitration proceedings can be nuanced, particularly when considering its implications for extrajudicial documents in such contexts. Although arbitration documents could theoretically fall under the ambit of this convention if judicial assistance is required, in practice, serving these documents according to party-agreed arbitration rules often means that requests for service under the Convention are infrequent. Consequently, some jurisdictions have concluded that the Hague Service Convention does not necessarily apply to arbitration documents.[20]

From this observation, two significant insights emerge. First, there is a dependence on arbitration institutional rules for the service process. Many arbitration institutions in China have adopted provisions for electronic service of process, and there is no recorded instance where a court has set aside or refused to enforce an arbitral award due to the electronic nature of the process. The efficacy of such service in arbitration is contingent not only on the rules of the arbitrating institution but also on the legal framework of the jurisdiction where the arbitration is seated and where the award is to be enforced. Courts in these jurisdictions interpret the service of documents and evaluate the validity of electronic service based on national laws. A notable case in point is where the High Court of Singapore upheld an arbitral award that was served via text message by the SCIA, despite the argument against the unreliability of service by electronic means.[21]

16 Civil Procedure Law of the People's Republic of China, Article 66.

17 Electronic Signature Law of the People's Republic of China, Article 14; Civil Code of the People's Republic of China, Article 469.

18 Civil Procedure Law of the People's Republic of China, Article 90.

19 The Hague Service Convention formally came into effect in China on January 1, 1992.

20 Hague Conference on Private International Law, "Revised Draft of the Practical Handbook on the Operation of the Service Convention," accessed July 31, 2024, https://assets.hcch.net/docs/37d9b7a9-f29f-4e43-9c8f-963d899631fa.pdf, 78.

21 *Wang Bin v. Zhong Sihui* [2024] SGHC 189. The judge stated: "Just as we have moved from communications by postal mail to faxes and then to email, so we should also be prepared to consider communications beyond email. Many jurisdictions have already done so with short messaging services displacing email as the main form of business communications. We should not fail to recognise this."

Second, there is no uniform convention on electronic service. While the Hague Service Convention is the primary international framework addressing the service of judicial documents, it does not explicitly cater to electronic service. Under the Convention, the possibility of serving judicial documents electronically across borders hinges on the specific legal provisions of the destination country. If a country has not opted out of Article 10 of the Hague Service Convention – which permits postal service of documents and, by extension, could allow for electronic service if equated with postal methods – then cross-border electronic service may be feasible. However, China has explicitly reserved against this provision, thus precluding the cross-border service of foreign judicial documents via electronic means, including email or facsimile.[22]

Beyond the aforementioned developments, the concept of "smart arbitration" is gaining traction in academic and practical circles in China. As an advanced iteration of internet arbitration, smart arbitration incorporates technologies such as artificial intelligence (AI), blockchain, and big data to pre-fix evidence and digitize case facts. This technological integration facilitates the intelligent organization of evidence and the automated generation of arbitration documents, thereby assisting arbitrators in conducting proceedings online. However, these advancements also raise new legal questions, such as the validity of arbitral awards generated through intelligent systems, necessitating further examination and alignment with existing legal frameworks.

China's current arbitration law, enacted in 1995, has not kept pace with the significant transformations witnessed in the theory and practice of international arbitration. In some instances, the rules adopted by Chinese arbitration commissions not only align with but also surpass global practices, occasionally contradicting the stipulations of the arbitration law. This phenomenon reflects a broader, more prominent characteristic of Chinese legal practice, where practical implementations often precede formal legislative recognition.[23] This is particularly evident in the realm of arbitration, which also benefits from being a private dispute resolution mechanism. The relative independence from the formal legal system grants arbitration the flexibility needed for institutional evolution. Simultaneously, as a service-oriented sector, arbitration institutions naturally strive to enhance their offerings. This competitive drive fosters the development of innovative arbitration methods aimed at satisfying the needs of the parties involved, thereby deriving benefits and advancing the field.

Moreover, the advancement of electronic and digital systems within the litigation frameworks of major countries and regions worldwide indirectly influences the arbitration sector. For instance, the digitalization of the Chinese litigation system can positively impact its international arbitration framework, as previously

22 Chenyang Zhang, *Win in Chinese Courts: Practice Guide to Civil Litigation in China* (Springer, 2023), 60, https://doi.org/10.1007/978-981-99-3342-6.

23 Lu Xu, *Chinese Legal Reforms: Transformations in a Decade* (Leiden: Brill, 2024), 28–30, https://doi.org/10.1163/9789004537125.

discussed. This interaction underscores the interconnected development of institutional practices and regulations, highlighting a trend where the evolution of arbitration norms and infrastructure often precedes formal legal adaptation.

Asynchronous online hearings

Concept and rules of asynchronous online hearing

Similar to traditional court procedures, arbitration typically employs a synchronous hearing model, where both parties appear simultaneously in front of arbitrators. However, advancement in technology and the move toward online arbitration have introduced an alternative approach in the form of asynchronous online hearing. In recent years, several Chinese arbitration institutions, such as the Wuhan Arbitration Commission, the Quzhou Arbitration Commission, and the Nanping Arbitration Commission, have adopted this concept in their arbitral practice. Furthermore, the acceptance of this novel approach by the Chinese court sheds light on the development of arbitration in the digitized environment that courts and arbitration institutions find themselves in.

The online arbitration rules issued by the Wuhan Arbitration Commission on August 1, 2019, define "online arbitration" as any form of dispute resolution conducted over the internet. These rules classify "online hearings" into two types: asynchronous electronic interactive hearings and synchronous video hearings. An asynchronous electronic interactive hearing allows the arbitral tribunal, claimant, respondent, and other participants to log onto a designated electronic platform at their convenience within a specified period to complete the arbitration proceeding asynchronously according to the rules. Following this approach, both the Quzhou Arbitration Commission and the Nanping Arbitration Commission introduced their cyber arbitration rules on January 1, 2020, and July 1, 2020, respectively, incorporating asynchronous electronic interactions as one of the modes for online hearings.

The cyber arbitration rules of the Quzhou Arbitration Commission, in its current version effective June 2024, provide a good illustration of the operation of asynchronous online hearing. Asynchronous hearings are now the preferred model of the Quzhou Arbitration Commission, while synchronous hearings are the exception. Article 27, paragraph 1 of its rules stipulates that cyber arbitration be conducted through asynchronous electronic interaction, except in two instances: (1) if the parties agree to conduct synchronous video hearings within three days of receiving the notice of arbitration or (2) if a party applies, and the arbitral tribunal deems it necessary based on the specific case circumstances, to hold the hearing online via synchronous video. Furthermore, paragraph 2 states that if the case is to be conducted asynchronously, the initiation of the first hearing is marked by the notification sent to the parties by the Commission regarding the online hearing. Within a prescribed time frame, the arbitral tribunal and all participants must complete the arbitration activities, including, but not limited to, evidence presentation, evidence examination, and debates, at individually chosen times, in accordance with these rules, using the electronic interactive format. Notification of the commencement of each phase of the hearing process is to be electronically conveyed to the parties. Paragraph 3 outlines the steps of asynchronous hearings: (1) The arbitral tribunal may send a questionnaire through the online platform for the parties to respond with evidence or views within 48 hours; (2) the parties are required to present their arguments within 72 hours of receiving the arbitration notice; and (3) the parties must submit their final statements within 24 hours of receiving the presentation notice. These submissions may be made by editing or uploading documents, and failure to submit within these time frames shall not impede the arbitration proceedings.

Empirical study of judicial acceptance of asynchronous arbitration

The emergence of asynchronous hearing poses a new question for the Chinese system, as the existing law takes no clear position on whether to recognize such an approach of arbitration. Under the arbitration law and related regulations, courts have the authority to supervise arbitration, by either setting aside arbitral awards or refusing enforcement. An extensive empirical study was conducted in order to evaluate the stance and attitude of Chinese courts when they are asked to enforce arbitral awards reached by asynchronous hearings.

This study was based on keyword searches of an extensive judicial judgments database in July 2024.[24] The search utilized keywords such as "asynchronous electronic interactions," "asynchronous electronic exchanges," and "asynchronous cyber-arbitration" to identify relevant judgments by Chinese courts. It identified a total of 139 court judgments related to non-labor arbitration and 12 judgments related to labor arbitration. In this context, Chinese law operates a "two-track system" that differentiates between arbitrations with foreign elements and those that are purely domestic. This distinction is often pivotal in understanding how Chinese courts handle arbitration cases. Regarding judicial supervision of arbitration, the grounds for setting aside or non-enforcement of foreign-related arbitral awards only pertain to procedural matters, whereas, in purely domestic cases, the court also supervises substantive issues, such as evidence.[25] However, as it turns out, all 151 cases uncovered in this study are purely domestic cases, and courts have set aside or not enforced arbitral awards only on the basis of procedural defects, rather than on any substantive grounds. Moreover, all 139 non-labor cases relate to arbitral awards made by the Quzhou Arbitration Commission in Zhejiang Province, while all 12 labor cases originated from Guangzhou.

Of these 139 non-labor cases, there are three types of claims raised by the plaintiffs, namely, applications for enforcement of the arbitral award, applications for non-enforcement of the arbitral award, and applications for setting aside the

24 The WK Priority Legal Information Database (accessed July 31, 2024, https://law.wkinfo.com.cn/), used for this study, contains the same range of judgment documents as the free public database China Judgments Online, operated by SPC. The former offers better search functionalities and greater stability in terms of the availability of cases than the official database.

25 Arbitration Law of the People's Republic of China (2017 Amendment), Articles 58, 63, 70 and 71; Civil Procedure Law of the People's Republic of China (2023 Amendment), Articles 248 and 291.

arbitral award. An overwhelming majority of 135 out of 139 cases related to the enforcement of arbitral awards obtained through asynchronous electronic interactions.[26] Remarkably, the court either declined to enforce or dismissed the applications in all these cases. Among the remaining four cases, three were applications to deny enforcement of arbitral awards, two of which successfully obtained a non-enforcement ruling,[27] and one resulted in the dismissal of the plaintiff's claim, thereby effectively upholding the arbitral award.[28] The last of the 139 cases was an application for the setting aside of an arbitral award, which was reviewed by the Quzhou Intermediate People's Court. The court rejected the party's request and upheld the arbitral award made by the Quzhou Arbitration Commission in the form of asynchronous electronic interactive hearings.[29] This data highlights a predominant judicial inclination to question asynchronously decided arbitral awards, especially regarding whether the process provided sufficient protection for the rights of the parties.

Substantive qualitative analysis of all judgments further reveals three distinct approaches to the issue of asynchronous online hearings by arbitral tribunals among the Chinese judiciary. These varied approaches by Chinese courts highlight the complexities and the evolving judicial perspectives toward the use of asynchronous electronic interactions in arbitration, reflecting a nuanced balance between adherence to procedural fairness and the efficiency offered by modern technological practices in arbitration.

The first approach is evasive, observed in 22 cases.[30] In these instances, the court avoided directly addressing the parties' concerns about asynchronous online hearings. Instead, the courts ruled on other grounds for non-enforcement of the arbitral awards. This type of judgment typically emerges when parties object to the asynchronous nature of the online hearings in their legal submissions, but the courts choose not to address these objections in their judgments.

26 These include 44 cases from Chongqing No. 2 Intermediate People's Court, 31 cases from Anhui Province Anqing Intermediate People's Court, 12 cases from Guangxi Autonomous Region Hechi Intermediate People's Court, 8 from Guangdong Province Yangjiang Intermediate People's Court, 7 cases from Anhui Province Fuyang Intermediate People's Court, 6 cases from Liaoning Province Dandong Intermediate People's Court, 5 cases from Hainan Province Haikou Intermediate People's Court, 3 cases each from three different courts, 2 cases each from three different courts, and 1 case each from seven different courts.

27 郭小博、深圳融信保非融资性担保有限公司借款合同纠纷案, (2019)豫11执异55号执行裁定书, Henan Province Luohe Intermediate People's Court (October 29, 2019); 蒋欣倩、广州万达普惠网络小额贷款有限公司借款合同纠纷案, (2021)川01执异2784号执行裁定书, Sichuan Province Chengdu Intermediate People's Court (December 14, 2021).

28 岳丹丹、万达齐富(杭州)投资管理有限公司民事执行异议案, (2022)吉07执异79号执行裁定书, Jilin Province Songyuan Intermediate People's Court (December 13, 2022).

29 高强、上海方达小额贷款有限公司申请撤销仲裁裁决案,(2020)浙08民特17号民事裁定书, Zhejiang Province Quzhou Intermediate People's Court (December 7, 2020).

30 For example, 上海快升金融信息服务有限公司、吴雪金融借款合同纠纷案，辽宁省丹东市中级人民法院（2021）辽06执236号执行裁定书, Liaoning Province Dandong Intermediate People's Court (April 25, 2021); 谢某方借款合同纠纷执行复议案, (2023)黔执复504号裁定书, Guizhou Province High People's Court (November 20, 2023).

The second approach is notably conservative against the new model, encompassing 115 cases. Here, the courts explicitly discussed the arbitration tribunal's use of asynchronous online hearings and concluded that such practices did not sufficiently protect the procedural rights of the parties involved. Consequently, the courts either denied enforcement of the arbitral awards or dismissed the applications for enforcement on these grounds. For example, the Fuyang Intermediate People's Court of Anhui Province found that the Quzhou Arbitration Commission's use of asynchronous electronic interactions, conducted by a sole arbitrator, did not adequately protect the party's fundamental procedural rights, including the right to challenge the arbitrator, provide evidence, and defend their case.[31]

The third approach is supportive of asynchronous hearings, evident in only two cases that eventually upheld the arbitral awards.[32] In the aforementioned ruling by the Quzhou Intermediate People's Court, the court noted that the Quzhou Arbitration Commission's use of asynchronous electronic interactions for online hearings and the delivery of arbitration documents via text messages were consistent with the terms of the contract involved in the case and the online arbitration rules of the Arbitration Commission. The court held that these methods did not infringe upon the procedural rights of the parties involved.

In addition to those 139 cases of non-labor arbitration, there are 12 judgments related to labor arbitration, all of which involved applications for setting aside arbitral awards.[33] It is noteworthy that all 12 cases originated in Guangzhou and arose against the backdrop of the Guangzhou Municipal Labor and Personnel Dispute Arbitration Commission issuing the "Notice on Launching the Guangzhou Municipal Labor and Personnel Dispute Arbitration Internet Asynchronous Hearing System" on March 1, 2020. On the same day, this asynchronous hearing system was formally launched. Initially a pilot program in Guangzhou,[34] the use of asynchronous online hearings for labor dispute arbitration was later expanded across Guangdong Province. On April 20, 2023, new functions were added to the online service platform for labor and personnel disputes, including remote video hearings,

31 上海万达小额贷款有限公司与杨震借款合同纠纷案, (2021)皖12执195号执行裁定书, Anhui Province Fuyang Intermediate People's Court (April 14, 2021).

32 高强、上海方达小额贷款有限公司申请撤销仲裁裁决案,(2020)浙08民特17号民事裁定书, Zhejiang Province Quzhou Intermediate People's Court (December 7, 2020); 岳丹丹、万达齐富(杭州)投资管理有限公司民事执行异议案, (2022)吉07执异79号执行裁定书, Jilin Province Songyuan Intermediate People's Court (December 13, 2022).

33 The claim for all 12 judgments relates to the application to annul labor dispute arbitration awards. These applications targeted awards made by several arbitration courts in Guangzhou: 8 cases were reviewed by the Guangzhou Arbitration Commission for Labor and Personnel Dispute Arbitration, 1 case by the Haizhu District Arbitration Commission for Labor and Personnel Dispute Arbitration, and 3 cases by the Tianhe District Arbitration Commission for Labor and Personnel Dispute Arbitration.

34 Guangzhou Municipal Human Resources and Social Security Bureau, "Notice on the Launch of the Guangzhou Municipal Labor and Personnel Dispute Arbitration Internet Asynchronous Hearing System 关于启用广州市劳动人事争议仲裁互联网异步审理系统的通知," March 1, 2020, https://rsj.gz.gov.cn/ywzt/ldgx/ldrszyzc/zcgg/content/post_7111815.html.

asynchronous hearings, and the online issuance and delivery of procedural arbitration documents within the centralized Guangdong Human Resources and Social Security Integration Information System.[35]

Following the implementation of these technological innovations, many labor arbitration cases employing asynchronous online hearings have been adjudicated. Subsequently, some employers, having received unfavorable arbitral decisions, initiated legal challenges in court to request the setting aside of these arbitral awards. Among the 12 judgments examined in this study, various courts in Guangzhou displayed a supportive stance toward the asynchronous arbitration process in 11 of them, while one adopted an evasive approach. In this latter case, the court rejected the plaintiff's request to set aside a labor dispute arbitral award due to the expiration of the time limit for litigation, without addressing the use of asynchronous electronic interactive hearings. This presents a strikingly different picture from other courts' treatment of asynchronous arbitration processes mentioned earlier, where almost no arbitral awards were successfully enforced.

Evaluation of asynchronous hearings

The issues associated with asynchronous online arbitral hearings can be delineated into several key areas, reflecting underlying procedural and operational inadequacies that impact their efficacy and fairness. More importantly, this highlights the various opportunities and challenges facing online arbitration and the use of technology as they interact with existing legal systems and traditional frameworks.

Firstly, the existing arbitration rules of major Chinese arbitration commissions are overly general regarding the conditions under which asynchronous online hearings are applied. The rules broadly categorize applicable disputes as either "arising from cyber transactions or not" or simply as "civil and commercial disputes," which overlooks the specific complexities and requirements of individual cases. In contrast, the three internet courts in China, examined in Chapter 5, only conduct pilot asynchronous hearings after intentionally narrowing their applicability to cases. These include "civil cases with clear facts and legal relationships suitable for online hearings" from the Hangzhou Internet Court,[36] "small-claims cases ascertainable without a hearing" from the Guangzhou Internet Court,[37] or situations where "simultaneous hearings present genuine difficulties" from the Beijing Internet Court.[38]

35 Guangdong Provincial Department of Human Resources and Social Security, "Comprehensive Initiation of Online Case Handling Modes for Labor and Personnel Dispute Mediation and Arbitration in the Province 我省劳动人事争议调解仲裁全面启动在线办案模式," April 20, 2023, https://hrss.gd.gov.cn/zwgk/xxgkml/gzdt/content/post_4158235.html.

36 Hangzhou Internet Court, "Provisions on Asynchronous Trial of Internet-Related Cases (Trial Implementation) 涉网案件异步审理规程(试行)," May 31, 2018, Article 2.

37 Guangzhou Internet Court, "Guangzhou Internet Court Provisions on Online Trial (Trial Implementation) 广州互联网法院在线审理规程(试行)," October 22, 2019, Article 83.

38 Beijing Internet Court, "Beijing Internet Court Provisions on Online Hearing (Trial Implementation) 北京互联网法院电子诉讼庭审规范(试行)," February 21, 2020, Article 20.

Arbitration institutions aiming to implement asynchronous hearings need to adopt a more meticulous approach in defining eligibility criteria. For instance, the Wuhan Arbitration Commission issued its Online Arbitration Hearing Regulations on December 10, 2021, which provided additional operational details for asynchronous online hearings. Article 5(2)(3) of the regulations specifies that, following a change request by the parties, the arbitral tribunal should decide the hearing method based on the dispute's characteristics, the hearing's duration, and other relevant factors, opting for asynchronous interactions or transitioning to offline or synchronous video hearings as appropriate.

Secondly, the procedural rights of parties are often inadequately protected in asynchronous hearings. Arbitration rules typically stipulate that parties must select their preferred online hearing method within three days of receiving the arbitration notice. If parties do not make a selection or make inconsistent choices, the hearing defaults to an asynchronous format. The Quzhou and Nanping Arbitration Commissions grant the arbitral tribunal the authority to opt for synchronous video hearings if deemed necessary.

However, such mandates do not sufficiently safeguard the parties' rights to determine their preferred procedural methods and deviate from the practices of the internet courts, which predicate the use of asynchronous methods on party consent. This approach underscores that asynchronous hearings should be based on parties' procedural discretion and judicial oversight to ensure fairness and efficiency. Failure to adhere to such principles has led to serious difficulties in the enforcement of arbitral awards. As explained earlier, several courts, such as the Anqing and Fuyang Intermediate People's Courts of Anhui Province, have explicitly refused to enforce arbitral awards by the Quzhou Arbitration Commission reached via asynchronous processes, highlighting issues of procedural justice.

Thirdly, the operational design of asynchronous online arbitration is flawed. Unlike traditional hearings, which involve a continuous process of examination, questioning, and debate, asynchronous hearings fragment these interactions into separate stages. Participants are required to fulfill their designated roles according to the arbitral tribunal's instructions within specified time frames for each part of the process. This segmented approach can disrupt the natural flow of argumentation and evidence presentation, potentially compromising the integrity and thoroughness of the proceedings.

The examination of asynchronous hearings in arbitration reveals several nuances, particularly regarding their efficacy in providing an accurate portrayal of the facts and capturing the parties' attitudes and subjective views about the dispute. Traditional face-to-face interactions during hearings often present the most authentic picture, where parties' immediate responses and spontaneous reactions are crucial. In contrast, asynchronous electronic interactive hearings lack this direct exchange, as participants do not engage in real-time dialogue via network equipment but rather transmit and receive only text or audiovisual recordings. These limitations inherently reduce the efficacy of these hearings in terms of direct examination and defense, and the detachment from real-time interaction may fail to meet the procedural demands of arbitration.

Furthermore, if excessive time is allowed for responses during stages like tribunal investigations, there exists a potential for parties to seek external assistance to fabricate or alter the facts, thereby increasing the likelihood of dishonesty. This setup is less conducive to a fair and proper resolution of disputes, as it compromises the integrity of testimonial exchanges and evidence presentation.

In China, the application of asynchronous arbitration has unfolded differently across sectors. In commercial disputes, where the Quzhou Arbitration Commission has employed asynchronous hearings, the predominant judicial stance has been one of disapproval. Courts have consistently ruled against the enforcement of such arbitral awards, criticizing the format for failing to ensure adequate procedural rights. This is evident from the substantial number of cases where courts have rejected arbitration awards due to the inadequacies in procedural safeguards provided by asynchronous hearings.

It should be noted that the arbitral awards of the Quzhou Arbitration Commission that were not upheld by the courts were all based on private loan disputes, mostly between microfinance companies and consumer borrowers. The legitimacy of many of these loans from microfinance companies is often questionable and involves complex public policy issues. Typically, the situation involves a loan company obtaining an arbitral award from the Quzhou Arbitration Commission in its favor and then requesting the court to enforce the arbitral award. The court then ruled that it would not be enforced. A common reason for non-enforcement is that the arbitral tribunal used asynchronous online hearings which did not adequately safeguard the procedural rights of the parties. In addition to procedural reasons, another possibility is that, rather than the Quzhou Arbitration Commission doing a poor job with asynchronous online hearings, the court may have been inclined to protect the borrower due to the unique nature of these cases.

In contrast, in the realm of labor arbitration, where the Guangzhou Municipal Labor and Personnel Dispute Arbitration Commission has pioneered the use of asynchronous hearings, the courts have shown overwhelming support. This is largely due to the perceived procedural safeguards, which are deemed sufficient under the conditions of labor disputes. This sectoral support can be attributed to a top-down push by officials in Guangdong Province and Guangzhou City. Notably, in these labor arbitration cases, employees generally emerge as the beneficiaries of the awards, suggesting a tilt in favor of the weaker party – the employee – thus aligning with broader labor protection goals.

The reluctance to overturn labor arbitration awards based solely on the asynchronous nature of hearings reflects a judicial recognition of their practicality and necessity in certain contexts. Not setting aside these awards on procedural grounds underscores an intent to effectively protect employee rights. However, the ongoing judicial criticism in commercial arbitration contexts indicates that the current procedural framework for asynchronous hearings requires significant refinement to better safeguard the rights of the parties and align more closely with the standards of fairness and legitimacy expected in arbitration processes. It is intriguing how much of the differences in judicial attitude toward the two arbitration regimes can be attributed to the different policy considerations behind the subject matters of disputes.

Consumer arbitration

Dispute resolution mechanisms for online platforms

Arbitration offers a broad spectrum of applications, extending well beyond commercial disputes to encompass those involving individuals. It can facilitate resolution between both parties of equal standing and those of unequal power, as evidenced in consumer, labor, and sports arbitration contexts. In such contexts, however, issues frequently arise concerning the validity of arbitration clauses and the enforceability of standard terms, which are typically unilaterally imposed by organizations or service providers.

Once deemed valid, these arbitration clauses bind the parties to resolve their disputes through arbitration, precluding the option of litigation. This stipulation becomes particularly significant in the digital era, where it is increasingly commonplace for web applications to offer goods or services through online platforms, accompanied by user agreements that include arbitration clauses for dispute resolution.

This section delves into the legal implications of these clauses, specifically those designed to resolve consumer disputes through arbitration. To shed light on the current landscape in China, Table 4.2 lists the dispute resolution clauses embedded within the user agreements of 18 prominent Chinese online platforms. This analysis examines the prevalence and variation of arbitration clauses within digital platforms, offering insight into their legal standing and practical impact on consumer rights.

For business models where the platform provides services or sells goods directly to users (B2C), it is essential for these platforms to establish clear protocols for resolving disputes that may arise between the platform and its users. Typically, most platforms mandate that disputes be initially addressed through negotiation, and if this fails, the user may submit the dispute to a court of competent jurisdiction. For instance, the Tencent WeChat software license and service agreement stipulates that any dispute or controversy between the user and Tencent should first be resolved through friendly consultation; if the consultation fails, the user agrees to submit the dispute to the jurisdiction of the people's court of competent jurisdiction in the place where the agreement is signed. Another common practice is to litigate in the defendant's location, which is most likely the operator of the internet application, and consistent with the jurisdictional rules of Chinese civil law.[39] Such a clause is observed, for instance, in Xiaohongshu's user service agreement, which stipulates that in the event of failed negotiations, the people's court of the location of the defendant of the dispute shall have jurisdiction.

39 Civil Procedure Law of the People's Republic of China, Article 22.

Table 4.2 Dispute resolution clauses of leading internet applications in China

Platform		*Dispute resolution mechanism*		
Name	*Category*	*Parties to the dispute*	*Category of dispute*	*Methods of dispute resolution*
WeChat	Basic application (instant messaging)	Users vs. platform operators	Disputes between users and the platform	Negotiation, litigation (court where the agreement was signed)
Taobao	Business transactions (online shopping)	Users vs. platform operators	Disputes arising from the use of platform services and related matters	Negotiation, litigation (court of the defendant's location)
		Users vs. users	Transaction disputes	Negotiation, platform dispute resolution service, mediation by consumer associations or other organizations, administrative complaints, arbitration, litigation
Tmall Global	Business transactions (online shopping)	Users vs. platform operators	Disputes arising from or related to the agreement	Hong Kong International Arbitration Centre arbitration (HKIAC rules, 3 arbitrators, arbitration in English, arbitration in Hong Kong)
		Users vs. users (buyers vs. sellers)	Transaction disputes	Negotiation, platform dispute resolution service (applying Tmall Global dispute resolution rules, 20 days to submit for HKIAC arbitration if disputed), litigation, others
Pinduoduo	Business transactions (online shopping)	Users vs. platform operators	Disputes arising from or related to the agreement	Negotiation, litigation (court where the agreement was performed)
		Users vs. users	Disputes arising from the use of platform services	Platform dispute resolution service, others

(*Continued*)

Table 4.2 (Continued)

Platform		*Dispute resolution mechanism*		
Name	*Category*	*Parties to the dispute*	*Category of dispute*	*Methods of dispute resolution*
JD.com	Business transactions (online shopping)	Users vs. platform operators	Disputes arising from the content or performance of the agreement	Negotiation, litigation (court where the agreement was signed)
		Users vs. users	Transaction disputes	Negotiation, platform dispute resolution service, mediation by consumer associations or other organizations, administrative complaints, arbitration, litigation
Vipshop	Business transactions (online shopping)	Users vs. platform operators	Disputes arising from the fulfilment of the obligations stipulated in the agreement and its supplements	Negotiation, litigation (court where the agreement was signed)
Kaola	Business transactions (online shopping)	Users vs. platform operators	Disputes arising from and related to platform services	Negotiation, CIETAC arbitration (CIETAC rules, 3 arbitrators)
		Users vs. users	Transaction disputes	Negotiation, platform dispute resolution service, mediation by consumer associations or other organizations, administrative complaints, arbitration, litigation
Sina Weibo	Network entertainment (social media)	Users vs. platform operators	Disputes arising from the content or performance of the agreement	Negotiation, litigation (Haidian District People's Court, Beijing)
Douyin	Network entertainment (video, live streaming)	Users vs. platform operators	Disputes between users and the platform	Negotiation, litigation (Haidian District People's Court, Beijing)

(Continued)

Table 4.2 (Continued)

Platform		*Dispute resolution mechanism*		
Name	*Category*	*Parties to the dispute*	*Category of dispute*	*Methods of dispute resolution*
Bilibili	Network entertainment (video, live streaming)	Users vs. platform operators	Disputes arising from the content or performance of the agreement	Negotiation, SHAC arbitration (SHAC rules, arbitration in Shanghai)
NetEase Cloud Music	Network entertainment (music)	Users vs. platform operators	Disputes arising from the use of platform services	Negotiation, litigation (court of the defendant's location)
Xiaohongshu	Network entertainment (social media)	Users vs. platform operators	Disputes between users and the platform	Negotiation, litigation (court of the defendant's location)
Keep	Network entertainment (fitness)	Users vs. platform operators	Disputes between users and the platform	Negotiation, BAC arbitration (arbitration in Beijing)
Didi Chuxing	Public services (transportation)	Users vs. platform operators	Disputes arising from or related to the agreement, disputes arising from the use of platform services	Negotiation, litigation (court of the defendant's location)
58.com	Public services (job hunting)	Users vs. platform operators	Disputes arising from the agreement	Negotiation, litigation (court where the agreement was signed)
NetEase Youdao Dictionary	Public services (translation)	Users vs. platform operators	Disputes arising from or related to the agreement	Negotiation, litigation (court of the defendant's location)
Zhiwen	Public services (job hunting)	Users vs. platform operators	Disputes arising from or related to the agreement	Chengdu Arbitration Commission arbitration (CDAC rules, arbitration in Chengdu)
Ofo	Public services (transportation)	Users vs. platform operators	Disputes arising from or related to the agreement	CIETAC arbitration (CIETAC rules, arbitration in Beijing)

A minority of apps and websites choose arbitration as their preferred dispute resolution method. The Ofo user service agreement, for example, mandates that disputes between users and the platform be submitted directly to CIETAC for arbitration in Beijing. Similarly, Keep's user agreement requires arbitration by BAC in Beijing. In the realm of cross-border e-commerce, Tmall International, in its user service agreement, stipulates that disputes between users and the platform shall be submitted to HKIAC for arbitration, any Hong Kong "conflict of laws" rules or principles shall not apply, the number of arbitrators shall be three, and the language of arbitration shall be English.

Moreover, third-party trading platforms such as Taobao also delineate how disputes between users should be resolved. Taobao's service agreement provides that users in Taobao platform transactions who encounter disputes with each other have the right to choose the following ways to resolve the disputes: (1) negotiating directly with the other party; (2) using the Taobao platform's dispute mediation services; (3) requesting mediation from consumer associations or other legally established mediation organizations; (4) filing a complaint with the relevant administrative departments; (5) submitting to an arbitration institution for arbitration according to any arbitration agreement reached with the other party in the dispute; and (6) filing a lawsuit with the people's court. Another example is the Tmall International dispute handling guidelines, which state that "after a buyer applies for a refund, the buyer and seller can choose to resolve the dispute by negotiating on their own, requesting Tmall International to intervene, or through judicial means." However, Article 48 stipulates that if the parties opt for Tmall International's intervention and disagree with the resolution, they "must take the dispute to the HKIAC for arbitration within 20 days after Tmall International has finished its resolution process."

Court judgments on the validity of arbitration clauses involving consumers

The validity of arbitration clauses in consumer disputes often hinges on whether such clauses are upheld by the courts. Under the Law of the People's Republic of China on the Protection of Consumer Rights and Interests (Consumer Protection Law), arbitration, along with negotiation, mediation, and litigation, is recognized as a valid dispute resolution mechanism. The courts assess the validity of consumer-related arbitration clauses based on the formal and substantive requirements in the arbitration law. Article 16 of the arbitration law specifies the formal and substantive elements of arbitration clauses, while Article 17 outlines grounds for invalidating such clauses.

A notable case that exemplifies judicial attitudes toward consumer arbitration clauses is the series of disputes involving Ofo, a bike-sharing company. In 2018, a user named Chen Shuaishuai filed a lawsuit in the Haidian District People's Court in Beijing against the operator of Ofo, Beijing Bikelock Technology Co., over a bicycle rental fee of RMB 3 (less than 1 USD). The court initially dismissed the lawsuit, citing an existing arbitration clause that directed disputes to CIETAC. Upon appeal by Chen, the Beijing No. 1 Intermediate People's Court reaffirmed the validity of the arbitration clause, despite Chen's claims that the clause was non-negotiable in a standard terms contract and that Ofo failed to reasonably highlight to consumers. The court, invoking Article 26 of the arbitration law, held that Chen and Ofo had already agreed to submit disputes to CIETAC for arbitration, and that the dispute should be arbitrated by CIETAC, thereby upholding the first-instance decision.[40]

From 2019 to 2020, as Ofo faced increasing operational issues and user demands for deposit refunds intensified, numerous users sought legal recourse to challenge the arbitration agreement. However, the Beijing No. 4 Intermediate People's Court consistently upheld the validity of the arbitration clauses in Ofo's service agreement in all five cases it adjudicated, rejecting claims from users. Ofo, which had once expanded its business to Singapore, the United Kingdom, the United States, and Australia, abruptly ceased operation in China in mid-2020.

There have always been notable divergences in judicial attitudes toward what constitutes reasonable notice to consumers in relation to arbitration clauses in standard terms contracts. In a 2020 case involving NetEase, a major Chinese cyber company, the Nanjing Intermediate People's Court ruled an arbitration clause invalid. The court criticized the online sales platform for only using bold font to highlight the clause on the order confirmation page, which it deemed as insufficient notice for consumers.[41] This contrasts with a 2016 ruling by the Beijing No. 2 Intermediate People's Court which affirmed a similarly presented arbitration clause in the NetEase Kaolai service agreement.[42]

These cases underscore a critical judicial scrutiny of the presentation and fairness of arbitration clauses in consumer agreements, reflecting a nuanced approach to ensuring consumer protection in arbitration processes. Furthermore, they illustrate the varied approaches Chinese courts take in determining the validity of arbitration clauses. The core issue arises from the common practice in app-based consumer interactions, where arbitration clauses are typically presented as predefined standard terms by the merchant. This practice raises critical questions about the validity of these clauses – specifically, whether they are accompanied by reasonable notice, and whether there is adequate consent for the binding nature of such clauses. In particular, courts examine whether the provider of the standard terms has fulfilled its obligations to adequately notify or explain the terms, and whether it has unfairly excluded or limited its liability, increased the liability of the other party, or restricted the rights of the other party.

40 陈帅帅与北京拜克洛克科技有限公司车辆租赁合同纠纷二审民事裁定书, (2018)京01民终6155号, Beijing No. 1 Intermediate People's Court (July 25, 2018).

41 杭州优买科技有限公司与张哲、广州网易计算机系统有限公司网络购物合同纠纷案, (2020)苏01民辖终422号民事裁定书, Jiangsu Province Nanjing Intermediate People's Court (June 18, 2020).

42 徐高峰与上海网之易网络科技发展有限公司申请确认仲裁协议效力，上海市第一中级人民法院（2020）沪01民特622号民事裁定书, Shanghai No. 1 Intermediate People's Court (December 21, 2020)；王璇与北京中公教育科技有限公司申请确认仲裁协议效力案，沈阳市中级人民法院（2022）辽01民特203号民事裁定书, Shenyang Intermediate People's Court (January 12, 2023).

Moreover, consumer disputes typically involve large numbers of participants with relatively minor individual stakes, yet the legal costs and logistical challenges of pursuing arbitration can be considerable. This often results in a situation where the practical ability to pursue litigation is effectively eliminated, potentially depriving parties of their fundamental right to legal recourse.

In another case involving Ofo, the plaintiff consumer, Wang, contested the validity of Ofo's arbitration agreement on several grounds.[43] Wang argued not only that Ofo did not make the arbitration clause sufficiently conspicuous but also that the costs associated with arbitrating a typical consumer dispute, like those over rental fees or deposits, could be disproportionately and prohibitively expensive. Such high costs could deter an average consumer from defending their rights, placing an undue burden on the consumer and making the clause substantively unfair in violation of Article 26 of the Consumer Protection Law.

The Beijing No. 4 Intermediate People's Court, however, determined that the plaintiff, as a long-time user and twice-registered user of Ofo bike-sharing, genuinely accepted the arbitration clause. It also noted that the defendant had emphasized the dispute resolution clause in a section designed for careful review and underlined the text advising users to "please be sure to carefully read . . ., " which indicated adequate notification. Regarding the question of whether the arbitration clause constituted an exemption or limitation of liability, the court observed that litigation and arbitration are distinct mechanisms, each with inherent advantages and disadvantages. It highlighted that arbitration, known for its efficiency and finality, allows an arbitral tribunal to apportion the final arbitration costs based on each party's responsibility and to require the losing party to cover reasonable costs incurred by the winning party. Therefore, choosing arbitration was seen as offering an equitable option for all contract parties, not as a limitation of one party's rights. Furthermore, the court addressed the plaintiff's concern regarding the high costs of arbitration relative to litigation and the value of the disputed goods, stating that this issue does not stem from the arbitration agreement itself. The court also rejected the claim that the arbitration clause unfairly increased the cost burden on the consumer, as outlined in Article 26 of the Consumer Protection Law, finding no basis to support the claim for invalidity. Such an interpretation was largely consistent with the court's other decisions in the context of consumer arbitration.[44]

The analysis of arbitration clauses in consumer contracts within China reveals two key issues with the judicial approach, as illustrated in the discussed cases. First, while courts assess the formal legality of arbitration clauses, they often overlook the significant imbalance in bargaining power between consumers and network service providers. Consumers, typically in a weaker position, are seldom afforded the opportunity to negotiate or modify the terms set forth by operators.

43 王子安与北京拜克洛克科技有限公司申请确认仲裁协议效力案, (2019)京04民特44号民事裁定书, Beijing No. 4 Intermediate People's Court (July 5, 2019).

44 蒋志雄与北京学慧网络科技有限公司申请确认仲裁协议效力案, (2022)京04民特422号民事裁定书, Beijing No. 4 Intermediate People's Court (August 22, 2022).

This "take it or leave it" approach results in agreements that appear fair and balanced yet are inherently unequal and unfair, limiting the weaker party's rights to claim. Furthermore, the courts rarely scrutinize the contracting process of arbitration clauses in depth. This oversight potentially neglects the significant unfairness that may arise from the technical setup of signing agreements on apps or the lack of digital and legal literacy among consumers under online transaction modes.

Second, practically speaking, the costs associated with arbitration can be prohibitively high compared to litigation. Under the current "Litigation Expenses Payment Measures" for people's court, the court fees for a property dispute not exceeding 10,000 RMB is merely 50 RMB. In comparison, a similar dispute submitted to CIETAC arbitration incurs the total fee of 6,100 RMB; even with the application of CIETAC online arbitration rules, the fee remains at a minimum of 4,000 RMB. This disparity in costs suggests that the arbitration clause effectively precludes parties from seeking redress through more economical means, thus violating the restrictions on form clauses outlined in Article 497 of the Civil Code and Article 26 of the Consumer Protection Law. It also contravenes the principle of fairness under civil law, as it imposes an undue financial burden on consumers seeking to assert their rights.

In conclusion, despite the existing legal framework and judicial practices, China fails to offer special consideration to arbitration clauses involving consumers, nor does it classify such clauses as "unfair," in contrast to other jurisdictions, such as the European Union, which exempt consumers from binding arbitration clauses.[45] Furthermore, some judicial bodies fail to recognize the passive and vulnerable position of consumers regarding information access and contract conclusion, a stance that is not conducive to protecting consumer rights and interests. This gap in legal protection suggests a need for a more nuanced and consumer-friendly approach in judicial reviews of arbitration clauses within consumer contracts.

Observations and reflections on consumer arbitration

Exploring the effectiveness of arbitration in resolving consumer disputes in China reveals several challenges and underscores the need for alternative dispute resolution mechanisms that are better suited to the nature of consumer transactions. A significant concern is the lack of awareness among average consumers about arbitration, including a lack of knowledge on how to initiate an arbitration proceeding, or even complete unawareness of the arbitration process and its implications. This issue is compounded by the cost implications, as the procedures and rules set forth by arbitration institutions in China do not specifically cater to the unique attributes of consumer disputes, which are generally characterized by smaller monetary values compared to other types of cases involving substantial financial sums.

45 Council Directive 93/13/EEC (April 5, 1993) on unfair terms in consumer contracts, Article 3 and Annex 1(q).

There is notable complexity in designing specific provisions for online consumer jurisdiction, involving both litigation and arbitration.[46] A key question to be answered in the design of mechanisms for online arbitration from a perspective of institutional analyses is what alternatives exist to the current system of arbitration.

This concern has two main aspects: First, in parts of China, there are efforts to establish specialized arbitration centers for consumer disputes under arbitration commissions or to integrate arbitration services within consumers association. However, these local solutions are not typically recognized in the arbitration agreements instigated by nationally operating, app-based services, which rarely list these bodies as options for dispute resolution. Furthermore, the relationship between these arbitration committees and local consumer associations is often so intertwined – sharing offices and personnel – that their ability to function as neutral and impartial entities is questionable at best.

Second, the rise of the internet and cross-border activities, especially in e-commerce, necessitates mechanisms capable of managing international disputes effectively. Operators of cross-border e-commerce platforms frequently choose to specify arbitration in their consumer agreements. Although this approach may not represent the ideal solution from a consumer perspective, it serves as a compromise that balances the varied interests of both domestic and foreign markets, domestic regulations, consumer protection, and the platform's investment priorities. Within the institutional framework proposed in earlier discussions, there are other ODR mechanisms available besides arbitration. Platforms often develop their own endogenous dispute resolution mechanisms, discussed in Chapter 3, which are continually refined under the pressures of market competition to better serve consumer needs. For example, Tmall International has implemented a mediation mechanism for managing after-sale disputes and has set up a dedicated professional customer service and after-sales team. Additionally, it has established clear platform rules, such as the "seven days refund without reason" policy, and detailed its dispute resolution procedures in the "Tmall International Dispute Handling Specification." These provisions allow consumers to provide feedback on transaction disputes through two accessible methods: online consultation and a dedicated hotline.

Therefore, although traditional arbitration presents numerous obstacles, particularly in terms of accessibility and affordability for consumers, alternative models and ODR systems are emerging as more adaptable and potentially more effective solutions. These systems are evolving in response to the specific needs of internet-based transactions and the global nature of contemporary consumer markets, with the goal of balancing efficiency, fairness, and the protection of consumer rights.

46 Current debates include, for example, whether to allow jurisdiction by agreement, without directly stipulating that the court at the consumer's place of residence has jurisdiction. This could lead to consumers bypassing the platform's mechanisms and directly seeking court resolution. Table 4.2 includes platform rules that stipulate court jurisdiction. The effectiveness of this arrangement is relatively complex and is still under discussion.

Ideally, disputes should be resolved internally by the platform or through mutual negotiation between the parties involved. If these methods prove ineffective, disputes should then be escalated to more formal ODR systems, such as online arbitration or litigation. According to arbitration theory, arbitration and litigation are mutually exclusive; once an arbitration clause is deemed valid and enforceable, it is the arbitral tribunal – and not the courts – that should exercise jurisdiction over the case. The interaction between arbitration and litigation largely hinges on the legal recognition of the arbitration system in resolving specific consumer disputes. If an arbitration agreement is judicially found to be invalid, consumers must resort to litigation as their final means to settle disputes.

The response of China's judicial system to disputes arising from internet transactions will be further discussed in the forthcoming chapter (Chapter 5). From an institutional analysis perspective, examining ODR, including arbitration, involves assessing the accessibility of different ODR mechanisms and their ability to interconnect and complement one another. This analysis is crucial for understanding the inherent value of ODR systems both individually and as a collective whole for any legal system or any specific domain, such as consumer protection.

Information technology in international arbitration

Integration of artificial intelligence and digital technologies

The ICC's report titled "Information Technology in International Arbitration – Report of the ICC Commission on Arbitration and ADR" examines the application of information technology in international arbitration. It outlines the stages involved in the application of information technology and highlights the issues that arise, including six key aspects: compatibility issues, electronic exchange of exhibits and other submissions, data integrity issues, proof of service, confidentiality and data security, and intellectual property.[47]

A 2023 International Arbitration Survey Report titled "Artificial Intelligence in International Arbitration," published by Bryan Cave Leighton Paisner, provides an in-depth analysis of the current use of AI tools in international arbitration, their integration with specific arbitration procedures, and the issues related to disclosure and regulation of AI tools. Looking ahead, the future calls for the continued promotion of the integration of technology and law, through multi-party collaboration and rulemaking, to effectively regulate the application of AI in arbitration. This will ensure the judicious use of AI technology and enhance the fairness, transparency, and reliability of the arbitration process.[48]

47 International Chamber of Commerce, "Information Technology in International Arbitration-Report of the ICC Commission on Arbitration and ADR," 2017, https://iccwbo.org/news-publications/arbitration-adr-rules-and-tools/information-technology-international-arbitration-report-icc-commission-arbitration-adr/.

48 Bryan Cave Leighton Paisner, "Annual Arbitration Survey 2023," accessed July 31, 2024, https://www.bclplaw.com/a/web/tUW2SW6fjHrpXVrA7AfWkS/102932-arbitration-survey-2023-report_v10.pdf.

Indeed, major international arbitration institutions, including some in China, are increasingly adopting AI and digital technologies for tasks such as document management, case management, evidence review, and even the drafting of orders and decisions. Specifically, these tasks encompass document filing, storage, management, disclosure, review, and sharing; case management by arbitration institutions; preparatory work, including research, drafting, and preparation for cross-examination, by parties and experts; preparation of transcripts and translations; and the preparation and drafting of orders, decisions, and awards by the tribunal. While these technologies improve efficiency, they also introduce challenges, such as security risks, lack of transparency, privacy concerns, bias and discrimination, ethical concerns, concentration of power, and dependence or overreliance on AI. Thus, there is an urgent need for regulatory frameworks.[49]

Significant developments are ongoing in the legal and regulatory frameworks governing the use of AI and other digital technologies. In March 2024, the European Parliament passed the AI Act, the first comprehensive attempt to regulate AI globally. In China, the Supreme People's Court's (SPC) 2022 Opinions on Regulating and Strengthening the Applications of AI in the Judicial Fields lay out the basic principles for the judicial application of AI. Notably, Article 5 of the Opinions stipulates AI must not make judicial decisions substituting for the judge in any case, regardless of technological advancements. The results from AI shall be for supplemental reference only, for adjudication or judicial supervision and management. Although there are currently no official documents on how to use AI in arbitration, it is probable that AI-based arbitration awards will be treated similarly.

Enhanced cybersecurity and data privacy in China

With the growth of online arbitration, there has been a corresponding increase in the emphasis on cybersecurity and data privacy. Arbitration institutions and legal frameworks are evolving to address these concerns, stressing the need for secure data handling and compliance with data protection regulations. Data protection and cybersecurity are key topics in international arbitration. The majority of respondents in the 2018 Queen Mary International Arbitration Survey listed "security of electronic communications and information" as an issue that should be addressed in arbitration rules. This demonstrates that users of arbitration are deeply concerned about data security.[50]

49 UNCITRAL Colloquium on Possible Future Work on Dispute Settlement, March 28 to April 1, 2022. The colloquium discussed four topics, including developments in dispute resolution in the digital economy, online platforms for dispute resolution, technology-related dispute resolution, and adjudication. All these topics are closely linked with the development of digitalization and data. See also UNCITRAL Working Group II, "Technology-related dispute resolution and adjudication: Model clauses and guidance texts," A/CN.9/WG.II/WP.236, December 4, 2023, https://undocs.org/en/A/CN.9/WG.II/WP.236.

50 Pierre Bienvenu and Benjamin Grant, "Data Protection and Cyber Risk Issues in Arbitration: Dealing with Regulation, Cyber-Attacks and Hacked Evidence," *International Arbitration Report* 13 (September 2019): 19, https://www.nortonrosefulbright.com/-/media/files/nrf/nrfweb/knowledge-pdfs/emea_15747_newsletter__international-arbitration-report-_issue-13.pdf.

China has recently enacted three major pieces of data-related legislation: the Cybersecurity Law (effective November 7, 2016), the Data Security Law (effective September 1, 2021), and the Personal Information Protection Law (effective November 1, 2021, PIPL). These laws impose restrictions and mandate security assessments on the cross-border transfer of data. Among them, the Data Security Law is the first comprehensive legislation in the field of data security in China, which mandates security management of cross-border transfer of data as specified by subsequent regulations and administrative rules.[51] The Cybersecurity Law governs the transfer of important data collected and generated by "operators of key information infrastructure" when it needs to be transferred abroad.[52] Cross-border transfer of important data collected and generated by "other data processors" within China are governed by the relevant security management measures established by the Cyberspace Administration of China. In the context of arbitration, the specifics depend on the nature of the claimants or respondents, the type of data involved in the cross-border transfer, and whether it falls under the scenarios outlined in the two laws. Currently, this topic has received limited attention in Chinese academia.

The Data Security Law has specific rules on dealing with requests for data from foreign judicial or law enforcement authorities. Only competent authorities in China may approve such request in accordance with relevant laws and international treaties and agreements, while any domestic organization or individual shall not provide data stored in China to any foreign judicial or law enforcement authority without official approval.[53] Currently, courts, law enforcement agencies, and securities regulatory bodies outside mainland China (excluding Hong Kong, Macau, and Taiwan) are generally considered "foreign judicial or law enforcement authorities." However, it remains uncertain in practice whether international arbitration institutions and tribunals fall under this category. In one case, the Ministry of Justice of China deemed an arbitration tribunal to be a "foreign judicial authority," requiring approval for the disclosure of important data to it.[54]

The PIPL aims to balance the reasonable use of personal information with the protection of personal data rights. Its scope of application includes not only activities processing personal information of natural persons within the territory of China

51 Data Security Law of the People's Republic of China, Article 31. On July 7, 2022, the "Measures for the Security Assessment of Outbound Data Transfer" were issued, clarifying three scenarios that require outbound security assessments: The first category is the outbound transfer of important data, the second category is the outbound transfer of personal information collected and generated by the critical information infrastructure operator, and the third category is the outbound transfer of personal information collected and generated by non-critical information infrastructure operators that meet certain conditions.

52 Cybersecurity Law of the People's Republic of China, Article 37.

53 Data Security Law of the People's Republic of China, Article 36.

54 Fu Jiamian 傅嘉绵, Yang Chunlei 杨春雷 and Zhou Jiashu 周家树, "Guoji minshangshi zhengyi jijue changing xia Zhongguo jingnei zhengju de kuajing chuanshu 国际民商事争议解决场景下中国境内证据的跨境传输," Mayer Brown, January 23, 2024, https://www.mayerbrown.com/zh-hans/insights/publications/2024/01/cross-border-transfer-of-evidence-from-mainland-china-under-international-commercial-dispute-resolution-scenarios.

but also activities processing personal information of natural persons outside the territory of China under specified circumstances, such as for the purpose of providing products or services to natural persons within China or analyzing or assessing the behavior of natural persons within China.[55]

The PIPL may therefore apply to international arbitration involving the processing of personal information within China and under certain conditions to the processing of personal information outside China, regardless of the identity of the data processor. At any stage of information disclosure, evidence collection, and use in the international arbitration process occurring within China, compliance with the PIPL is required. If the arbitration institution processes personal information to provide products or services to natural persons within China, or to analyze or assess their behavior, or if there are other circumstances provided by law or administrative regulations, the PIPL will likewise apply.[56]

This law is set to impact the entire international arbitration process. For example, a party may initially not raise data protection issues during the first procedural meeting but might later claim that disclosing documents would violate the PIPL, thereby refusing to produce them. At the 2022 Hong Kong Arbitration Week, several Hong Kong lawyers noted that Chinese parties increasingly rely on China's data protection laws to resist requests from opposing parties or to significantly delay proceedings, by claiming the need for self-assessment and/or approval from relevant Chinese authorities.[57] If the parties do not address personal information protection issues, the tribunal should consider including them in the agenda of the first case management meeting or procedural meeting/hearing and issue directions if no consensus is reached.

Moreover, given the nature of international arbitration, legislation from other jurisdictions will also influence international arbitration involving China. For example, the EU's General Data Protection Regulation (GDPR) may apply to arbitrations involving China, depending on the parties involved and the arbitration location. "Ultimately, the applicability of the GDPR to an international arbitration will depend on the facts and circumstances of the case, the applicable rules of the tribunal, and (perhaps) the whims of arbitrators."[58]

55 Personal Information Protection Law of the People's Republic of China, Article 3.

56 The specific type of arbitration does not determine the applicability of data protection law. Instead, the applicability of one nation's data protection law is determined by whether the data processing activities within the arbitration procedure fall under the jurisdiction of the that law. International Council for Commercial Arbitration, "ICCA-IBA Roadmap to Data Protection in International Arbitration," 2022, at 3, https://cdn.arbitration-icca.org/s3fs-public/document/media_document/ICCA_Reports_No_7_ICCA-IBA_Joint_Task_Force_on_Data_Protection_in_International_Arbitration.pdf.

57 Yi-Jun Kang and Rong Gu, "Hong Kong Arbitration Week Recap: Implications of PRC's Evolving Data Protection Laws in International Arbitration," *Morrison Foerster*, October 27, 2022, https://www.mofo.com/resources/insights/221027-hong-kong-arbitration-week-recap.

58 Paul Weiss, Rifkind Wharton and Garrison LLP, "GDPR Issues in International Arbitration," August 10, 2020, https://www.paulweiss.com/practices/litigation/international-arbitration/publications/gdpr-issues-in-international-arbitration?id=37691.

Finally, data-related disputes are steadily increasing in arbitration. The Chinese government has been actively promoting the construction of a data-based regime in various fields. As data exchanges evolve and the scale of data transactions expands, the number and complexity of data-related disputes continue to rise. However, China has not yet established laws addressing data ownership issues, and the data property rights system is not fully developed. The circulation and trading of data are still in the early stages, lacking specific regulations, which increases the likelihood of data-related disputes. The Shanghai International Economic and Trade Arbitration Commission (Shanghai International Arbitration Center) has introduced the "Data Arbitration Rules," which came into effect on January 1, 2024. These rules position data disputes as the core subject of arbitration. To more effectively resolve data disputes, the arbitration commission even established a new data arbitration center.

Summary and analysis

In the early days of ODR, arbitration was expected to be a key method for resolving commercial disputes, and significant attention was devoted to the study of online arbitration. This focus encompasses not only the development of online arbitration itself but also the complexity of the associated issues involved and the variations in online arbitration practices across different countries. However, despite these efforts, online arbitration did not see significant advancement for a considerable period. The unexpected arrival of the COVID-19 pandemic, though, highlighted how exogenous factors could dramatically influence institutional development. The pandemic undeniably provided a substantial boost to online arbitration, and the effects of this shift are likely to be lasting.

After summarizing the latest developments in online arbitration in China over the past year and detailing the promotion of online proceedings, this chapter elaborates on the findings of several empirical studies, including a comprehensive overview that compiles a list of all current arbitration commissions in China, offering unique insights into the evolution of online arbitration within the country. It then explores the use of asynchronous hearings in arbitration, a practice still surrounded by significant uncertainty, largely due to flaws in the initial mechanism design. Refining, and improving, asynchronous hearings remains a crucial area for future research and practical application. In the realm of online litigation, similar concerns arise regarding whether asynchronous hearings adhere to the principle of oral debate commonly discussed in civil litigation. This discussion facilitates a comparative analysis between the arbitration and litigation systems, fostering a deeper understanding of the distinct characteristics of different dispute resolution systems.

Additionally, this chapter explores the issue of consumer arbitration, which, while not new, presents unique challenges in the internet environment when leveraging online platforms to resolve consumer disputes. Consumer protection and dispute resolution regulations vary significantly from country to country, necessitating a detailed analysis of the current legal and judicial practices regarding consumer arbitration clauses in China. Furthermore, the traditionally high costs associated with using commercial arbitration to resolve disputes involving consumers underscore the need for a variety of ODR systems. Specifically, this chapter concludes that relying on endogenous mechanisms within platforms to resolve consumer disputes is a practical approach. In summary, this chapter not only provides an update on the state of online arbitration in China but also sets the groundwork for ongoing improvements and adaptations in ODR practices aimed at enhancing the effectiveness, affordability, and accessibility of dispute resolution in the digital age.

This chapter also explores the increasingly important topic of the use of AI and data protection in international arbitration. As online arbitration becomes more prevalent, AI and digital technologies are being integrated into various aspects of the arbitration process. These technologies are employed in document management, case management, evidence review, and even in drafting orders and decisions. Such technological advancements undoubtedly boost efficiency but also introduce a range of challenges. These challenges include security risks stemming from potential data breaches, a lack of transparency in how AI algorithms make decisions, concerns over privacy and how personal data is handled, potential biases and discrimination resulting from imperfect algorithms, ethical issues surrounding the fairness and impartiality of AI-driven processes, issues related to the centralization of power when decision-making is delegated to technology, and a general overreliance on technology, which may undermine human oversight in critical decision-making processes.

Because of these challenges, there has been a marked increase in the emphasis on cybersecurity measures and data privacy within the sphere of online arbitration. Arbitration institutions are proactively evolving their legal frameworks to address these concerns, with a particular focus on the secure handling of data and compliance with rigorous international data protection regulations. Notably, the GDPR plays a significant role, affecting not only entities within the EU but also those outside the EU, including China, that process data pertaining to EU-based individuals. This broad scope of regulation impacts how data is managed during the arbitration process, necessitating careful adherence to legal standards to avoid penalties and ensure procedural integrity.

Moreover, the versatility of arbitration enables its application across various domains, reflecting its adaptability to evolving commercial and legal landscapes. This chapter addresses not only commercial and consumer arbitration but also includes other forms of arbitration that closely align with digital ODR systems or are endogenous to specific sectors. Examples highlighted include the Aragon platforms, discussed in Chapter 3, as well as the domain name dispute resolution system. While these systems are structured similarly to traditional arbitration, they operate more like digital ODR mechanisms, being designed to be more seamlessly integrated with the technological environments in which they function.

In conclusion, online arbitration has undergone significant evolution to both coexist with and complement traditional offline arbitration, establishing itself as a robust option for parties engaged in disputes. While the foundational legal framework of traditional international arbitration has not drastically changed, the ongoing digitization trend is poised to drive incremental changes in legal systems, gradually aligning the legal regime of arbitration more closely with contemporary arbitration practices. Online arbitration, as a digital variant of the international arbitration system, continues to play a critical role in resolving international commercial disputes, whether they arise from online or offline activities.

Despite the advantages offered by online arbitration, many arbitrators involved in international cases express a preference for conducting hearings in person whenever possible. They emphasize the value of direct interactions and the cultural exchanges that occur during in-person proceedings, which are considered irreplaceable aspects of the arbitration experience. This preference underscores the enduring importance of face-to-face communication in the legal profession and highlights the persistent appeal of international arbitration as a career path, where personal engagement and global interaction play pivotal roles.

Bibliography

Arsic, Jasna. "International Commercial Arbitration on the Internet: Has the Future Come Too Early?" *Journal of International Arbitration* 14, no. 3 (1997): 209–21.

Bienvenu, Pierre, and Benjamin Grant. "Data Protection and Cyber Risk Issues in Arbitration: Dealing with Regulation, Cyber-Attacks and Hacked Evidence." *International Arbitration Report* 13 (September 2019): 19–21. https://www.nortonrosefulbright.com/-/media/files/nrf/nrfweb/knowledge-pdfs/emea_15747_newsletter__international-arbitration-report-_issue-13.pdf.

Bonnet, Vincent, Karima Boudaoud, Michael Gagnebin, Jürgen Harms, and Thomas Schultz. "Online Dispute Resolution System as Web Services." *ICFAI Journal of Alternative Dispute Resolution* 3 (2004): 57–73.

Bryan Cave Leighton Paisner. "Annual Arbitration Survey 2023." Accessed July 31, 2024. https://www.bclplaw.com/a/web/tUW2SW6fjHrpXVrA7AfWkS/102932-arbitration-survey-2023-report_v10.pdf.

Fu, Jiamian 傅嘉绵, Yang Chunlei 杨春雷, and Zhou Jiashu 周家树. "Guoji minshangshi zhengyi jijue changing xia Zhongguo jingnei zhengju de kuajing chuanshu 国际民商事争议解决场景下中国境内证据的跨境传输." *Mayer Brown*, January 23, 2024. https://www.mayerbrown.com/zh-hans/insights/publications/2024/01/cross-border-transfer-of-evidence-from-mainland-china-under-international-commercial-dispute-resolution-scenarios.

Hörnle, Julia. "Online Dispute Resolution: The Emperor's New Clothes?" *International Review of Law, Computers and Technology* 17, no. 1 (2003): 27–37. https://doi.org/10.1080/1360086032000063093.

International Chamber of Commerce. "Information Technology in International Arbitration – Report of the ICC Commission on Arbitration and ADR." 2017. https://iccwbo.org/news-publications/arbitration-adr-rules-and-tools/information-technology-international-arbitration-report-icc-commission-arbitration-adr/.

International Council for Commercial Arbitration. "ICCA-IBA Roadmap to Data Protection in International Arbitration." 2022. https://cdn.arbitration-icca.org/s3fs-public/document/media_document/ICCA_Reports_No_7_ICCA-IBA_Joint_Task_Force_on_Data_Protection_in_International_Arbitration.pdf.

Kang, Yi-Jun, and Rong Gu. "Hong Kong Arbitration Week Recap: Implications of PRC's Evolving Data Protection Laws in International Arbitration." *Morrison Foerster*, October 27, 2022. https://www.mofo.com/resources/insights/221027-hong-kong-arbitration-week-recap.

Miller-Moore, Debi. "ODR at the AAA: Online Dispute Resolution in Practice." *University of Toledo Law Review* 38 (2006): 395–402.

Paul, Weiss, Rifkind Wharton and Garrison LLP. "GDPR Issues in International Arbitration." August 10, 2020. https://www.paulweiss.com/practices/litigation/international-arbitration/publications/gdpr-issues-in-international-arbitration?id=37691.

Schultz, Thomas. "Online Arbitration: Binding or Non-Binding?" *ADR Online Monthly*, November 2002. http://www.ombuds.org/center/adr2002-11-schultz.html.

Turner, Rachel I. "Alternative Dispute Resolution in Cyberspace: There Is More on the Line, Than Just Getting 'Online'." *ILSA Journal of International & Comparative Law* 7 (2000): 133–48.

Xu, Lu. *Chinese Legal Reforms: Transformations in a Decade*. Leiden: Brill, 2024. https://doi.org/10.1163/9789004537125.

Zhang, Chenyang. *Win in Chinese Courts: Practice Guide to Civil Litigation in China*. Springer, 2023. https://doi.org/10.1007/978-981-99-3342-6.

5 The court in the internet era

Introduction: digitization of justice in China

The deep involvement of the court in ODR is one of the most important developments in recent years, challenging the early theorists' view that ODR should be understood as non-court dispute resolution.[1] Today, almost all legal systems are now engaged in digitization, despite significant differences of the underlying framework for justice.

The digitization of justice in China is notable not only for the scale of its implementation across the world's largest court system and to the world's largest online population but also for the multidimensional development, including administration, organization, and procedure.[2] On the administration front, years of dedicated efforts have driven the court's informationization, integrating a wide variety of technologies into judicial practice, such as artificial intelligence (AI), big data, and blockchain. Organizationally, China has established the world's first and, to date, only specialist internet courts to exclusively deal with online disputes on online judicial platforms. Procedurally, China has promulgated rules for online courts and expanded its scope to include all of the more than 3,500 courts, encompassing both online litigation and online mediation. Informationization and digitization are now integral to the foundation of Chinese judicial practice.

This chapter opens by setting out the status of and key factors driving the digitization of justice in China. It then explores the three internet courts as a significant advancement of ODR in judicial practice, including their achievements and challenges. The role of the court as a service provider, integrating both online litigation and online mediation, is explained next as an integral part of the Supreme People's Court's (SPC) strategy to establish a comprehensive, diversified, one-stop litigation service center and dispute resolution service. This chapter concludes with a summary and critical analysis of the digitization of justice in China.

1 Julia Hörnle, *Cross-Border Internet Dispute Resolution* (Cambridge: Cambridge University Press, 2009), 75, https://doi.org/10.1017/CBO9780511576102.

2 Wang Fuhua 王福华, "Huliangwang sifa de zhengyi tixi 互联网司法的正义体系," *Zhongguo Faxue* 中国法学 237 (2024): 125.

DOI: 10.4324/ 9781003594512-5

"Internet plus court" and the status of digitization of justice

The deep integration of internet technology with modern economic and societal dynamics has led to the emergence of numerous new types of internet-related disputes, posing significant challenges to the capability of judicial systems to effectively address these novel internet cases. The conventional judicial framework struggles to adapt to the escalating workload driven by societal advancements. Consequently, leveraging internet and information technology to modernize judicial processes and enhance the quality of legal proceedings has become an urgent and practical necessity in contemporary society.

The evolution of digital initiatives in China's judicial system exemplifies a "building blocks innovation" approach, which can be divided into three evolutionary phases: court informatization, smart court construction, and digital court construction. The genesis of court informatization dates back to the 1990s, characterized primarily by the initial development of infrastructure and networks. This phase saw the gradual incorporation of computers, the internet, and other information and communication technologies into the operational framework of the courts. Court informatization primarily served as a judicial public service, aimed at streamlining traditional business processes through data generation. It was generally auxiliary, service-oriented, and transactional, without significantly impacting the core functions of judicial powers, such as adjudication or enforcement.

In 2017, the SPC formally promulgated the concept of "smart courts" (*zhihui fayuan*), which had been around various discussions by judicial leadership since 2015.[3] By mandating the comprehensive integration of networking, transparency, and intelligence across all judicial activities, the official "Opinions" from the SPC marked the transition into the smart court era.[4] In the ensuing years, people's courts have developed a comprehensive system for online litigation, mediation, and procedural regulations that encompasses all areas of trial processes, enabling a seamless, parallel, and orderly connection between online and offline judicial activities. Significantly, the world's first internet courts were established in 2017 and 2018, with the intention of pioneering and testing the fully digital and online operation of judicial processes.

Despite these advancements, the modernization journey, under the banners of court informatization and smart court construction, still exhibits pronounced internal, localized, and sector-specific characteristics. While these technologies have successfully facilitated the transfer of case filing, adjudication, execution, and administrative tasks from offline to online platforms, these technologies primarily enhance public accessibility to online litigation and judicial efficiency in case management. Nonetheless, the overarching progress has largely remained at the stages of data generation and data storage.

3 Deng Heng 邓恒, "Ruhe lijie zhihui fayuan he hulianwang fayuan 如何理解智慧法院和互联网法院," *People's Court Daily* 人民法院报, July 25, 2017.

4 Supreme People's Court, "Opinions of the Supreme People's Court on Accelerating the Construction of Smart Courts 关于加快建设智慧法院的意见" (SPC Issue 2017/No. 12), April 12, 2017.

More recently, the concept of "digital courts" has gained further traction within the court system and academia.[5] In summary, this concept aims to better leverage previously accumulated big data and AI, unlocking greater potential through the integration of digital technology and the judicial system and realizing new possibilities.

Table 5.1 illustrates the pivotal initiatives in the digital transformation of the Chinese judicial system over the last decade, highlighting the tangible efforts and progression in merging information technology with judicial operations within China. Throughout this transformative period, several key milestones from an institutional perspective stand out.

Initially, the introduction of the world's first-ever internet courts marked a groundbreaking development. This began with the establishment of the Hangzhou Internet Court in 2017, followed by the Beijing Internet Court and the Guangzhou Internet Court in 2018. These pioneering institutions symbolized the seamless integration of the internet into judicial processes. Subsequently, in 2019, the SPC elevated the development of a comprehensive diversified dispute resolution and litigation service system as a key priority for all courts. This initiative emphasized the role of court informatization, outlining detailed protocols for the diversified dispute resolution mechanism, litigation service system, and cross-jurisdiction case filing services. Innovatively, it proposed two "one-stop" construction objectives: a "one-stop diversified dispute resolution mechanism" and a "one-stop litigation service center."

By 2021, leveraging advanced information technologies such as big data, cloud computing, artificial intelligence, and the Internet of Things, judicial bodies across all four hierarchical levels in China vigorously advanced the establishment of online mediation platforms. These platforms enabled the implementation of litigation service reforms, including the delegation of mediation and adjudication processes and the distinction between complex and straightforward cases. This approach aimed to systemically construct a comprehensive and evolving, multifaceted dispute resolution system that integrates various stages of the dispute resolution process, from the initial dispute origin through pre-litigation stages and throughout the entire litigation life cycle. The empirical insights gained from the operation of the three internet courts have significantly enhanced the development of the one-stop diversified dispute resolution mechanism and litigation service centers. In March 2021, the SPC announced the near completion of the comprehensive diversified dispute resolution and litigation service system for the people's courts, which demonstrated resilience through the severe challenges of the COVID-19 pandemic in 2020, ensuring the effective operation of the judicial system.[6]

5 Li Zhanguo 李占国, "'Quanyu shuzi fayuan' de goujian yu shixian '全域数字法院'的构建与实现," *Peking University Law Journal* 34, no. 1 (2022): 5; Jia Yu 贾宇, "Lun shuzi fayuan 论数字法院," *Chinese Journal of Law* 法学研究 46, no. 4 (2024): 3.

6 Zhou Qiang 周强, "Work Report of the Supreme People's Court 最高人民法院工作报告," presented to the 4th Meeting of the 13th National People's Congress, March 8, 2021, http://gongbao.court.gov.cn/Details/342529c11d2af722964a6b1c961105.html.

Table 5.1 Informationization and digitization of Chinese courts (2012–2022)

2012 and earlier	Some online functions for litigation record inquiries, access to certain court judgments, limited online case filing, electronic document service, and remote hearings
2013	Developed three major platforms: public access to trial processes, court judgments, and judicial enforcement information
	Formulated the *Five-Year Development Plan for Informatization of the People's Courts (2013–2017)*
2014	Implemented the *Tianping Project*, ensuring full tracking of trial and enforcement processes to drive judicial transparency and fairness through systemic reforms
2015	Achieved full connectivity of 3,512 court networks, integrating case trial processes into informatization management
	Launched "electronic courts" in Jilin and Zhejiang Provinces
2016	Started the "smart courts" initiative
	Established platforms for judicial big data management and services to reshape trial and enforcement processes through informatization
2017	Established the initial framework for "smart courts"
	Implemented online processing for all activities, full-process legal transparency, and intelligent services
	Founded the Hangzhou Internet Court
2018	Launched intelligent case recommendation and smart voice cloud platforms for judicial assistance
	Implemented online case file review, evidence exchange, hearings, and electronic service
	Piloted the Micro Court mobile application for all aspects of litigation
	Founded the Beijing Internet Court and the Guangzhou Internet Court
2019	Explored the new internet judiciary models: expanded online case hearings, refined online litigation rules, and promoted Mobile Micro Courts
	Advanced the application of big data, blockchain, and voice recognition in judicial practice
2020	Implemented online case filing across all courts, and online first-instance filing rate reached 54% in 2020
	Refined rules for online hearings, electronic evidence, and asynchronous trials
2021	Facilitated 11.439 million online case filings and 1.275 million online hearings during the pandemic with "smart courts"
	Led globally by introducing the *Rules for Online Litigation in People's Courts*, *Rules for Online Mediation in People's Courts*, and *Rules for Online Operations in People's Courts*, transitioning from technology-led to rule-led advancements
2022	Advanced intelligent services, trials, enforcement, and management, creating an intelligent court system with full online processing, legal transparency, and smart services
	Completed the world's largest judicial information database
	Highlighted the "smart court" as a defining feature of China's judiciary on the global stage
Summary	Transition from isolated instances to a holistic system; from a technology-oriented approach to a rule-oriented approach; from existing resources to new developments
	Significant progress in judicial techniques and online justice achieved despite technological deficiencies, lack of skilled personnel, and financial constraints

The foundational premise behind the establishment of the internet courts was to leverage regions with robust internet industries, abundant internet-related legal cases, advanced technological infrastructure, and substantial talent pools to pioneer and advance the innovative judicial mechanism of "online trial of online cases." As specialized "functional courts," the internet courts primarily assume this experimental role. In contrast, other courts focus largely on providing litigants with a variety of litigation services. The expansion of comprehensive online litigation services across courts nationwide aims to simplify the litigation process for the public and proactively respond to their demand for more efficient methods of litigation. This approach is demand-driven, with courts striving to enhance their capacity to meet the ever-increasing societal need for justice and dispute resolution, moving away from the traditional expectation for litigants to conform to the court's operational mechanisms in their interaction with the judicial system.

A third major milestone in the digitization of Chinese courts was the codification of online litigation rules, particularly after 2020, when online courts became standard across China. All 3,504 courts across all four levels of the judicial pyramid now actively engage in online litigation. The COVID-19 pandemic acted as a pivotal catalyst, accelerating the institutionalization of this digital transformation. During a time when courts were compelled to function within a "contactless litigation" framework, the model demonstrated its efficacy and gained acceptance from both the judiciary and litigants. The SPC swiftly institutionalized online courts as a permanent fixture in every court's operation in China, thereby establishing, for the first time, a legal framework for the application of technology in judicial processes. The foundational rules include the Rules for Online Litigation, commencing in August 2021;[7] the Rules for Online Mediation, effective January 2022;[8] and the Rules for Online Operation, implemented in March 2022.[9] These rules encapsulate the accumulated experience and best practices of the courts over the preceding years.

The scope of online courts is now remarkably expansive, encompassing all courts in China and covering various categories and procedures of litigation.[10] With the exception of most criminal cases, any court can potentially engage in online litigation and online mediation for all or parts of civil, administrative, and enforcement

7 Supreme People's Court, "Rules of People's Courts for Online Litigation 人民法院在线诉讼规则" (Judicial Interpretation 2021/No. 12, June 16, 2021) (Online Litigation Rules).

8 Supreme People's Court, "Rules of the People's Courts for Online Mediation 人民法院在线调解规则" (Judicial Interpretation 2021/No. 23, December 30, 2021) (Online Mediation Rules).

9 Supreme People's Court, "Rules of the People's Courts for Online Operation 人民法院在线运行规则" (SPC Issue 2022/No. 8, January 26, 2022). Unlike the other two sets of rules, these rules do not have the status of judicial interpretations.

10 The term "online courts" is used in this book to encapsulate the online operation of courts, including both online litigation and online mediation in the Chinese context. However, official documents from the Supreme People's Court and other senior courts rarely use such a term (*zaixian fayuan*). The only official document that contains this term is a joint report produced by the Supreme People's Court and courts from Shanghai, Jiangsu, Zhejiang, and Anhui: "Renmin fayuan fuwu he baozhang Changsanjiao yitihua fazhan sifa baogao 人民法院服务和保障长三角一体化发展司法报告," November 2, 2021, https://www.chinacourt.org/article/detail/2021/11/id/6344918.shtml.

cases.[11] Innovations pioneered by the internet courts, such as the use of blockchain for evidence, have been formalized and are now accessible to all courts.[12] The rules have been comprehensively refined across different facets of online courts, including new procedures that recognize both synchronous and asynchronous exchanges and challenges of evidence.[13] Furthermore, these developments have an international dimension, as demonstrated by the launch of the online dispute resolution platform by the SPC in July 2021 for the China International Commercial Court, which envisions the involvement of foreign mediators in disputes that include foreign entities.[14] In under half a decade, the Chinese judicial system has progressed from its initial, unregulated experiments in online hearings and adjudications to the formal establishment of three specialized internet courts, and now to the nationwide authorization for conducting online litigation and mediation in all courts across the country.

Contributing factors for the digitization of justice

The international attention and analysis of China typically focus on its population or economy, both of which are the world's second largest. However, there is relatively limited scholarly interest in China's politics, governance, or legal system, beyond the stereotypical view of it as a powerful authoritarian, socialist, or communist party state. What is far less discussed are many other equally important characteristics of China in the information era, such as the fact that it has the largest number of courts, the largest number of judges, the largest online database of court judgments, the largest number of live broadcast and recording of court hearings, the largest number of online hearings, the world's only internet courts to date, the widest range of online courts, and so on. In line with the global trend where the court becomes integral to ODR,[15] members of the Chinese judiciary are evidently some of the most enthusiastic practitioners. As shown earlier in Figure 5.1, the Chinese court system has swiftly and fundamentally transformed in the digital realm since 2013, surpassing many of the more established jurisdictions in the world in terms of progress in digitization despite their earlier start.

There are two important contributing factors underlying the Chinese legal system's swift and large-scale digitization. First, policy experimentation, which has proved to be invaluable in China's economic reforms, has again been effectively employed in the digitization of justice. Second, the traditionally weak legal system has readily embraced digitization, displaying little resistance, and with significant expectations of gaining influence and legitimacy. Each of these factors will now be explored.

11 Online Litigation Rules, Article 3; Online Mediation Rules, Article 3.

12 Online Litigation Rules, Articles 16–19.

13 Online Litigation Rules, Article 14.

14 Online Mediation Rules, Article 6.

15 Orna Rabinovich-Einy and Ethan Katsh, "Lessons from Online Dispute Resolution for Dispute System Design," in *Online Dispute Resolution: Theory and Practice*, eds. Daniel Rainey, Ethan Katsh, and Mohamed S. Abdel Wahab, 2nd ed. (The Hague: Eleven, 2021), 50.

Policy experimentation

Heilmann has carefully analyzed the approach of "decentralized experimentation" in Chinese policymaking and elucidated how it reduces resistance and mitigates political risks.[16] Important national policies in China are typically preceded by a number of local experiments and pilots, which differ substantively in their approaches, seeking innovative policy instruments. Experiences extracted from the more successful experiments are then gradually disseminated across an increasing number of regions before finally being refined and adopted at national level.[17] Such experimentation was once conducted on legally uncertain grounds, but this approach has largely been institutionalized in recent years through legislative changes and the growing use of formal authorization from the National People's Congress.[18]

The digitization of the court system since 2012 has once again demonstrated the application of this experimental approach in action. The three internet courts, for example, were established at different times, with the Hangzhou Internet Courts launching one year ahead of the other. The plan to establish internet courts in Beijing and Hangzhou specifically referred to the perceived success of Hangzhou as a reason for the expansion to other parts of China.[19] Even after the establishment of the three internet courts and the creation of unified rules, they each pursued different experiments of key initiatives independently of one another. For instance, asynchronous hearings were trialed at the Hangzhou Internet Court.[20] Conversely, the Beijing Internet Court had its own unique initiatives, such as the "e-Copyright" system.

Beyond the three internet courts, much larger-scale experiments and adoptions have taken place. The online litigation platform known as "Mobile Micro Court" (*yidong wei fayuan*, MMC), which takes the form of a mobile phone app, originated as a spontaneous initiative by the Ningbo Intermediate People's Court in October 2017, among various other similar ideas across dozens of other courts in different provinces. However, the MMC gained favor of the SPC due to its superior design and technical advantages, which promoted its wider adoption by other courts from 2018 onward. The MMC eventually covered all provinces and all of the more than 3,500 courts in 2020.[21] From its origin as a mobile app developed by

16 Sebastian Heilmann, "Policy Experimentation in China's Economic Rise," *Studies in Comparative International Development* 43 (2008): 21, https://doi.org/10.1007/s12116-007-9014-4.

17 Sebastian Heilmann, "From Local Experiments to National Policy: The Origins of China's Distinctive Policy Process," *The China Journal* 59 (2008): 2.

18 Lu Xu, *Chinese Legal Reforms: Transformations in a Decade* (Leiden: Brill, 2024), 33, https://doi.org/10.1163/9789004537125.

19 Supreme People's Court, "Plan to Additionally Establish the Beijing Internet Court and the Guangzhou Internet Court关于增设北京互联网法院、广州互联网法院的方案" (SPC 2018/No. 216, August 9, 2018).

20 Hangzhou Internet Court, "Rules and Procedures for Asynchronous Trial of Internet-related Cases (Trial Implementation) 涉网案件异步审理规程(试行)," April 2018.

21 Liyuan Wang, "Application of Information Technology in Judicial Field: The Development Model of Online Litigation in China," *Computer Law & Security Review* 52 (2024): 105936, 3, https://doi.org/10.1016/j.clsr.2024.105936.

one of the over 300 intermediate people's courts, the MMC has become the default means for all litigation and court mediation in China, used in 99.7% of cases in 2022.[22] Even cases which are substantively dealt with almost entirely offline are nevertheless logged on to the MMC, to enable efficient case management and logistical arrangements.

Although experimentation in the digital age is not unique to Chinese practice and policymaking, China's vast size and the significant diversity of its legal system offer a wide range of possibilities for developing various initiatives and approach. Meanwhile, the customary resolve and efficiency in implementing policies once they are decided upon by national or judicial leadership also enhance the productivity of this approach. In other words, both the bottom-up and top-down channels are exceptionally well-suited to decentralized experimentation and centralized implementation, making this strategy highly effective in the fast-evolving internet society.

A legal system seeking influence and legitimacy

Changes on the scale such as the Chinese online courts understandably encountered considerable obstacles in practice. Measures such as "asynchronized litigation," where each litigant and the judge deal with different components of the litigation, such as exchange and challenge of evidence, at their own time, can cause much unease.[23] Despite these concerns, there is notedly little hesitation, let alone resistance, shown by the court system institutionally toward these significant changes and new measures of digitization being experimented and implemented. The willingness, even enthusiasm, that the judiciary collectively has shown in embracing the online court and digitization may be better explained and understood when examined against the traditionally "weaker" position of the court in the Chinese political system and society.

China's judiciary has long been under criticism, such as the lack of judicial independence,[24] lack of transparency in the judicial process,[25] poor training and professionalism,[26] and so on. The local courts have always been seen by critics as weak, lacking independence, poorly resourced, and occupying much less influential positions than other institutions, such as the Communist Party, the government,

22 Chen Guoping 陈国平 and Tian He 田禾, *Annual Report on Informationization of Chinese Courts No. 7 (2023)* 中国法院信息化发展报告(2023) (Beijing: Social Science Academic Press China, 2023), 23.

23 Online Litigation Rules, Articles 14 & 20; Zuo Weimin 左卫民, "Online Litigation in the Post-Epidemic Era: Where to Go 后疫情时代的在线诉讼: 路向何方," *Xiandai Faxue* 现代法学 43, no. 6 (2021): 45.

24 Graig R. Avino, "China's Judiciary: An Instrument of Democratic Change," *Penn State International Law Review* 22, no. 2 (2003): 381.

25 Benjamin L. Liebman, "Assessing China's Legal Reforms," *Columbian Journal of Asian Law* 23, no. 1 (2009): 24, https://doi.org/10.7916/cjal.v23i1.3284.

26 William Fairbairn, "An Examination of Judicial Independence in China," *Journal of Financial Crime* 23, no. 4 (2016): 824, https://doi.org/10.1108/JFC-12-2015-0068.

the procuratorate, and so on.[27] Chinese courts have been seen to strive for "legitimacy" from their traditionally weaker position.[28] In this context, the imperatives for digitization of justice comes with strong political endorsement from both the leadership of the Communist Party and the central government.[29] Armed with both centrally driven policy imperatives and technological capabilities, the SPC finds itself in a very strong position to convince the lower courts to accept its digitization initiatives and methods.

Moreover, judges in Chinese courts, particularly those in many basic courts and their subsidiary tribunals, are accustomed to working under physically challenging conditions. Some judges and their staff have traveled to remote areas for circuit court hearings, conducted proceedings on fishing boats or in tents. There is little concern for preserving "the majesty of the court" in the transition to online operation, unlike in some other jurisdictions,[30] as this shift is generally perceived as an improvement by both litigants and the judiciary. More importantly, the Chinese judiciary has never been viewed as being above litigants or the general population. Foreign scholars have observed that many judges struggle to maintain a clear division between their private and professional lives, as litigants can approach them at almost any time, referring to them as "comrade," "cadre," "uncle," "elder sister," and so on.[31] This closeness between the judiciary and the population is actively promoted by state and judicial leadership as part of the tradition of legal practice in the communist People's Republic.[32] As the general population increasingly moves toward online operations in almost every aspect of life, judges both expect and are expected to embrace the latest technologies and digital methods.

In this context, the traditionally "weak" position of the Chinese court has facilitated the widespread acceptance of digitization throughout the legal system. It has been suggested that developing nations might leapfrog more advanced jurisdictions in the global movement of online courts by bypassing many of the traditional

27 Stanley B. Lubman, *Bird in a Cage: Legal Reform in China After Mao* (Stanford, CA: Stanford University Press, 1999), 292–95; Randall Peerenboom, "Judicial Independence in China," in *Judicial Independence in China*, ed. Randall Peerenboom (Cambridge: Cambridge University Press, 2010), 78–84.

28 Peter C. H. Chan, "Do the 'Haves' Come Out Ahead in Chinese Grassroots Courts? Rural Land Disputes Between Married-Out Women and Village Collectives," *Hastings Law Journal* 71, no. 1 (2019): 72.

29 Opinions of the General Office of the CPC Central Committee and the General Office of the State Council on Improving the Diversified Resolution Mechanism of Conflicts and Disputes (Central Office Issue 2015/No. 60).

30 Lord Justice Briggs, *Civil Courts Structure Review: Interim Report* (Judiciary of England and Wales, December 2015), 4, https://www.judiciary.uk/wp-content/uploads/2016/01/ccsr-interim-report-dec-15-final1.pdf.

31 Stéphanie Balme, "Local Courts in Western China: The Quest for Independence and Dignity," in *Judicial Independence in China*, ed. Randall Peerenboom (Cambridge: Cambridge University Press, 2010), 168.

32 "'Ma xiwu shenpan fangshi' de zairenshi zaishijian '马锡五审判方式'的再认识、再实践," *People's Court Daily* 人民法院报, June 19, 2023, https://www.chinacourt.org/article/detail/2023/06/id/7347625.shtml.

challenges to legal reforms.[33] The rapid embrace of online courts and digitization by over 3,500 courts in China is an illuminating example in this context. A further exploration in what follows of how the internet courts and online courts operate in the Chinese legal system will shed more light on the achievements and challenges of these significant changes.

Internet courts: endogenization of exogenous dispute resolution

Overview of internet courts

China's internet courts are the world's first "cyber court" and the world's first "online court," both distinctions of considerable significance that warrant further explanation. Regarding the "cyber court" aspect, the internet courts are empowered to deal with only and all disputes arising in cyberspace, encompassing areas such as contract, tort, intellectual property, administrative enforcement, and more. As for the "online court" aspect, these courts function as comprehensive, fully operational civil and administrative courts with a conventional judicial operational structure based on an established physical entity, complete jurisdiction, and a full range of judicial powers and remedies at their disposal, all while operating almost entirely online. In many regards, the internet courts are prime examples and pioneers for achieving fairness, technological trust, and competence expected of online courts.[34] Although the initial excitement over the internet courts has subsided somewhat since their inception in 2017 and 2018, as of 2024, no other court anywhere in the world has met either one of these criteria, let alone both.

Some scholars have seemingly overlooked the significance of these characterizations, for example, in drawing comparisons to the Civil Resolution Tribunal (CRT) in British Columbia, Canada, and implying that the CRT predates the internet courts.[35] This, however, is a misconception. The CRT explicitly identifies itself on its own website as an "independent, quasi-judicial tribunal,"[36] indicating that it operates as a tribunal rather than a court, as typically construed. Even among civil courts, this distinction crucially differentiates China's internet courts from other conceptions of online courts globally. For instance, the Federal Court of Australia's eCourt functions as a virtual courtroom or platform, essentially an email service within a secure environment, combined with a message board system, rather than a

33 Richard Susskind, *Online Courts and the Future of Justice* (Oxford: Oxford University Press, 2019), 300, https://doi.org/10.1093/oso/9780198838364.001.0001.

34 Larry W. Bridgesmith, "ODR and the Justice System," in *Online Dispute Resolution: Theory and Practice*, eds. Daniel Rainey, Ethan Katsh, and Mohamed S. Abdel Wahab, 2nd ed. (The Hague: Eleven, 2021), 145–47.

35 Meirong Guo, "Internet Court's Challenges and Future in China," *Computer Law & Security Review* 40 (2021): 105522, 2, https://doi.org/10.1016/j.clsr.2020.105522.

36 Civil Resolution Tribunal, "About the CRT," accessed July 31, 2024, https://civilresolutionbc.ca/about-the-crt/.

full court or courthouse.[37] Similarly, other initiatives, such as Money Claim Online, Possession Claim Online, and Online Civil Money Claims in the UK, discussed in Chapter 1, are designed to handle a specific category of cases with clear limitations, such as the maximum sum of claim or the remedies sought. In Singapore, the Subordinate Courts of eAlternative Dispute Resolution (e@dr), despite the name, is primarily an online mediation platform dealing with e-commerce disputes, restricted to cases that do not enter litigation.

In contrast, China's three internet courts are fully established courts with physical courthouses, where judges and staff conduct daily operations, fundamentally differing from purely online hearing mechanisms imposed over multiple courts dealing with specific types of cases. The internet courts have comprehensive jurisdiction over all civil disputes and some administrative law disputes, just like any other basic people's court. The only limit to the internet courts' jurisdiction is that any civil or administrative law dispute must have some substance that relates to the online world, which is practically always satisfied in any dispute involving computers and digitization nowadays.

Before the establishment of the internet courts, various courts in China had already begun utilizing online hearings to adjudicate cases, though these hearings were often conducted on an ad hoc basis, without clear legal grounding.[38] In contrast, the internet courts are specifically designed to conduct the entire litigation process – ranging from case acceptance, service of documents, mediation, evidence exchange, pre-trial preparations, trial to the handing down of judgment – online as a matter of general principle.[39] However, based on the parties' requests or the trial's requirements, certain parts of the proceedings may be conducted offline. Should an appeal arise from a case adjudicated by an internet court, the appellate court should, in principle, also conduct the hearing online, unless all parties involved request an offline trial or if the appellate court determines that an online hearing would be ineffective in establishing facts or evaluating evidence, in which case an offline hearing may be considered.[40]

The internet courts stand out as significant pioneers in the empirical practice of delivering justice online, achieving an exceptionally high online engagement rate of well over 90% across hundreds of thousands of cases since their establishment. Taking the Guangzhou Internet Court as an example, from its inception until December 2022, an impressive 99.93% of cases were filed online; 99.97% of cases utilized electronic service of documents, with 93% of services being successful;

37 Nicolas W. Vermeys and Karim Benyekhelf, "ODR and the Courts," in *Online Dispute Resolution: Theory and Practice*, eds. Mohamed S. Abdel Wahab, Ethan Katsh, and Daniel Rainey (The Hague: Eleven, 2012), 312.

38 Gao Wei 高薇, *Institutional Analysis of Dispute Resolution in Cyberspace* 网络空间争议解决的制度分析 (Beijing: Peking University Press, 2022), 180.

39 Supreme People's Court, "Provisions of the Supreme People's Court on Several Issues Concerning the Trial of Cases by Internet Courts 最高人民法院关于互联网法院审理案件若干问题的规定" Judicial Interpretation 2018/No. 16, September 6, 2018 (Internet Court Provisions), Article 1.

40 Internet Court Provisions, Article 22.

98.49% of cases were resolved at the first instance; and 89.04% of judgments were voluntarily complied with by litigants.[41] In 2022, the rate of online court hearings reached 99.72% in the over 50,000 cases resolved by the court.[42] This level of online integration is unprecedented compared to the numerous other courts globally that are adopting or considering ODR process. Larson identified 57 individual courts (primarily in the United States and Canada) that are progressing toward ODR, including China's three internet courts.[43] However, only the internet courts are predominantly online, with others still falling short of achieving such a high level of digital engagement.

As mentioned earlier, the internet courts exclusively handle internet-related disputes, in line with major national directives and strategies.[44] The jurisdiction of these courts currently encompasses 11 specific categories of internet-related civil or administrative law issues, including disputes over online shopping contracts, online service contracts, online financial loan contracts, copyright ownership of works published online, and internet domain names.[45] Administrative litigation, such as lawsuits over sanctions imposed by government for illegality in online operation, is rare in practice, with civil disputes dominating the caseload of all three internet courts.

This strategic positioning establishes the internet courts as significant trendsetters in the jurisdiction over online disputes, regularly taking precedence in deciding nearly all relevant cases before other courts intervene. This stands in stark contrast to some other jurisdictions, such as the United States, where online litigation is most advanced in handling types of cases unrelated to cyberspace, such as traffic disputes.[46] The unique format of "ODR tailored to internet disputes" utilized by China's internet courts, combined with their substantial innovative impact, underscores their critical importance and the broader attention they rightfully command.

The wide adoption of innovative technologies has been a hallmark of the internet courts, particularly in the realm of electronic evidence management. Most notably, these courts have piloted the use of blockchain technology as a method

41 Chen and Tian, *Annual Report 2023*, 21.

42 "2022 annual self-evaluation report of the Guangzhou Internet Court on overall expenditure and performance 2022年度广州互联网法院部门整体支出绩效自评报告," Guangzhou Internet Court, October 16, 2023, at 7 and 9, https://www.gz.gov.cn/attachment/7/7465/7465600/9259645.pdf.

43 David Allen Larson, "ODR Accessibility for Person with Disabilities: We Must Do Better," in *Online Dispute Resolution: Theory and Practice*, eds. Daniel Rainey, Ethan Katsh, and Mohamed S. Abdel Wahab, 2nd ed. (The Hague: Eleven, 2021), 151.

44 General Office of the Central Committee of the Communist Party of China and General Office of the State Council, "Outline of the National Strategy for the Development of Informatization 国家信息化发展战略纲要," July 2016; Central Committee of the Communist Party of China, "Implementation Outline for Constructing the Rule of Law Society (2020–2025) 法治社会建设实施纲要(2020–2025年)," December 2020.

45 Internet Court Provisions, Article 2.

46 Avital Mentovich, J. J. Prescott, and Orna Rabinovich-Einy, "Legitimacy and Online Proceedings: Procedural Justice, Access to Justice, and the Role of Income," *Law & Society Review* 57, no. 2 (2023): 190, https://doi.org/10.1111/lasr.12653.

for parties to fix, preserve, collect, and extract evidence, in addition to leveraging electronic evidence collection and preservation platforms. This approach substantially enhances traditional methods, such as notarization for confirming electronic evidence, significantly increasing its evidentiary value. Blockchain technology offers distinct advantages in terms of being tamperproof and providing traceability, which are crucial in legal settings, where the integrity of evidence is paramount. By incorporating blockchain into their processes, the internet courts have pioneered new methods for confirming electronic evidence. This technological integration not only strengthens the reliability of electronic evidence but also facilitates cross-examination procedures during trials.[47] Such innovations underscore the role of technology in modernizing judicial processes and ensuring that evidence handling meets the highest standards of security and verifiability.

Positioning internet courts from an institutional analysis perspective

Chapter 2 of this book distinctly differentiates between endogenous and exogenous ODR mechanisms, observing a trend toward the endogenization of exogenous ODR. In this context, the internet courts serve as a prime example of this trend, exhibiting significant characteristics of endogenous ODR within what initially emerged as an exogenous framework from the traditional formal legal system.

The internet courts function within the structure of conventional courts, originating as an exogenous mechanism – external to the spontaneous developments within the internet industry. Starting from an exogenous design and motivation, these courts adapt existing judicial frameworks to the digital realm, maintaining the conventional litigation pattern from case filing to decision-making. While innovative, this approach still represents the digitization of distinct segments rather than a holistic technological integration across all judicial processes, indicating partial digitization, which is typical of many exogenous initiatives and reforms. However, unlike other exogenous mechanisms, the internet courts are intrinsically tied to the internet, explicitly designed by outsiders to address and resolve disputes arising from cyberspace. Thus, this orientation is not merely an adaptation of traditional courts to the digital environment but a deliberate institutional effort to promote a novel conception of the rule of law in cyberspace through technological advancements and integration. This distinctive positioning redefines their institutional attributes, making them fundamentally different from conventional courts.

From an institutional analysis perspective, several aspects underscore the unique role of the internet courts and the endogenization of an exogenous mechanism. Following the framework outlined in Chapter 2, the internet courts display notably different characteristics in terms of incentives, agents, and methodology.

Firstly, the incentive structure is different for the internet courts. Unlike conventional courts, whose operations are driven by general legal demands in society,

47 Internet Court Provisions, Article 11.2.

the internet courts are specifically incentivized by the needs of cyberspace. Their primary goal is to address and resolve online disputes, directly reflecting the core challenges and dynamics of the digital age. Specialized in cyber-related disputes, the courts serve as the designated judicial venue for virtually all internet-related legal issues within China's vast legal system. This specialization enables them not only to resolve disputes but also to establish judicial precedents that enhance legal certainty and exert preemptive and preventative effects on future disputes.

The internet courts lead the way in pioneering new judicial concepts and practices. They play a critical role in shaping the future of judicial activity, setting benchmarks for how legal systems can adapt to and integrate with the digital world. Through landmark cases, they have asserted judicial sovereignty in cyberspace, tackled illegal online activities, and upheld rights related to personal information security, minors' protection, and overall network information security. These attributes illustrate the transformational impact of internet courts, making them more than just venues for online litigation – they are critical models for the evolution of legal systems in the digital era. Their approach and outcomes not only address immediate legal disputes but also pave the way for broader judicial reforms and the advancement of rule of law within and beyond cyberspace.

The significance and expectations placed on the internet courts by the Chinese legal system and society are best illustrated by an example. After generative artificial intelligence (GAI) surged to the forefront of global discourse in November 2022, each of China's three internet courts promptly delivered landmark judgments on GAI, demonstrating their responsiveness and relevance compared to conventional courts, both domestically and internationally.

1. In April 2023, the Hangzhou Internet Court ruled that any "virtual person" created with GAI on the basis of real-time motion capture technology did not possess legal personality or any intellectual property rights. However, the human being that this "virtual person" was based on qualified as a "performer" under Chinese law and could rightfully prevent others from using their performance.[48]
2. In November 2023, the Beijing Internet Court issued one of the world's first rulings on the intellectual property rights of images created by GAI.[49] The plaintiff utilized GAI graphic generation software to create an image, which was subsequently used by the defendant in its online business activities without permission. The court conducted a thorough examination of the various factors involved in the creation process, including the selection of templates, the input of prompt words, and the repeated modification of parameters. The court concluded that the image constituted graphic artwork with aesthetic value, characterized by an original composition of lines and colors resulting from human intellectual effort, and was therefore eligible for legal protection as artwork.

48 (2022)浙0192民初9983号, Hangzhou Internet Court (April 25, 2023); upheld by (2023)浙01民终4722号, Hangzhou Intermediate People's Court (August 8, 2023).

49 (2023)京0491民初11279号, Beijing Internet Court (November 27, 2023).

3. In February 2024, the Guangzhou Internet Court decided that original images created by a GAI service following explicit user instructions bore a strong resemblance to the popular Japanese science-fiction character Ultraman, thereby infringing upon the rights-holder's intellectual property.[50] The GAI service provider was found liable for failing to take active steps to prevent such infringements and for not exercising reasonable care, such as not alerting users to the risks of copyright infringement and not establishing complaint mechanisms for reporting such violations.

Since their establishment, the internet courts have delivered judgments that defend judicial sovereignty in cyberspace, combat illicit online activities, safeguard personal information, protect minors' rights, and ensure network information security. Numerous landmark cases on novel issues in cyberspace underscore the broader, intrinsic value and purposes of the internet courts as an institution beyond pioneering ODR methods. Rather than simply responding to the disputes before them, the internet courts are incentivized to proactively address the newest and emerging issues at the intersection of cyberspace and law, functioning much like an endogenous ODR system tailored for the internet era.

Secondly, judges at the internet courts demonstrate a higher level of specialization in handling internet-related cases and possess a deeper understanding of technology compared to their peers in other courts. This expertise is evident not only in their adept use of technology to resolve disputes but also in their continuous education on emerging types of issues and disputes in cyberspace. Judges at the internet court regularly engage in training focused on cyber technology, fostering an environment that is often likened to that of an internet start-up company or a university.[51] Additionally, the internet courts enhance their knowledge base by collaborating with various social resources and institutions, including large internet companies and administrative agencies.

However, it is essential to recognize the inherent challenges within this system. Given that judges resolve disputes as outsiders, there is a notable gap in information access compared to insiders of the internet communities. This gap underscores the problems with the endogenization of an exogenous mechanism, sparking discussions about how to evolve internet courts into entities genuinely suited to cyberspace. Such evolution necessitates shifting the focus away from merely recognizing the information gap between outsiders and insiders and, instead, towards acknowledging the inherent constraints of human-led dispute resolution. This shift in perspective encourages further exploration into how technology can be more effectively utilized to either supplement or replace human adjudicators in resolving disputes online.

50 (2024)粤0192民初113号, Guangzhou Internet Court (February 8, 2024).

51 Jin Hao 靳昊 and Sun Mingxi 孙铭溪, "'Hulianwang faguan' shi ruhe liancheng de '互联网法官'是如何炼成的," *Guangming Daily* 光明日报, September 10, 2019, https://epaper.gmw.cn/gmrb/html/2019-09/10/nw.D110000gmrb_20190910_3-06.htm.

Thirdly, from a methodological perspective, the internet courts have reshaped traditional notions of judicial proceedings, introducing significant innovations and experiments within the judicial system. While maintaining an online activity rate of around 99%, the internet court's contributions go beyond simply replicating traditional litigation forms. Their experimental approach involves innovations in trial organization and a departure from the structure of other specialized courts in China, such as intellectual property courts or financial courts. Notably, during the COVID-19 pandemic, many of these innovations ensured the continuity of judicial processes, showcasing the adaptability and resilience of this model.

Furthermore, the trial model at the internet courts has evolved from offline to online, from face-to-face to remote interactions, and from synchronous to asynchronous proceedings. Before the establishment of internet courts, such a transformation would have been unimaginable. This shift not only highlights the potential for judicial innovation but also reflects the advantages of centralized jurisdiction, marking a significant evolution in how justice is administered in the digital age.

The exceptional efficiency demonstrated by the internet courts is a testament to the effective integration of ODR within the judicial framework, offering the largest and most comprehensive empirical data currently available globally. Significantly, court hearing durations in the internet courts are typically reduced by up to 75% compared to those in conventional courts.[52] This increased efficiency, however, is not solely attributed to the online nature of the litigation process but also results from a deliberate and strategic shift in institutional configuration.

According to the "ODR Quadrant Diagram" presented in Chapter 3, internet courts are positioned as the most "bottom-left" model of ODR worldwide, highlighting their significant global relevance. This positioning emphasizes the proactive and experimental nature of these courts, characterized by their readiness to test and refine various procedural innovations. It is crucial to recognize that the operations of internet courts are marked by endogenous mechanisms. They serve as both experimental platforms and benchmarks for broader judicial practices, allowing for the trial-and-error application of various measures. This adaptability means that ineffective strategies can be promptly identified and discarded, ensuring the system remains dynamic and responsive to the needs of dispute resolution in the digital era.

Critical analysis of the internet courts

The COVID-19 pandemic prompted and accelerated the adaptation of online litigation across all courts, diminishing, to some extent, the distinctiveness of the internet courts. Once other courts incorporated the pioneering methods of the internet courts, the line between conventional and internet courts began to blur. A pivotal

52 "Zuigaofa: hulianwang fayuan shenjie anjian 19.4 wan jian 最高法: 互联网法院审结案件19.4万件," China Internet Information Center, September 23, 2020, http://news.china.com.cn/txt/2020-09/23/content_76733305.htm.

question arises regarding the ongoing role and value of internet courts: If all courts are equipped to handle cases online, what becomes of the internet court's exemplary function? This question touches on the existential purpose of internet courts in a future where their pioneering attributes may be universally adopted, prompting a re-evaluation of their unique contributions and possibly redefining their role within China's judicial landscape. It is also relevant to consider whether the internet courts, as experimental entities, have outlived their innovative purposes. Could they then be abolished or reverted to the conventional court structure? These considerations are essential as they will determine the future trajectory of the internet courts in sustaining their relevance and leadership in the evolving realm of judicial processes.

In the meantime, certain challenges facing the internet courts have become increasingly apparent. Firstly, one major concern is the persistent imbalance of "heavy caseload and shortage of personnel" (*an duo ren shao*), a problem prevalent for all Chinese courts but particularly pronounced in the internet courts. According to the work report of the SPC, from 2012 to 2022, the number of cases handled by courts nationwide skyrocketed from 13 million to 33.7 million, while the number of judges has remained largely unchanged. As a result, in 2022, the average annual caseload per quota judge soared to 242.[53]

Amidst this challenge, the Beijing Internet Court, as an example, has been facing a tremendous caseload. The court dealt with around 55,000 cases annually, with only 48 quota judges on its roster and fewer than 40 actively presiding over cases. This figure far exceeds the national average and the average for Beijing, with internet court judges each handling almost 1,000 cases per year.[54] This stark disparity underscores the urgent need for structural and resource adjustments within the internet court system to maintain efficiency and justice.

The escalating workload of individual judges points to a fundamental limitation: There is a finite capacity for human dispute resolution. With potentially hundreds of thousands of copyright infringements, online tors, and online contractual disputes being taken to court,[55] despite efforts to mitigate these disputes at the source, the stark imbalance between the number of cases and available judges remains a fundamental challenge in the current judicial landscape. This imbalance underscores the inherent limitations of any systemic design that failed to address this central issue.

53 Zhou Qiang 周强, "Work Report of the Supreme People's Court 最高人民法院工作报告," *Presented to the 1st Meeting of the 14th National People's Congress*, March 7, 2021, http://gongbao.court.gov.cn/Details/0cf2ab48a3d2a9cd604af4991aa7d7.html.

54 The statistics for 2022 is 991 cases per judge. Beijing Internet Court, "Jianzheng 2022! Qihang 2023! 见证2022! 启航2023!," January 3, 2023, https://news.bjd.com.cn/2023/01/03/10286377.shtml.

55 The Beijing Internet Court resolved 182,000 cases in the first five years of its operation. Of these cases, 71.57% involved copyright infringements, 11.27% pertained to other online torts, and 8.65% were related to online contract disputes. "Beijing hulianwang fayuan: wunian shenjie 18.2 wan anjian 北京互联网法院: 五年审结18.2万案件," *People.com.cn* 人民网, September 9, 2023, http://society.people.com.cn/n1/2023/0909/c1008-40073886.html.

In considering whether the integration of technology has made the administration of justice more convenient, the heavy workload across the judiciary, characterized by prevalent overtime and overwork, exposes major difficulties in the design and practice of the Chinese legal system.[56] The conventional adjudication model and traditional court operations are strained under the weight of increasing demands, leading to a potential decline in the quality of justice. This situation begs the question of whether technology or institutional reforms can alleviate these pressures.

The path to resolving these systemic issues likely lies in the deeper digital transformation of the courts, a process that extends beyond mere technological adoption.[57] Achieving what might be termed "digital justice" requires not only advanced technological tools but also a significant shift in mindsets about how justice is administered. This transformation involves reimagining judicial processes and the role of judges in a digital age, envisioning a system where technology augments and enhances human capacities rather than simply adding to the workload. The successful realization of digital justice hinges on a holistic approach that combines technological innovation with strategic, systemic reforms aimed at improving both efficiency and fairness in the judicial process.

The evaluation of internet courts in terms of their functional and value-based roles necessitates a critical reassessment of their case jurisdiction and institutional positioning. Currently, the internet courts are not specialized courts per se but hold centralized jurisdiction over specific types of cases within designated geographical areas. This model has led to some ambiguities within the broader jurisdiction system, potentially causing conflicts with other courts over jurisdictional authority in internet-related cases.

The three internet courts are responsible for handling first-instance internet dispute cases that would otherwise fall under the jurisdiction of local basic courts in the areas where the internet courts are located. The three cities of Hangzhou, Beijing, and Guangzhou are strategically chosen, as they are the hubs of the Chinese internet and digital industries, with the majority of China's leading internet companies headquartered in these three cities or in nearby Shanghai and Shenzhen, which are close to Hangzhou and Guangzhou, respectively. However, this arrangement has led to a scenario where the internet courts are overwhelmed with a vast number of cases, many of which involve straightforward, repetitive, and technical non-legal issues of minimal legal significance or complexity. This situation primarily serves to facilitate litigation rather than advancing the broader goal of enhancing cyberspace governance.

There are further issues with internet courts being positioned as basic people's courts. An appeal case filed against a judgment or ruling rendered by the Beijing, Guangzhou, or Hangzhou Internet Court shall be tried by their respective

56 Cheng Jinhua 程金华, "A Cross-Country Comparison of 'Too Many Cases, Too Few Judges' in Courts 法院'案多人少'的跨国比较," *Social Science Journal* 社会科学辑刊 262 (2022/5): 82.

57 Jia Yu, "Lun shuzi fayuan," 16–20.

higher-level intermediate people's courts, that is, the Fourth Intermediate People's Court of Beijing Municipality, the Intermediate People's Court of Guangdong City, and the Intermediate People's Court of Hangzhou City. However, there are specialized intermediate-level people's courts on cases concerning intellectual property rights in Beijing and Guangzhou, namely, Beijing Intellectual Property Court and Guangzhou Intellectual Property Court. As such, an appeal case against a judgment or ruling rendered by the Beijing Internet Court and Guangzhou Internet Court in a dispute over the ownership of or infringement upon any online copyright, or a dispute over any internet domain name, shall respectively be tried by the Beijing Intellectual Property Court and Guangzhou Intellectual Property Court instead.

For a more effective and purposeful future, it is advisable for internet courts to shift their focus toward adjudicating new and complex types of cases that carry demonstrative significance. By delegating the resolution of routine disputes, such as online shopping issues, to ordinary basic courts, internet courts could then concentrate on major, novel, internet-related cases at both the first and second instances. This strategic focus would enable them to fulfill their foundational purpose more effectively, aligning more closely with the intent behind their establishment.

At the same time, the criteria for case acceptance by internet courts should also undergo reassessment. The current jurisdiction requires a clear, initial determination of the types of civil disputes involving online matters.[58] As digital elements increasingly permeate all aspects of social activities and new types of internet-related cases continuously emerge, often not fitting neatly into predefined categories, determining the appropriate court for these disputes from the outset presents a significant challenge.

These considerations suggest that an optimal potential solution is to elevate the level of abstraction in the jurisdictional rules of internet courts, making them more adaptable to the evolving landscape of internet-related cases. Additionally, considering the inherently trans-territorial nature of internet-related disputes, it would be beneficial to incorporate provisions for trans-territorial jurisdiction within the operational scope of internet courts. This approach would not only address the current jurisdictional ambiguities but also enhance the courts' capacity to effectively manage the complexities of modern digital disputes.

Moreover, elevating internet courts to the level of intermediate people's courts and giving them appellate jurisdiction also addresses some current limitations in the focus but expertise of internet court judges. The conceptualization of internet courts as specialized entities initially included professional thresholds intended to create barriers that emphasize expertise in specific legal areas. However, these courts face challenges related to the breadth and depth of case exposure that judges receive compared to their counterparts in traditional courts. Judges at intermediate courts, for example, typically handle more than 200 types of civil disputes. Judges at internet courts currently handle only eight civil cases, excluding public interest or administrative litigation. This narrow focus can limit judges' exposure to a broader

58 Internet Court Provisions, Article 2.

spectrum of legal issues and diminish their ability to develop a well-rounded judicial expertise.

The rapid evolution of technology, such as AI, blockchain, and crowdsourcing, presents formidable challenges to judges at internet courts, as they grapple with complex new types of cases that span multiple legal domains. These judges wield significant influence over many emerging issues from cyberspace, including their practical implications for society and the digital economy, being among the first members of the judiciary to express their views on these quickly evolving matters. As discussed in Chapter 3, a first-instance decision from the Hangzhou Internet Court effectively halted the operation of the most successful crowdsourced ODR in China to date, even if that might not have been the intention of the judge at all.

Another illustrative example is the first case on AI-generated voice technology adjudicated by the Beijing Internet Court in April 2024. A voice actress sued five defendant technology companies over AI-generated voice that was synthesized on the basis of her natural voice and widely used commercially.[59] Judges face a delicate balancing act in such cases. Protecting traditional sound and personality rights might undermine intellectual property and data rights, potentially stifling innovation in the data and AI sectors. Conversely, favoring the protection of the AI and copyright industries could weaken the enforcement of individual personality rights. Such decisions are pivotal, as they not only resolve individual disputes but also set precedents that delineate the boundaries of application for emerging technologies and industries. In the end, the court held that human voice could be recognizable due to its distinctiveness, uniqueness, and stability, as determined by whether the general public was able to associate the voice with the natural person. Moreover, intellectual property rights over the recording of human voice do not extend to its use for AI voice generation. Three of the defendants were therefore found liable for infringing upon the voice of the plaintiff.

These cases underscore the complex challenges that internet court judges must navigate. They are tasked not only with applying existing laws to new technologies but also with actively shaping the legal landscape in which these technologies operate. This dual responsibility requires a deep understanding of both the legal implications of new technologies and the potential societal impacts of their judicial decisions.

Six to seven years after the establishment of the world's internet courts, they stand as the only internet courts and entirely online courts globally. Yet even in this short period of time, internet courts are already facing pressures to potentially reinvent and reposition themselves in the fast-evolving internet society and ODR landscape. Ultimately, perception of the internet courts' role and effectiveness is nuanced and varies among those involved or affected by its decisions. Stakeholders, ranging from judges and legal professionals to technology companies and the

59 "Beijing Internet Court delivered first instance judgment on AI-generated voice case 北京互联网法院对一起AI生成声音人格权侵权案进行一审宣判," *The Paper* 澎湃, April 23, 2024, https://www.thepaper.cn/newsDetail_forward_27137070.

general public, may hold differing opinions about the courts' current capabilities and alignment with their expectations of an ideal judicial body capable of addressing the complexities introduced by technological advancements. Meanwhile, the internet courts, as an important stepstone in China's digitization of justice, continue to search for their distinctive role and values in the legal system and the digital age.

Court as service provider

One-stop diversified dispute resolution

The concept of a one-stop diversified dispute resolution mechanism (*yizhanshi duoyuan jiufen jiejue*) in Chinese courts originated in the Second Five-Year Reform Program for the People's Courts, which emphasized

> [s]trengthening and perfecting the system of mediation in litigation, attaching importance to guiding the work of people's mediation, and supporting and supervising arbitration activities in accordance with the law. Collaborate with other departments and organizations to explore new methods of dispute resolution, and promote the establishment of a sound and diversified dispute resolution mechanism.[60]

Scholars identify two primary reasons for the adoption of such a mechanism. Firstly, the rapid pace of economic development has resulted in litigation inadequate to manage the sheer volume and diversity of disputes. Secondly, mediation is considered a significant "Eastern experience," deeply embedded in China's historical approach to dispute resolution.[61] In essence, Chinese courts have traditionally not viewed themselves as the ultimate authority in dispute resolution. The expression to "explore dispute resolution with other departments" reflects a uniquely Chinese perspective. This approach is underpinned by the relatively weaker influence of the courts, mentioned earlier, and a cultural aversion to litigation,[62] making it both desirable and necessary for the judiciary to collaborate with various mechanisms in resolving disputes. This philosophy supports the broader integration of traditional and modern methods to create a more comprehensive and culturally attuned dispute resolution landscape.

The concept of one-stop diversified dispute resolution mechanisms extends beyond merely integrating information technology into the adjudication process. It involves a comprehensive re-engineering of the entire case management and adjudication framework, utilizing internet technology and embedding the idea of

60 Supreme People's Court, "Second Five-Year Reform Plan of People's Courts (2004–2008)," (SPC Issue 2005/No. 18, October 26, 2005), Point 7.

61 Wenhua Shan and Yunya Feng, "The China International Commercial Court: Towards an Integrated Dispute Resolution System," *Asia Pacific Law Review* 29, no. 1 (2021): 115.

62 Qingxiu Bu, "Will Chinese Legal Culture Constrain Its Corporate Governance-Related Laws?," *Journal of Corporate Law Studies* 15, no. 1 (2015): 108.

"smart courts" throughout all phases of dispute management and case resolution. Key components of the one-stop multi-dispute resolution mechanisms include governance of litigation sources, diversified dispute resolution, separation of cases into simple cases and complicated ones, and separation of simple cases into pre-trial mediation, fast-tracking, and summary procedures, all of which underscore the dual goals of dispute avoidance and efficient dispute resolution.

"Governance of litigation sources" emphasizes the use of judicial big data to identify, assess, and mitigate potential risks and conflicts before they escalate into full-blown disputes. This proactive approach aims to reduce the incidence of conflicts and disputes at their source, thereby alleviating the overall burden on the judicial system.

"Diversified dispute resolution" encourages disputing parties to opt for non-litigation methods to settle their disputes, adhering to the principles of voluntariness and legality. This facet of the mechanism promotes the development of trial process management systems or online mediation platforms for courts, enhancing the judicial confirmation of mediation agreements. It also advocates for the establishment of pre-litigation mediation case management systems, which involve meticulous case-by-case registration and comprehensive recordkeeping, ensuring that all mediation efforts are well-documented and legally binding where applicable.

The "separation of cases into simple and complicated ones" is a refined strategy that involves several critical steps. Initially, systematic algorithms combined with manual identification are employed to categorize cases based on their complexity. This allows for a more structured and efficient approach to case management. Firstly, litigation service centers are equipped with fast-track adjudication judges or teams who utilize an array of procedural tools, such as supervisory proceedings, judicial confirmation proceedings, small-claims proceedings, summary proceedings, and ordinary proceedings. These teams are specifically tasked with handling simpler cases swiftly and efficiently. To support this process, mechanisms for centralized handling of these cases are established, standardized litigation models are set up, document templates are created, and intelligent voice and online hearings are extensively used to enhance efficiency.

Additionally, a specialized team is designated to manage cases that escalate from simple to complex, ensuring a smooth procedural conversion. The ultimate goal is to ensure that simple cases are resolved through summary procedures and more complex cases receive the thorough examination they require.

Furthermore, the internal management mechanisms of courts are also undergoing reform to better accommodate the development of online dispute resolution systems. A notable reform is "intensive management." For instance, since 2019, Beijing Xicheng District People's Court has progressively removed clerks from the trial teams, establishing a clerk management office for centralized oversight. According to statistics from Xicheng Court, this intensive management reform has significantly reduced the average length of court hearings by nearly 40%, increased courtroom utilization by 30%, and enhanced the punctuality rate of court sessions from 59% to 92%. Moreover, the Xicheng Court's Electronic Service Center and

Electronic File Generation Center have also adopted an intensive working model by separating court records, case services, filing, and scanning from the trial teams, achieving intensive management of trial support services and saving judges an average of more than nine hours per case. The court has also embraced outsourcing of services to further advance court management reforms and reduce the workload on the trial teams, aligning with the goals of the one-stop mechanism.

However, it is crucial to note that, despite these innovations, currently the outsourcing service model of courts nationwide tends to remain relatively simplistic, with scarce institutional rules, inadequate financial support, and a lack of specialization of services. Additionally, internal management mechanisms are often underdeveloped and require further strengthening and regulation to fully realize the potential of these reforms.[63]

Together, these strategies carried out by courts are designed not just to handle disputes as they reach the court but to proactively manage potential sources of litigation and offer multiple pathways for dispute resolution, thereby fostering a more efficient and responsive judicial environment.

The development of China's one-stop litigation service system is a strategic initiative orchestrated by the SPC to modernize and streamline judicial processes across the country. This top-down reform aims to integrate and automate litigation service information resources and big data management across the four levels of the judiciary, ensuring uniformity and efficiency in the delivery of judicial services nationwide.

In June 2019, the SPC took a significant step forward by launching the Litigation Service Guidance Center Information Platform. This platform encompasses five critical business modules: "diversified dispute resolution," "case classification, mediation, and adjudication," "case filing service," "trial assistance," and "complaints and petitions."[64] Each module is designed to cater to different aspects of the litigation process, providing a comprehensive suite of services that enhance the efficiency and accessibility of judicial procedures.

The platform also integrates with several key information technology application systems, such as the aforementioned Mobile Micro Court mobile application, the People's Court mediation platform, and the unified nationwide court service platform. This integration facilitates a seamless flow of information and enables the SPC to visually display and quantitatively assess the litigation services provided by courts in various regions. By doing so, it allows for targeted guidance and support to courts at all levels, promoting consistency and quality in judicial services across the country. For underdeveloped regions, such as Xizang, which may

63 "Beijing Xichengqu renmin fayuan linghuo zujian guifan guanli qianghua baozhang youhua shenpan tuandui yunxing jizhi shifang shenpan xiaoneng 北京市西城区人民法院 灵活组建 规范管理 强化保障 优化审判团队运行机制 释放审判效能," *People's Court Daily* 人民法院报, December 3, 2020.

64 "Integrated Online Management System Enhances the Quality of Litigation Service 一网统管提升诉讼服务工作水平," *Supreme People's Court*, June 1, 2020, https://www.court.gov.cn/zixun/xiangqing/232951.html.

lack sufficient judicial resources and have relatively lower levels of information technology development, the SPC takes a more hands-on approach. It deploys special teams to conduct in-depth research and provide one-on-one guidance to local courts. This tailored support ensures that even the most resource-constrained areas are not left behind in the nationwide push for judicial modernization and efficiency.

Overall, the establishment of the one-stop litigation service system under the leadership of the SPC represents a significant advancement in China's judicial reform efforts. It exemplifies the judiciary's commitment to leveraging technology to enhance the accessibility and effectiveness of the legal system, ensuring that all regions, regardless of their level of development, benefit from improved litigation services.

Online mediation

One of the cornerstones of one-stop multidisciplinary dispute resolution is the integration of the well-established non-judicial mediation mechanisms and the mediation culture inherent in Chinese society with formal court-based dispute resolution processes. The system of "people's mediation" (*renmin tiaojie*) is a distinctly Chinese feature.[65] Historically, the utilization of people's mediation, along with administrative mediation and other non-litigation dispute resolution mechanisms, originated before the founding of the People's Republic, in areas under the control of the Communist Party during the Yan'an period. This approach was instrumental in mitigating social conflicts and addressing disputes at the grassroots level in the absence of any established formal legal system, eventually leading to the development of a governance-oriented judiciary that prioritizes harmony over strict legal principles.

Mediation has traditionally been central to, and often the primary function of, the Chinese legal system, as reflected in the SPC's stated principle of "prioritizing mediation and combining mediation with adjudication."[66] The goal of this approach is to resolve disputes in a manner that is less costly, is more efficient, and minimizes conflict that is often experienced in adjudication. The application of mediation within the litigation process can be categorized into pre-litigation mediation and mediation during litigation. Pre-litigation mediation occurs before a case is officially filed and can be facilitated either by the court itself or a people's

65 "Zhongguo tese renmin tiaojie zhidu de chuancheng yu fazhan 中国特色人民调解制度的传承与发展," *Ministry of Justice of China*, November 7, 2019, https://www.moj.gov.cn/pub/sfbgw/zlk/201911/t20191108_174221.html: "People's Mediation refers to the activities conducted by the People's Mediation Committees through methods such as persuasion and guidance, prompting parties to voluntarily reach a mediation agreement based on equal negotiation, thereby resolving civil disputes. People's mediation is an important method outside of litigation for resolving conflicts and eliminating disputes. It is known as the 'first line of defence' in maintaining social harmony and stability and is acclaimed by the international community as the 'Eastern Experience'" (translation by the author).

66 Supreme People's Court, "Several Opinions on Further Implementation of the Work Principles of 'Prioritizing Mediation and Combing Mediation with Adjudication' 关于进一步贯彻'调解优先、调判结合'工作原则的若干意见," (SPC Issue 2010/No. 16, June 7, 2010).

mediation organization. In instances where the court conducts and successfully concludes the mediation by all parties reaching agreement, it issues a "mediation order" (*tiaojie shu*), which is enforceable as a judicial judgment. Conversely, when a people's mediation organization conducts a successful mediation, the parties involved may apply for judicial confirmation (*sifa queren*) from the court to render the mediation results enforceable, or they may voluntarily perform the agreement without judicial compulsion.

Mediation during litigation refers to mediation that occurs after a case has been filed, which can take place at any point before, during, or after court hearings, up until the final judgment is handed down. Similar to pre-litigation mediation, this can be conducted either by the presiding judges or a people's mediation organization as assigned by the court, with the outcomes subject to the same enforceability conditions as pre-litigation mediation.

In summary, courts are actively encouraged to promote mediation at any stage of the litigation process to facilitate effective dispute resolution. This process is fundamentally grounded in the voluntary participation of the parties involved. Should mediation fail, it is imperative that the litigation proceed without delay. This is particularly important in scenarios where mediation and litigation processes are closely intertwined during online litigation and online mediation.[67]

The "governance of litigation sources" (*suyuan zhili*) of Chinese courts mainly refers to the resolution of cases through mediation and other means after filing a lawsuit and before formal acceptance by the court. This includes the establishment of litigation service centers by the courts with a view to accommodate a large number of mediation organizations, arbitration institutions, notary institutions, mediators, lawyers, and volunteers, who can provide parties with various dispute resolution methods.[68] In 2023, courts across the country resolved a total of 11.998 million disputes through pre-litigation people's mediation assigned by the court, administrative mediation, and industry-specific professional mediation, accounting for 40.2% of the total volume of civil and administrative cases filed in courts during the same period.[69]

To advance dispute resolution and improve access to justice, the SPC has taken a leading role in implementing and promoting a nationwide, unified online mediation platform for courts, along with standardized online mediation rules. The People's Court Mediation Platform, developed by the SPC, was launched in 2018.[70]

67 Online Mediation Rules, Article 21.

68 "Zhua qianduan zhi weibing zuohao 'suyuan zhili' wenzhang 抓前端治未病 做好'诉源治理'文章," *People's Court Daily* 人民法院报, March 10, 2024, http://society.people.com.cn/n1/2024/0310/c1008-40192662.html.

69 "Supreme People's Court: Advancing Diversified Dispute Resolution最高法：深化矛盾纠纷多元化解," *China Court*中国法院网, March 8, 2024, https://www.chinacourt.org/article/detail/2024/03/id/7838547.shtml.

70 "Renmin fayuan tiaojie pingtai shangxian dangshiren ke wangshang shenqing tiaojie 人民法院调解平台上线 案件当事人可网上申请调解," *People.com.cn* 人民网, February 28, 2018, http://legal.people.com.cn/n1/2018/0228/c42510-29840160.html.

This platform enables parties to initiate online mediation proceedings seamlessly. Users can submit applications for mediation, provide electronic service addresses, and upload evidentiary materials directly through the platform. Mediations are conducted by qualified mediators, and outcomes, such as mediation agreements and transcripts, can be validated through electronic signatures and other online methods. Significantly, the platform integrates directly with the courts' case filing systems, thereby enhancing the efficiency and coherence of the mediation process.

The SPC has also been a vigorous advocate for the expansion and utilization of online mediation platforms by lower courts, emphasizing the importance of comprehensive mediation efforts and the acceleration of platform development by courts nationwide.[71] These individual mediation platforms established by lower courts are designed to integrate seamlessly with the SPC's centralized online mediation platform, creating a cohesive framework for handling various types of mediation cases across the country. As seen in other jurisdictions, such as the United States, court-led ODR has become increasingly important and integral to legal practice, evolving from technology-assisted processes to online processes.[72]

SPC's online mediation platform has had significant reach and impact since its launch in February 2018. By the end of 2020, all of the over 3,500 courts in China were connected to the SPC's online mediation platform. The platform had handled a cumulative total of 13.6 million mediation cases, with a success rate of 65%, and an average mediation duration of 23 days. Following successful pre-litigation mediation, only 12.3% of cases required judicial confirmation, while 3% resulted in the issuance of a mediation order. Notably, the majority of pre-litigation mediation cases were resolved through subsequent voluntary performance by parties. On a typical working day, the platform mediated 66 disputes per minute, equating to 17,000 cases each day, effectively reducing the need for adjudication and judgment.

Effective January 1, 2022, the promulgation of online mediation rules marked a significant advancement in the standardization of mediation procedures across China. Before the establishment of these rules, local courts operated without uniform provisions, primarily relying on advocacy, guidance, and recommendations that lacked enforceable and binding standards. The introduction of the online mediation rules has instituted comprehensive guidelines for online mediation activities conducted through the court's mediation platforms. Online mediation can be employed for disputes legally amenable to mediation or conciliation, including civil, administrative, enforcement, and private criminal prosecutions. The rules facilitate the use of modern audio-video mediation technologies, allowing courts to conduct online mediation via video, telephone, WeChat, and other audio-video

71 "Opinions of the Supreme People's Court on Building One-Stop Diversified Dispute Resolution Mechanisms and One-Stop Litigant Service Centers最高人民法院关于建设一站式多元解纷机制一站式诉讼服务中心的意见," (SPC Issue 2019/No. 19, July 31, 2019).

72 Noam Ebner and Daniel Rainey, "ODR and Mediation," in *Online Dispute Resolution: Theory and Practice*, eds. Daniel Rainey, Ethan Katsh, and Mohamed S. Abdel Wahab, 2nd ed. (The Hague: Eleven, 2021), 409–10.

communication methods.[73] These guidelines detail the protocols for various aspects of the mediation process, including the qualifications of mediators, selection of mediation organizations, initiation of online mediation, creation of mediation agreements, integration of litigation and mediation processes, and termination of mediation.

As of August 2024, according to real-time data from the People's Court Mediation Platform (tiaojie.court.gov.cn), the platform had connected to 3,504 courts nationwide, involved 109,587 mediation organizations, and included 447,767 professional mediators. A total of 69 million cases had been mediated on the platform, with a pre-litigation mediation success rate of 66%. Underlying these figures is the extensive network of 630,000 mediation organizations across the country being connected in the platform's rapid and effective integration of various social mediation resources and personnel, which underscores the dynamic and impactful nature of the court's modernization efforts.

The Chinese leadership and the central government have repeatedly stated that, given China's national conditions, the country could not afford becoming a litigious society.[74] Instead, the emphasis should remain on preventing conflicts and disputes at their source, positioning non-litigation mechanisms at the forefront of "litigation source governance." This approach aligns with the broader strategic goal of building rule of law in China, which prioritizes the minimization of disputes through proactive measures. Mediation, therefore, continues to be a critical component of the judicial process in Chinese courts and is integral to the Chinese-style diversified dispute resolution mechanism.[75] This enduring commitment highlights the role of mediation as not just a tool for resolving disputes but as a fundamental aspect of the judicial philosophy that seeks to harmonize societal relations and reduce judicial burdens.

New hybrid model for online litigation and online courts

This continuing emphasis of mediation by the Chinese legal system does not hinder major development in relation to online litigation. In fact, alongside internet courts and online mediation, China has also advanced with the largest operation of online litigation and online courts, covering all of the over 3,500 courts nationwide. Effective from August 2021, all Chinese courts can utilize online litigation for civil and administrative lawsuits of any kind, including enforcement cases, as well as a small number of criminal cases, such as summary procedures and parole hearings.[76] The

73 Online Mediation Rules, Article 3.

74 Xi Jinping 习近平, "Jianding buyi zou Zhongguo tese shehuizhuyi fazhi daolu 坚定不移走中国特色社会主义法治道路 为全面建设社会主义现代化国家提供有力法治保障," *Qiushi* 求是 2021/5, http://www.qstheory.cn/dukan/qs/2021-02/28/c_1127146541.htm.

75 Supreme People's Court and the Ministry of Justice, "Opinions on Maximizing the Basic Role of People's Mediation in Promoting Litigation Source Governance 关于充分发挥人民调解基础性作用推进诉源治理的意见" (*Si Fa* 2023/No. 1, September 27, 2023).

76 Online Litigation Rules, Article 3.

2021 amendments to the Civil Procedure Law further reinforced the legislative foundation for online litigation, confirming that civil litigation proceedings can be conducted online and ensuring that online litigation activities hold the same legal validity as their offline counterparts.[77]

In response to the COVID-19 pandemic, most jurisdictions adapted by switching to some form of online operation. However, what makes the Chinese approach to online litigation and online courts unique is not only that it has institutionalized this transition on a permanent basis but also that it has established a new hybrid model of online courts never before envisioned or experimented with in China or elsewhere.

Among all the implemented or envisioned models of online courts, be it the Civil Resolution Tribunal in Canada (CRT), the Online Civil Money Claim (OCMC) in the United Kingdom, and others mentioned previously in this book, there are always eligibility criteria for online litigation. Typically, these restrictions could be the type of cases, for example, money-only claims up to a certain limit in OCMC, or strata disputes in CRT. Thus, the legal system would only permit certain predetermined types of cases to be subject to online litigation. In sharp contrast to this conventional approach, the Chinese online courts movement immediately opened all civil and administrative lawsuits to online litigation.

Such a comprehensive adoption of online courts could have been a highly problematic move, as not all litigants are accustomed to or have access to online litigation. Many questions have been asked of the internet courts before based on what-ifs, such as what if litigants have no access to computers or what if they live in areas with poor internet connection.[78] In the context of access to justice, concerns are not only over physical or technological availability of internet access, the so-called "first digital divide," but also people's understanding and capacities of undertaking activities online, the so-called "second digital divide."[79] It could have been grossly counterproductive if the Chinese online courts movement had compromised access to justice of the population by expanding in such an extensive manner.

The solution offered by the SPC is to make this selection between online or offline litigation a free choice for each party at each stage of any litigation, including case filing, mediation, exchange of evidence, questioning, court hearing, and document servicing.[80] Crucially, the choice by one party to undertake activities online does not affect or preclude the choice by other parties to participate online or offline. If, for example, the plaintiff decides to take part in the court hearing online, while the defendant opts to attend in person, the hearing is then conducted

77 Civil Procedure Law of the People's Republic of China, Article 16.

78 Huang-Chih Sung, "Can Online Courts Promote Access to Justice? A Case Study of the Internet Courts in China," *Computer Law & Security Review* 39 (2020): 105461, https://doi.org/10.1016/j.clsr.2020.105461.

79 Catrina Denvir and Amanda Darshini Selvarajah, "Safeguarding Access to Justice in the Age of the Online Court," *Modern Law Review* 85, no. 1 (2022): 29, https://doi.org/10.1111/1468-2230.12670.

80 Online Litigation Rules, Article 1.

as a hybrid of online and offline attendance.[81] While the court may decide that certain cases or certain stages of particular cases are to proceed offline, there is no authority for any court to demand any litigant to undertake activities online.[82] Only litigants can decide for themselves to do anything online, thereby preventing any undermining of the access to justice mentioned previously.

The reforms establishing online courts have rapidly become a cornerstone of legal practice in China. In 2021, the courts accepted 11.439 million cases online, conducted evidence exchanges for 2.601 million cases digitally, and held 1.275 million court hearings online.[83] As expected, more developed regions have led the expansion of online courts, exemplified by Beijing, where 67.4% of all court hearings were conducted online in 2021.[84] Meanwhile, other areas are also advancing rapidly; 37.3% of all court hearings nationwide were held online in 2022, a significant increase from just 1.1% in 2018.[85]

The promotion and acceptance of online litigation and online courts are not merely about technology, as most courts in most countries nowadays are technically capable of managing hearings and other litigation activities remotely. The real question is about the conception of justice in the digital era and the role of the court in such a configuration. As mentioned earlier, Chinese courts have firmly placed them as service providers, catering for the needs of litigants, rather than expecting the latter to navigate through the physical and structural framework of conventional courts. This free-choice hybrid model of online courts is a prime example of the distinctive and, as of today, unique approach adopted by the Chinese courts. Together with mechanisms such as online mediation and one-stop litigation service centers, it contributes to the Chinese conception of the digitization of justice, examined next.

Conclusion: Chinese conception of the digitization of justice

The chapter traces the evolutionary trajectory of integrating the internet, technology, and the judicial system in China, providing a thorough analysis of the country's online litigation system. The forthcoming phase in the evolution of judicial processes in China is centered on the concept of digital justice, often referred to as "digitized justice." There is currently a vibrant discussion in China regarding the idea of "digital courts" and what the future of a digitized justice system might look like. While the exact contours and operational specifics of digital courts are still emerging and open to interpretation, the trend is unmistakably toward a more technologically integrated judicial system.

81 Online Litigation Rules, Article 4(3).
82 Online Litigation Rules, Article 2(2).
83 Chen Guoping 陈国平 and Tian He 田禾, *Annual Report on Informationization of Chinese Courts No. 6 (2022)* 中国法院信息化发展报告(2022) (Beijing: Social Science Academic Press China, 2022), 5.
84 Chen and Tian, *Annual Report 2022*, 96.
85 Chen and Tian, *Annual Report 2023*, 23.

The advancement of deep learning and large language model technologies, hallmarks of a new generation of AI, is rapidly becoming a cornerstone of this transformation. The development of digital courts will likely extend far beyond the current applications of big data for supervision, error correction, and early warning systems. Instead, the future is expected to feature more advanced integrations, such as superintelligent humanoid bionics and human–computer coupled interactions, which will significantly influence the direction of judicial reforms. Ultimately, the deeper integration of technology and data with the judicial system is set to fundamentally reshape structure and functionality.

In exploring the nature of justice in the internet era and the potential shape of digital justice, China's response to Richard Susskind's question "Is court a service or a place?"[86] reflects a transformative vision. China asserts that, in the digital age, litigation should be viewed primarily as a service, similar to platforms that are as ubiquitous and user-friendly as online taxi-hailing. This shift emphasizes that judicial services ought to be inclusive, convenient, low-cost, and easily accessible, mirroring the ethos of consumer-centric digital services. This redefinition aims to make justice highly digitized and machine-readable. As litigation costs decrease, access to justice can expand to meet the growing legal needs of ordinary people, which is a necessity in an era characterized by a rise in the number of disputes.

To address this escalating demand, there is a pressing need to leverage and enhance the capabilities of technology. The future trajectory of justice is likely to evolve from a judge-driven framework to one that is predominantly driven by machines and data. This transition will not only streamline but also compartmentalize the judicial process. Certain aspects of case management and judicial support could be automated and executed by machines, while others will continue to be overseen by human judges. This compartmentalization will also facilitate the potential socialization of judicial functions – tasks traditionally handled within the judiciary could be delegated to specialized service providers in society.

The concept of "inclusive justice" further entails the democratization of legal language. This raises the discussion of judicial specialization versus popularization of justice. In the digital age, these concepts are not mutually exclusive; indeed, both perspectives contribute meaningfully to the conceptualization of justice. Popularization aims to demystify legal terminologies and procedures for the general public, enhancing their understanding and engagement with the law. Conversely, specialization addresses the inherent complexity of legal issues, highlighting the necessity of expert knowledge in the administration of justice.

Consider, for example, the scenario of a physical altercation. A legally trained individual might search online for terms such as "negligent injuring" or "intentional injuring," employing a vocabulary rich in legal jargon. In contrast, an individual without legal training might simply query restitution or incarceration, asking, "Who should pay, and should the person go to jail or not?" The future popularization of the language of justice entails a system where common

86 Susskind, *Online Courts and the Future of Justice*, 95.

language, rather than legalistic expressions, is inputted into technological platforms. These systems will then function as intermediaries, translating everyday language into the formal language of the law, effectively bridging the gap between lay understandings and legal standards. This capacity of technology to simultaneously professionalize and popularize justice represents a pivotal development in the trajectory of digital justice. It embodies the potential to make the legal system more accessible, while maintaining the rigor required for precise and equitable adjudication. This duality will undoubtedly shape the future landscape of digital justice, ensuring it is both inclusive and precise, thereby broadening its reach and deepening its impact.

Furthermore, under China's paradigm of one-stop litigation services and diversified dispute resolution, the digitization of justice assumes distinct functionalities and values compared to other countries. Within the Chinese framework, an additional and equally significant concept emerges – that the court transcends its traditional roles to become not merely a venue or service but a "platform," a "connection point," a "hub," and an "infrastructure" integral to social governance.

Viewing the court as a *platform* introduces a multi-layered structure. At the core of this structure lies the foundation of judicial technology, which supports and enhances judicial functions. Encircling this core is a network that provides access to specialized systems, such as adjudication and mediation, along with a self-sustaining ecosystem of various litigation services. Encompassing this is a broader layer where parties involved in dispute resolution – including service providers and other stakeholders – interact regularly within the platform's framework.

This platform concept also extends to the formulation of rules. It encompasses the development of detailed protocols for participation, including the establishment of security measures, privacy safeguards, access criteria, as well as incentives and penalties. The court in China serves not only as a judicial body but also as a platform for national and social governance, acting as a crucial connector among various organizations, social actors, and resources. It is positioned at the center of national governance, promoting the integration of courts with diverse social resources. Beyond the traditional combination of litigation and mediation, China has pioneered innovations in judicial enforcement to address specific challenges.

For instance, in response to enforcement difficulties, the Beijing Internet Court has developed a multi-party credit system for micro-discipline online. This innovative approach collaborates with numerous internet platforms to impose micro-disciplinary measures, such as restricting access to online shopping and online car-hailing services. These measures aim to incentivize debtors to honor their obligations in good faith. Additionally, the area of judicial auctions has seen significant advancements through leveraging social resources, including technology, funds, and personnel, to enhance the digitization and modernization of judicial processes. Currently, all courts in China delegate judicial auction tasks to major online platforms, such as Tmall, effectively utilizing social resources to conduct judicial operations. Tmall, part of Taobao, examined in Chapters 2 and 3, and a pioneer in this initiative, currently provides its services without charging fees, contributing to social resources and public welfare. This strategy not only addresses historical issues of corruption associated with court-managed judicial auctions but also advances judicial reform and practice.

In summary, the vision for China's future digital courts and digital justice encapsulates a diverse array of mechanisms, fusing modern and traditional justice in a hybrid model that integrates online and offline elements. Digitization of justice is fundamentally about creating institutional advancements (justice plus technology), building upon existing frameworks. Moreover, the integration of technology into the judicial system is a transformative process that influences not only the technology itself but also societal norms, individual behaviors, and attitudes. Throughout this transformation, it is imperative for practitioners within the justice system to adapt to and address the challenges posed by new technologies, shaping a future where digital justice improves both accessibility and efficacy.

Within the court system, there exists a dual structure comprising technical staff and judicial personnel. Technical staff often embrace the introduction of new technologies with enthusiasm, while judicial personnel typically respond with skepticism and resistance to new terms and technologies that extend beyond their existing knowledge frameworks.[87] Moreover, the preservation of traditional, offline trial procedures allows some judges, particularly older ones, to continue adjudicating cases in familiar ways. Across different contexts, there is nevertheless a perceived consensus that some disputes ae better suited to be handled offline, especially those with serious consequences for parties.[88] Judicial systems may incorporate both machine-based and human adjudicators, adjusting the mix of adjudicative mechanisms and systems depending on the case type. Investment in human resources and training represents a substantial societal cost, necessitating careful consideration during the judiciary's digital transformation.

Furthermore, the digital divide impacts legal professionals, such as lawyers, who are not proficient with IT systems or who oppose online litigation methods. These lawyers risk becoming obsolete, facing potential exclusion from the profession due to handling a greatly reduced number of cases – an exclusion not reflective of their professional ethics or competence. This type of exclusion based on procedural elements can be perceived as unjust.[89]

Technology itself is also in a state of evolution; for instance, blockchain technology, which has been a focal point in internet court applications, has seen minimal advancements or expansions in understanding since 2018.[90] Its application in the judiciary remains limited, primarily used for evidence deposition and verification, despite its potential to ensure the immutability of case materials and the

87 Chen and Tian, *Annual Report 2023*, 12.

88 Linda Mulcahy and Anna Tsalapatanis, "Exclusion in the Interests of Inclusion: Who Should Stay Offline in the Emerging World of Online Justice," *Journal of Social Welfare and Family Law* 44, no. 4 (2022): 458, https://doi.org/10.1080/09649069.2022.2136713.

89 Chen and Tian, *Annual Report 2023*, 13.

90 Xuhui Fang, "Recent Development of Internet Courts in China," *International Journal of Online Dispute Resolution* 5 (2018): 50, https://doi.org/10.5553/IJODR/235250022018005102006.

authenticity of evidence. These are critical applications in practice across the wider legal system involving the police, the procuracy, and the court.[91] The challenges associated with blockchain in the judiciary – including its underdeveloped infrastructure, limited application scenarios, and the lack of comprehensive measures for legal risk prevention[92] – highlight the ongoing need for further development and better integration of such technologies into the judicial framework.

In envisioning the future justice system within a digital society, the overarching goal is to achieve "access without barriers," a paradigm shift made possible by advancements in the internet era. This vision is rooted in the justice system's enhanced capacity to meet people's needs more effectively, driven by technological innovation, rather than relying solely on human capabilities.

As digital courts evolve and artificial intelligence gains greater power, the foundational principles of justice and efficiency must remain unwavering. The judicial ethos, which prioritizes the pursuit of justice, dictates that technology serve as a tool to facilitate legal processes, not as an end in itself. This understanding is evident in the position taken by the SPC, which emphasizes the principle that AI should not supplant human judges in making judicial decisions, regardless of the technological advancements or their potential for providing to assist the judiciary.[93] At the pinnacle of digital court development, the fundamental human pursuit of fairness and justice must still rely on the discernment and professional wisdom of judges. Even with extensive digital support and AI capabilities, the ultimate safeguarding of justice remains firmly a human responsibility. Judges are indispensable in ensuring that the application of justice is consistently balanced, fair, and aligned with the ethical standards and values of society.

Bibliography

Avino, Graig R. "China's Judiciary: An Instrument of Democratic Change." *Penn State International Law Review* 22, no. 2 (2003): 369–92.

Balme, Stéphanie. "Local Courts in Western China: The Quest for Independence and Dignity." In *Judicial Independence in China*, edited by Randall Peerenboom, 154–79. Cambridge: Cambridge University Press, 2010.

Bridgesmith, Larry W. "ODR and the Justice System." In *Online Dispute Resolution: Theory and Practice*, edited by Daniel Rainey, Ethan Katsh, and Mohamed S. Abdel Wahab, 2nd ed., 137–47. The Hague: Eleven, 2021.

91 Jiangxi Courts Project Team 江西法院政法协同课题组, "区块链助力政法机关在线协同办案调研报告," in *Annual Report on Informatization of Chinese Courts No. 7 (2023)* 中国法院信息化发展报告(2023), eds. Chen Guoping and Tian He (Beijing: Social Science Academy Press China, 2023), 337.

92 Jiangsu Province High People's Court Project Team 江苏省高级人民法院课题组, "数字经济背景下区块链技术的司法应用调研报告," in *Annual Report on Informatization of Chinese Courts No. 7 (2023)* 中国法院信息化发展报告(2023), eds. Chen Guoping and Tian He (Beijing: Social Science Academy Press China, 2023), 106.

93 "Opinions of the Supreme People's Court on Regulating and Strengthening the Judicial Applications of Artificial Intelligence 关于规范和加强人工智能司法应用的意见" (SPC Issue 2022/No. 33, December 8, 2022).

Briggs, Lord Justice. "Civil Courts Structure Review: Interim Report." *Judiciary of England and Wales*, December 2015. https://www.judiciary.uk/wp-content/uploads/2016/01/ccsr-interim-report-dec-15-final1.pdf
Bu, Qingxiu. "Will Chinese Legal Culture Constrain Its Corporate Governance-Related Laws?" *Journal of Corporate Law Studies* 15, no. 1 (2015): 103–25.
Chan, Peter C. H. "Do the 'Haves' Come Out Ahead in Chinese Grassroots Courts? Rural Land Disputes Between Married-Out Women and Village Collectives." *Hastings Law Journal* 71, no. 1 (2019): 1–78.
Chen, Guoping 陈国平, and Tian He 田禾. *Annual Report on Informationization of Chinese Courts No. 6 (2022)* 中国法院信息化发展报告 (2022). Beijing: Social Science Academic Press China, 2022.
Chen, Guoping 陈国平, and Tian He 田禾. *Annual Report on Informationization of Chinese Courts No. 7 (2023)* 中国法院信息化发展报告 (2023). Beijing: Social Science Academic Press China, 2023.
Cheng, Jinhua 程金华. "A Cross-Country Comparison of 'Too Many Cases, Too Few Judges' in Courts 法院'案多人少'的跨国比较." *Social Science Journal* 社会科学辑刊 262 (2022/5): 72–84.
Denvir, Catrina, and Amanda Darshini Selvarajah. "Safeguarding Access to Justice in the Age of the Online Court." *Modern Law Review* 85, no. 1 (2022): 25–68. https://doi.org/10.1111/1468-2230.12670.
Ebner, Noam, and Daniel Rainey. "ODR and Mediation." In *Online Dispute Resolution: Theory and Practice*, edited by Daniel Rainey, Ethan Katsh, and Mohamed S. Abdel Wahab, 2nd ed., 409–49. The Hague: Eleven, 2021.
Fairbairn, William. "An Examination of Judicial Independence in China." *Journal of Financial Crime* 23, no. 4 (2016): 819–32. https://doi.org/10.1108/JFC-12-2015-0068.
Fang, Xuhui. "Recent Development of Internet Courts in China." *International Journal of Online Dispute Resolution* 5 (2018): 49–60. https://doi.org/10.5553/IJODR/235250022018005102006
Gao, Wei 高薇. *Institutional Analysis of Dispute Resolution in Cyberspace* 网络空间争议解决的制度分析. Beijing: Peking University Press, 2022.
Guangzhou Internet Court. "2022 Annual Self-Evaluation Report of the Guangzhou Internet Court on Overall Expenditure and Performance 2022年度广州互联网法院部门整体支出绩效自评报告." October 16, 2023. https://www.gz.gov.cn/attachment/7/7465/7465600/9259645.pdf.
Guo, Meirong. "Internet Court's Challenges and Future in China." *Computer Law & Security Review* 40 (2021): 105522. https://doi.org/10.1016/j.clsr.2020.105522.
Heilmann, Sebastian. "From Local Experiments to National Policy: The Origins of China's Distinctive Policy Process." *The China Journal* 59 (2008): 1–30.
Heilmann, Sebastian. "Policy Experimentation in China's Economic Rise." *Studies in Comparative International Development* 43 (2008): 1–26. https://doi.org/10.1007/s12116-007-9014-4.
Hörnle, Julia. *Cross-Border Internet Dispute Resolution*. Cambridge: Cambridge University Press, 2009. https://doi.org/10.1017/CBO9780511576102.
Jia, Yu 贾宇. "Lun shuzi fayuan 论数字法院." *Chinese Journal of Law* 法学研究 46, no. 4 (2024): 3–20.
Jiangsu Province High People's Court Project Team 江苏省高级人民法院课题组. "数字经济背景下区块链技术的司法应用调研报告. *Annual Report on Informatization of Chinese Courts No. 7 (2023)* 中国法院信息化发展报告 (2023), edited by Chen Guoping and Tian He, 101–13. Beijing: Social Science Academy Press China, 2023.
Jiangxi Courts Project Team 江西法院政法协同课题组. "区块链助力政法机关在线协同办案调研报告." In *Annual Report on Informatization of Chinese Courts No. 7 (2023)* 中国法院信息化发展报告(2023), edited by Chen Guoping and Tian He, 328–42. Beijing: Social Science Academy Press China, 2023.

Larson, David Allen. "ODR Accessibility for Person with Disabilities: We Must Do Better." In *Online Dispute Resolution: Theory and Practice*, edited by Daniel Rainey, Ethan Katsh, and Mohamed S. Abdel Wahab, 2nd ed., 49–79. The Hague: Eleven, 2021.

Li, Zhanguo 李占国. "'Quanyu shuzi fayuan' de goujian yu shixian '全域数字法院'的构建与实现." *Peking University Law Journal* 34, no. 1 (2022): 5–34.

Liebman, Benjamin L. "Assessing China's Legal Reforms." *Columbian Journal of Asian Law* 23, no. 1 (2009): 17–33. https://doi.org/10.7916/cjal.v23i1.3284.

Lubman, Stanley B. *Bird in a Cage: Legal Reform in China After Mao*. Stanford, CA: Stanford University Press, 1999.

Mentovich, Avita, J. J. Prescott, and Orna Rabinovich-Einy. "Legitimacy and Online Proceedings: Procedural Justice, Access to Justice and the Role of Income." *Law & Society Review* 57, no. 2 (2023): 189–213. https://doi.org/10.1111/lasr.12653.

Mulcahy, Linda, and Anna Tsalapatanis. "Exclusion in the Interests of Inclusion: Who Should Stay Offline in the Emerging World of Online Justice." *Journal of Social Welfare and Family Law* 44, no. 4 (2022): 455–76. https://doi.org/10.1080/09649069.2022.2136713.

Peerenboom, Randall Peerenboom. "Judicial Independence in China." In *Judicial Independence in China*, edited by Randall Peerenboom. Cambridge: Cambridge University Press, 2010.

Rabinovich-Einy, Orna, and Ethan Katsh. "Lessons from Online Dispute Resolution for Dispute System Design." In *Online Dispute Resolution: Theory and Practice*, edited by Daniel Rainey, Ethan Katsh, and Mohamed S. Abdel Wahab, 2nd ed., 49–72. The Hague: Eleven, 2021.

Shan, Wenhua, and Yunya Feng. "The China International Commercial Court: Towards an Integrated Dispute Resolution System." *Asia Pacific Law Review* 29, no. 1 (2021): 107–28.

Sung, Huang-Chih. "Can Online Courts Promote Access to Justice? A Case Study of the Internet Courts in China." *Computer Law & Security Review* 39 (2020): 105461. https://doi.org/10.1016/j.clsr.2020.105461.

Susskind, Richard. *Online Courts and the Future of Justice*. Oxford: Oxford University Press, 2019. https://doi.org/10.1093/oso/9780198838364.001.0001

Vermeys, Nicolas W., and Karim Benyekhelf. "ODR and the Courts." In *Online Dispute Resolution: Theory and Practice*, edited by Mohamed S. Abdel Wahab, Ethan Katsh, and Daniel Rainey, 307–24. The Hague: Eleven, 2012.

Wang, Fuhua 王福华. "Huliangwang sifa de zhengyi tixi 互联网司法的正义体系." *Zhongguo Faxue* 中国法学 237 (2024): 124–44.

Wang, Liyuan. "Application of Information Technology in Judicial Field: The Development Model of Online Litigation in China." *Computer Law & Security Review* 52 (2024): 105936. https://doi.org/10.1016/j.clsr.2024.105936.

Xi, Jinping 习近平. "Jianding buyi zou Zhongguo tese shehuizhuyi fazhi daolu 坚定不移走中国特色社会主义法治道路 为全面建设社会主义现代化国家提供有力法治保障." *Qiushi* 求是 (2021/5). http://www.qstheory.cn/dukan/qs/2021-02/28/c_1127146541.htm.

Xu, Lu. *Chinese Legal Reforms: Transformations in a Decade*. Leiden: Brill, 2024. https://doi.org/10.1163/9789004537125.

Zheng, George G. "China's Grand Design of People's Smart Courts." *Asian Journal of Law and Society* 7 (2020): 561–82. https://doi.org/10.1017/als.2020.20.

Zuo, Weimin 左卫民. "Online Litigation in the Post-Epidemic Era: Where to Go 后疫情时代的在线诉讼: 路向何方." *Xiandai Faxue* 现代法学 43, no. 6 (2021): 35–46.

6 ODR, China, and beyond

Institutional analysis of ODR

Online dispute resolution represents a cutting-edge area of internet research and dispute resolution that has consistently fueled diverse discussions and shaped perceptions since its inception. Unlike other texts in this field, this book adopts an institutional analysis approach to explore the mechanisms of dispute resolution in cyberspace. It delves into the driving forces behind institutional change from the perspective of mechanism design, addressing the inherent challenges and outlining the evolutionary patterns and dilemmas faced by various ODR systems. By providing a thorough analysis of major types of ODR, including private ordering, online arbitration, online mediation, and online litigation, this examination of the contemporary ODR landscape benefits from the doctrinal and practical experience within China and beyond.

Meanwhile, an examination through the lens of institutional economics does not represent a neglect of the significant role of the state and the rule of law. This book explicitly highlights the pivotal role the state plays in the development of ODR in China, examining the interconnection between the rule of law, the economy, and societal dynamics. Chapter 2 distinguishes between exogenous and endogenous ODR systems, noting that both theoretically permit state intervention. While acknowledging the influence of state intervention in shaping ODR, the book emphasizes that such intervention can profoundly transform the dispute resolution landscape.

In scenarios involving exogenous ODR, stakeholders may actively seek state involvement to enforce online arbitration or mediation through legislative or regulatory means, thereby shifting the dynamics from market-driven to policy-influenced competition and accelerating the integration of these systems. Conversely, key actors in endogenous ODR systems might resist state interference when these systems operate effectively independently. From a game theory perspective, while endogenous ODR may represent a stable Nash equilibrium,[1] it does not necessarily

1 A *Nash equilibrium* is defined as a solution in which each player evaluates the strategies of their competitors and decides that they gain no advantage by unilaterally changing strategy when all other players keep their own strategies unchanged; Jens David Ohlin, "Nash Equilibrium and International Law," *European Journal of International Law* 23, no. 4 (2012): 921, https://doi.org/10.1093/ejil/chs060.

DOI: 10.4324/ 9781003594512-6

achieve Pareto optimality.[2] The evolution of endogenous ODR is depicted as a transition from multiple potential equilibria to a conventional standard, where state influence could steer the selection toward a Pareto-optimal Nash equilibrium, supplanting the existing standard. However, identifying and implementing policies to achieve such optimal equilibria present substantial challenges.

Chapters 2 and 3 also introduce an original institutional analytical framework for examining ODR, visualized by the ODR Quadrant Diagram. This model positions existing and prospective ODR systems along two different dimensions, namely, one of endogenous or exogenous mechanisms and another of public, private, or technology-based dispute resolution. This provides a comprehensive theoretical foundation that differs from most existing theories, which typically focus on a single aspect of ODR, such as online litigation or arbitration. The introduction of this institutional axis and the broader analytical framework marks a significant theoretical advancement in the study of ODR, offering a fresh perspective for academic and practical exploration in the field. This unique contribution is particularly valuable as it provides a new lens for analyzing the complexities of ODR within the broader context of institutional economics, deepening the understanding of how such systems are integrated and function within various legal and societal frameworks.

One notable gap in the current international and domestic literature concerning China's ODR systems is the absence of any comprehensive analysis of the Chinese judicial system. Scholars such as Richard Susskind have predicted that developing nations possess a unique advantage in the digital era – they can leapfrog the developed countries in better overcoming traditional barriers that are entrenched in more established legal systems.[3]

In China, a critical juncture appears to be on the horizon for litigation modernization, driven by the concerted efforts of various stakeholders and the dynamic growth of the digital economy. Amid a societal transformation, and leveraging the firsthand experience as an academic fellow in the case filing division of the Supreme People's Court during 2020–2021, this author has had the unique opportunity to both observe and contribute to the implementation of ODR in Chinese courts. This experience has deeply informed Chapter 5 of this book, which details the recent advances in judicial digitization and modernization in China, particularly the development of one-stop dispute resolution and online courts.

The progressive efforts of Chinese courts to integrate technology with dispute resolution, including the advent of internet courts, smart courts, online courts, one-stop litigation services, and multidisciplinary dispute resolution mechanisms, have provided a robust foundation for theoretical examination. This expansive

2 *Pareto optimality* can be defined as the state where resources are allocated as efficiently as possible so that improving one criterion will not worsen other criteria; Nassir Ibrahim et al., "Multi-Objective Decision-Making Methods for Optimizing CO2 Decisions in the Automotive Industry," *Journal of Cleaner Production* 314 (2021): 128037, https://doi.org/10.1016/j.jclepro.2021.128037.

3 Richard Susskind, *Online Courts and the Future of Justice* (Oxford: Oxford University Press, 2019), 300, https://doi.org/10.1093/oso/9780198838364.001.0001.

material has facilitated the exploration of ODR beyond its initial focus on online arbitration and private ordering to encompass the judicial domain, ultimately culminating in a comprehensive view of the ODR ecosystem. This panoramic perspective is crucial in addressing the fundamental question "What exactly is ODR?" to be revisited later.

ODR and the internet society

Moreover, this book provides a chronological review of ODR's evolution, highlighting not only the challenges encountered during its early stages but also the most recent advancements. As the internet sector has burgeoned, reflecting on the past two decades of ODR worldwide reveals a significant ebb and flow – some ODR initiatives have vanished, while others have endured and thrived. This review also underscores the irreversible trend toward technologization and its transformative effects on how humans resolve disputes. The trajectory of ODR closely mirrors broader technological advancements; indeed, the evolution of ODR is emblematic of overall technological progression. China's early embrace of digital communications, which paved the way for the rise of its first tech giants and was followed by the boom in smartphone and mobile internet technologies, has established a solid foundation for subsequent innovations in cloud computing and artificial intelligence. This technological landscape has not only fueled the growth of commercial enterprises but also profoundly shaped the development of ODR frameworks within the country.

The integration of the internet into daily life in China has evolved dramatically over the years. The genesis of e-commerce in China dates back to the 1990s, a pivotal era marked by an iconic advertisement board erected in Beijing near Zhongguancun, often hailed as "China's Silicon Valley," which humorously read: "How far are the Chinese from the information superhighway? 1,500 meters north." This sign symbolized the dawn of China's journey toward digital connectivity.

The First Statistical Report on the Development Status of China's Internet Network, released in 1997, provides a snapshot of the initial stages of this transformation.[4] At that time, China had 299,000 computers connected to the internet. Of these, 49,000 were equipped for direct internet access, while the remaining 250,000 relied on dial-up connections. The total number of internet users was approximately 620,000, primarily relying on dial-up services, with the ratio of direct to dial-up users being about 1 to 3. This period was characterized by limited consumer engagement online, primarily because the internet service was not only slow but also prohibitively expensive for many users.

These early days were marked by a nascent user base and significant infrastructural limitations, reflecting the broader challenges of internet adoption. Despite

4 China Internet Network Information Center, "The 1st Statistical Report on the Development Status of China's Internet Network 第一次中国互联网络发展状况调查统计报告," December 1, 1997, https://www.cnnic.net.cn/NMediaFile/old_attach/P020120612485123735661.pdf.

these hurdles, this period laid the groundwork for the subsequent explosive growth and integration of digital technologies that would soon reshape the everyday life of millions across China, setting the stage for the country's rapid ascent as a global powerhouse in technology and e-commerce. By the time of the 53rd Statistical Report, released in 2024, the number of active internet users in China had reached 1.092 billion, with an internet access rate of 77.5%. Of these, the number of mobile internet users reached 1.091 billion. The scale of online shopping users in China is 915 million, accounting for 83.8% of the total internet users. Accompanying this surge in online shopping is the rapid development of China's electronic payment services. By December 2023, the scale of online payment users in China reached 954 million, accounting for 87.3% of the total internet users. Since 2013, China has been the world's largest online retail market for 11 consecutive years.[5]

In the final months leading up to the completion of this book, which coincided with the 2024 Summer Olympic Games in Paris, the pervasive influence of technology and the internet in Chinese society was distinctly highlighted by advertisements for major platforms like TikTok, Xiaohongshu, Tmall, Meituan, and Temu not only on Chinese television but also around venues in Paris. Meanwhile, one of the top-grossing films in China during August 2024, *Upstream* (*ni xing ren sheng*), portrayed the challenges and daily lives of Meituan delivery riders. This film and widespread discussions on the internet previously had highlighted how these riders are often trapped within the system, grappling with the platform's monopolistic tendencies and the rigid dictates of algorithmic management.[6]

These cultural touchstones underscore a critical observation: The integration of technology into everyday life has not only reshaped consumer behavior and employment paradigms but also established a foundational psychological and technical basis for using the internet and technology to resolve disputes. This broad acceptance and engagement with digital platforms indicate a societal readiness to embrace ODR mechanisms, which can leverage the widespread familiarity with and trust in technology to address and mediate conflicts. Therefore, the popularity of these platforms and the narratives emerging from them reflect a significant, ongoing shift in how technological solutions are perceived and utilized in managing societal and individual challenges in China.

The conception of ODR in China

The synthesis and institutional analysis of the various ODR systems discussed throughout this book revisit a fundamental question: What should ODR be? Susskind's distinction between IT-enabled conventional dispute resolution

5 China Internet Network Information Center, "The 53rd Statistical Report on China's Internet Development 第53次中国互联网发展状况统计报告," March 22, 2024, https://www.cnnic.net.cn/NMediaFile/2024/0325/MAIN1711355296414FIQ9XKZV63.pdf.

6 "Waimai qishou qun zai xitong li 外卖骑手，困在系统里," *RenWu* 人物, September 8, 2020, https://mp.weixin.qq.com/s/Mes1RqIOdp48CMw4pXTwXw.

and ODR is both instructive and thought-provoking in this context. He defines ODR as processes where the resolution of a dispute, especially the formulation of solutions, is conducted entirely or predominantly online.[7] This definition emphasizes the extent of online engagement, which Susskind acknowledges is not a "watertight dichotomy." But it is more meaningful than distinctions drawn on the basis of the non-involvement of courts, as proposed by other scholars.[8] The notion that minor judicial interactions, such as a judge notifying lawyers of schedule changes via email or social media, can constitute ODR is clearly unconvincing. Conversely, the presence of court involvement does not automatically preclude an activity from being classified as ODR. These perspectives are arguably too narrow and fail to capture the broader functionalities and implications of ODR.

ODR can both compete with and complement traditional court systems.[9] This interaction illuminates a crucial dimension of ODR's role within the broader legal framework. However, such a view may still be too Western-centric. Chinese courts, for instance, have long integrated alternative dispute resolution (ADR) methods, particularly mediation, into their judicial processes. This integration demonstrates that the understanding and implementation of ODR can vary significantly across different legal cultures.

At the outset of this book, the analogy of blind men feeling an elephant was employed to describe the varying perceptions of what constitutes ODR. If one were to ask Chinese judges, lawyers, or the public to define ODR, the responses would likely vary widely. Yet a common thread might be that ODR encompasses all the dispute resolution and prevention systems discussed in this book, including litigation.

Furthermore, as mentioned in Chapter 1, while ODR originated from ADR, its scope – as both a practical tool and an academic subject – has expanded considerably. The exploration of ODR now encompasses discussions on platforms, algorithms, and the interplay between private and public forms of ODR. It is crucial to recognize that the integration of algorithms and big data into dispute resolution is not solely beneficial or unidirectional. The rise of private platforms and the increasing complexity and opacity of algorithms introduce new challenges and barriers to traditional notions of judicial redress, necessitating a nuanced understanding and critical evaluation of these technologies' roles within the legal ecosystem.

7 Richard Susskind, *The End of Lawyers?: Rethinking the Nature of Legal Services* (Oxford: Oxford University Press, 2008), 219, https://doi.org/10.1093/oso/9780199541720.001.0001.

8 Julia Hörnle, *Cross-Border Internet Dispute Resolution* (Cambridge: Cambridge University Press, 2009), 75, https://doi.org/10.1017/CBO9780511576102; Suzanne Van Arsdale, "User Protections in Online Dispute Resolution," *Harvard Negotiation Law Review* 21 (2015): 110; Maxime Hanriot, "Online Dispute Resolution (ODR) as a Solution to Cross Border Consumer Disputes: The Enforcement of Outcomes," *McGill Journal of Dispute Resolution* 2 (2015): 2.

9 Nicolas W. Vermeys and Karim Benyekhelf, "ODR and the Courts," in *Online Dispute Resolution: Theory and Practice*, eds. Mohamed S. Abdel Wahab, Ethan Katsh, and Daniel Rainey (The Hague: Eleven, 2012), 309.

Indeed, foreign perspectives on China's ODR systems often suffer from cultural and linguistic barriers, leading to misunderstandings or skepticism of its development. For example, some commentators have expressed concerns about potential conflicts of interest, pointing out that companies like Alibaba have been involved in the design and implementation of systems for several internet courts in China. They argue that Alibaba's involvement might lead to conflicts of interest, given the company's significant online commercial presence.[10] However, such criticisms might neglect similar practices in other countries where judicial systems extensively utilize products from major tech companies like Microsoft, Google, and emerging technologies like ChatGPT. This raises the question: Is there not a similar potential for conflict of interest in these cases? In reality, not only Alibaba, but also other major tech firms, like Baidu, Tencent, and numerous smaller tech companies, are deeply integrated with the Chinese judicial system.[11] Excluding these major players from contributing to the development of ODR systems because of their size and influence would overlook the practical benefits they bring in terms of technology and innovation.

Furthermore, within China, there is a broad spectrum of discussions and evaluations regarding the mechanisms of ODR. Various stakeholders, including large internet platforms like Alibaba and Taobao, have diverse interests and concerns. These platforms often advocate for greater autonomy, fearing that strict legal regulations might hinder their growth and the evolution of the platforms themselves. In the realm of dispute resolution, these companies typically prefer to maintain control over their internal processes. Moreover, within the judiciary, judges and legal scholars are actively reflecting on the nature and future of the internet courts. There is a growing discourse on what constitutes Chinese-style digital justice and how it should be shaped to incorporate both local realities and broader technological advancements.

This book aims to bridge these gaps in understanding by offering a comparative law perspective. It seeks to enable researchers and readers from various countries to understand both the unique aspects and commonalities of China's ODR system, providing insights into the diverse ways in which ODR is perceived and implemented across different contexts. By presenting a balanced view, this work enhances a more nuanced discussion about the integration of technology in judicial processes globally, fostering a deeper appreciation of how different legal cultures address the challenges and opportunities presented by ODR.

10 Alison Xu, "Chinese Judicial Justice on the Cloud: A Future Call or a Pandora's Box? An Analysis of the 'Intelligent Court System' of China," *Information & Communications Technology Law* 26 (2017): 67, https://doi.org/10.1080/13600834.2017.1269873; Pablo Cortés, Aura Esther Vilata Nicuesa, and Chittu Nagarajan, "ODR For E-Commerce: Legal Standard and Developments in Asia and Europe," in *Online Dispute Resolution: Theory and Practice*, eds. Daniel Rainey, Ethan Katsh, and Mohamed S. Abdel Wahab, 2nd ed. (The Hague: Eleven, 2021), 262.

11 George G. Zheng, "China's Grand Design of People's Smart Court," *Asian Journal of Law and Society* 7 (2020): 576, https://doi.org/10.1017/als.2020.20.

Values and contributions of Chinese ODR

The final issue to be explored in this book is to evaluate the contributions of China's ODR mechanisms to the development of the rule of law online, by situating China's ODR practices within the broader context of global legal development.

Firstly, the internet and ODR originated in the Western context, yet they have profoundly taken root within the societal and judicial fabric of China. While the global community lacks a consensus on the precise definition of ODR, China's adoption of a comprehensive dispute resolution model now positions it as a leader in this field. Unlike Western models that predominantly derive from theoretical discourses emphasizing deductive logical coherence, Chinese institutional innovations are largely driven by pragmatic approaches shaped by socio-economic transformations. In the wake of its developmental phase, China encounters a greater volume and intensity of social conflicts compared to Western societies, necessitating a reliance on cost-effective and diverse practices for administering justice.

Within the traditional Chinese judicial framework, the principal aim has consistently been to resolve disputes by minimizing reliance on formal litigation and judicial rulings, thereby reducing the costs associated with formal legal proceedings and enhancing social harmony. This ethos is perpetuated in the construction of a diversified dispute resolution and litigation service system within the digital societal context, reflecting China's enduring judicial philosophy that emphasizes "conflict and dispute governance at the source" and "diversified dispute resolution," with mediation playing a pivotal role.

From a Western perspective, the mediation process should be distinctly separate from litigation, serving primarily to alleviate court burdens, and should remain independent from the formal legal system. However, viewing the justice system holistically and considering the practice of mediation within it, the strengths of the Chinese system become evident. It avoids categorizing disputes into a binary framework of winners and losers, as is common in Western systems. Instead, it employs a layered approach to disputes, addressing simpler cases through informal and semi-formal mediation processes, thus adhering to the traditional ethical mandate of "resolving disputes and fostering harmony." This not only aligns with traditional moral values but also significantly reduces judicial expenses and workload. The judicial system, when viewed comprehensively, is not synonymous with courtroom trials, which represent merely the final recourse in the pursuit of justice. This interpretative framework places preventive governance at the forefront and judicial adjudication as a subsequent measure. The promotion of a comprehensive, diversified dispute resolution and litigation system in China not only mirrors societal characteristics but also aligns with the global aspiration for justice in the digital age, demonstrating substantial institutional benefits and integration into Chinese society.

Secondly, the evolution of China's diversified dispute resolution mechanisms indicates a trend toward integrating and connecting social resources in the resolution of disputes. The Chinese model offers a comprehensive archetype of a pluralistic dispute resolution system for the internet era to the international community.

In China's ODR ecosystem, there are both grassroots-driven private dispute resolution mechanisms on digital platforms and government-promoted pluralistic mechanisms within the judicial system. Notably, China has excelled in advancing certain ODR concepts that were initially proposed but remained underdeveloped in other nations, including mobile ODR, crowdsourcing ODR, and online courts.

Gradually, the evolution of various ODR systems in China has facilitated an institutional interface between private mechanisms and the judicial framework, thereby endowing Chinese-style ODR with the capability to offer a diversified array of dispute resolution options for parties involved. The institutional analysis presented in this book transcends mere examination of individual ODR mechanisms; it aims to scrutinize the interplay among the judiciary, arbitration, and private ordering within Chinese society. The practice and underlying philosophy of ODR in China consistently highlight the principle of holistic social governance, a pivotal theme this book aims to elucidate.

For instance, judicial auctions have been entrusted to major platforms nationwide, illustrating how the courts' comprehensive, diversified dispute resolution initiatives integrate existing societal mechanisms – such as mediation and arbitration – within the litigation process. Furthermore, the integration of online litigation platforms with arbitration platforms exemplifies a seamless interface where court-assisted functions in arbitration, including the preservation of arbitration and judicial review of arbitration awards, are managed online through a unified portal. Previously, parties seeking arbitration preservation were required to apply or submit documents to the relevant arbitration institution or jurisdictional court separately. This process has now been streamlined, allowing all related activities to be conducted online through an integrated platform. This arbitration–adjudication interlinking platform significantly enhances the efficiency of document transmission and information exchange between arbitration institutions and courts, thereby improving case processing efficacy.[12]

Thirdly, in China, courts play a leading role in advancing the "litigation plus ODR" reform. This role encompasses not only judicial adjudication and dispute resolution but also the vital responsibility of fostering legal consciousness across society. In line with this perspective, Chinese courts continue to integrate legal education throughout the populace with the development of one-stop service infrastructure, thereby promoting the socialist "rule of law" spirit and core socialist values within the dispute resolution process. This approach not only guides the public toward relying on legal means to resolve conflicts but also enhances the "rule of law" consciousness, ultimately contributing to a more advanced level of socialist, rule-based governance.

Finally, an overview of the global development of judicial modernization and online dispute resolution in recent years reveals that the primary objective in the era of internet-based dispute resolution is not merely the theoretical pursuit

12 Guangdong High People's Court, "Jiri qi quan liucheng wangshang ban 即日起全流程网上办," August 5, 2024, https://www.163.com/dy/article/J8S1CJGG0514JA8E.html.

of enhanced justice but, rather, a concerted effort to mitigate injustices. Specifically, the "streamlining and simplifying" strategy of case management under the "one-stop diversified dispute resolution" framework in Chinese courts aims to accelerate the resolution of the majority of straightforward cases, effectively reducing and segmenting caseloads.

The concept of "separation of cases into simple cases and complicated ones" under the framework of "one-stop diversified dispute resolution" serves two key purposes. On the one hand, it aims to classify and streamline cases, expediting the resolution of simpler disputes. This approach ensures that litigants can access basic channels for dispute resolution efficiently and affordably, thereby reducing injustice. On the other hand, by fine-tuning the system for more complex cases, it leverages available human and material resources to enhance substantive justice. The effectiveness of any society's dispute resolution and justice system, regardless of its developmental path, is measured by its ability to adapt to contemporary trends and its effectiveness in making judicial processes accessible and efficient, thus allowing every individual in the internet era to experience fairness and justice. Achieving this goal will mark a significant step forward in the global development of the rule of law online.

Final reflections: ODR and justice

However, it is essential to recognize that the use of technology in justice systems can also impede the fulfillment of justice, primarily due to unequal access to technological resources. According to 2023 data, the internet access rate in China stood at 77.5%, but this figure dropped to just 66.5% in rural areas.[13] Furthermore, there is a significant disparity in how different demographics, particularly older age groups and those with lower education attainment, adapt to and utilize technology. These vulnerable individuals are at risk of being marginalized in the digital era.[14] Globally, the situation is even more concerning, with the Organisation for Economic Co-operation and Development (OECD) estimating that only 46% of the world's population lives under legal protection. Later figures indicate that the accessibility, impartiality, and effectiveness of ADR mechanisms have slightly deteriorated in OECD countries between 2016 and 2020.[15]

This digital and technological divide presents serious challenges to the fabric of justice in the internet era. The cases and developments discussed in this book represent only a fraction of the global scenario, focusing on regions with robust legal

13 China Internet Network Information Center, "53rd Report," 28.

14 Catrina Denvir and Amanda Darshini Selvarajah, "Safeguarding Access to Justice in the Age of the Online Court," *Modern Law Review* 85, no. 1 (2022): 48, https://doi.org/10.1111/1468-2230.12670; "Chao qicheng laoren wufa duli caozuo jiankangma 超七成老人无法独立操作健康码," *People.com.cn* 人民网, January 19, 2022, http://sh.people.com.cn/n2/2022/0119/c176737-35102220.html.

15 Susskind, *Online Courts*, 295; Organization for Economic Co-operation and Development, "Access to Justice", in *Government at a Glance 2021* (Paris: OECD Publishing, 2021), https://www.oecd-ilibrary.org/access-to-justice_8b8c48af-en.pdf.

systems and rapid technological advancements. Future research should expand its focus to monitor ODR developments in other regions and examine the interplay between technology and the rule of law more broadly. This will provide a deeper insight into how digital tools are reshaping legal systems worldwide and highlight areas where further development or regulation may be necessary to ensure that the benefits of technology-enhanced justice systems are accessible to all.

Bibliography

China Internet Network Information Center. "The 1st Statistical Report on the Development Status of China's Internet Network 第一次中国互联网络发展状况调查统计报告." December 1, 1997. https://www.cnnic.net.cn/NMediaFile/old_attach/P020120612485123735661.pdf.

China Internet Network Information Center. "The 53rd Statistical Report on China's Internet Development 第53次中国互联网发展状况统计报告." March 22, 2024. https://www.cnnic.net.cn/NMediaFile/2024/0325/MAIN1711355296414FIQ9XKZV63.pdf.

Cortés, Pablo, Aura Esther Vilata Nicuesa, and Chittu Nagarajan. "ODR for E-Commerce: Legal Standard and Developments in Asia and Europe." In *Online Dispute Resolution: Theory and Practice*, edited by Daniel Rainey, Ethan Katsh, and Mohamed S. Abdel Wahab, 2nd ed., 249–74. The Hague: Eleven, 2021.

Denvir, Catrina, and Amanda Darshini Selvarajah. "Safeguarding Access to Justice in the Age of the Online Court." *Modern Law Review* 85, no. 1 (2022): 25–68. https://doi.org/10.1111/1468-2230.12670.

Hanriot, Maxime. "Online Dispute Resolution (ODR) as a Solution to Cross Border Consumer Disputes: The Enforcement of Outcomes." *McGill Journal of Dispute Resolution* 2 (2015): 1–22.

Hörnle, Julia. *Cross-Border Internet Dispute Resolution*. Cambridge: Cambridge University Press, 2009. https://doi.org/10.1017/CBO9780511576102.

Ibrahim, Nassir, Sharon Cox, Robert Mills, Andrew Aftelak, and Hanifa Shah. "Multi-Objective Decision-Making Methods for Optimizing CO_2 Decisions in the Automotive Industry." *Journal of Cleaner Production* 314 (2021): 128037. https://doi.org/10.1016/j.jclepro.2021.128037.

Ohlin, Jens David. "Nash Equilibrium and International Law." *European Journal of International Law* 23, no. 4 (2012): 915–40. https://doi.org/10.1093/ejil/chs060.

Organization for Economic Co-operation and Development. "Access to Justice." In *Government at a Glance 2021*. Paris: OECD Publishing, 2021. https://www.oecd-ilibrary.org/access-to-justice_8b8c48af-en.pdf.

Susskind, Richard. *The End of Lawyers? Rethinking the Nature of Legal Services*. Oxford: Oxford University Press, 2008. https://doi.org/10.1093/oso/9780199541720.001.0001.

Susskind, Richard. *Online Courts and the Future of Justice*. Oxford: Oxford University Press, 2019. https://doi.org/10.1093/oso/9780198838364.001.0001.

Van Arsdale, Suzanne. "User Protections in Online Dispute Resolution." *Harvard Negotiation Law Review* 21 (2015): 107–42.

Vermeys, Nicolas W., and Karim Benyekhelf. "ODR and the Courts." In *Online Dispute Resolution: Theory and Practice*, edited by Mohamed S. Abdel Wahab, Ethan Katsh, and Daniel Rainey, 307–24. The Hague: Eleven, 2012.

Xu, Alison. "Chinese Judicial Justice on the Cloud: A Future Call or a Pandora's Box? An Analysis of the 'Intelligent Court System' of China." *Information & Communications Technology Law* 26 (2017): 59–71. https://doi.org/10.1080/13600834.2017.1269873.

Zheng, George G. "China's Grand Design of People's Smart Courts." *Asian Journal of Law and Society* 7 (2020): 561–82. https://doi.org/10.1017/als.2020.20.

Index

FSC
www.fsc.org
MIX
Papier | Fördert
gute Waldnutzung
FSC® C083411

Kolibri 360 GmbH
Ferdinand-Jühlke-Straße 7
99095 Erfurt, Deutschland
produktsicherheit@kolibri360.de